Nothing But
A Fine Nerve Meter

Nothing But
A Fine Nerve Meter
New Maps at the Planetary Turn

Natalie Rose Dyer

Copyright © 2025 Natalie Rose Dyer

All rights reserved. No part of this book may be reprinted or reproduced or utilised in any form or by any electronic, mechanical, or other means, now known or hereafter invented, including photocopying and recording, or in any information storage or retrieval system, without permission in writing from the publisher.

Paperback 978-1-7640782-3-8
eBook 978-1-7640782-4-5

Editor
Wallea Eaglehawk

Cover design
Wallea Eaglehawk

Cover art
'Neutralia Place' by Edvard Munch, 1915
Licensed under Unsplash courtesy of the Art Institute of Chicago

First published in 2025

Revolutionaries
Wonnarua and Gubbi Gubbi Country, Australia
www.revolutionaries.com.au

This book is dedicated to Jon, Marlene & Gabriel.

'Deeply and powerfully reflective, Natalie Rose Dyer's *Nothing But a Fine Nerve Meter* examines the urgency of poetics at the planetary turn. Braiding personal narrative with a finely crafted latticework of poets, artists, philosophers and scholars, Dyer provides an intricate map for surviving crisis and rupture. Indeed, at the heart of entropy, Dyer finds companionship in the application of her incredible internal library to the sublimity and uncanniness of living.'

Distinguished Professor Cassandra Atherton
School of Communication and Creative Arts
Faculty of Arts and Education
Deakin University

CONTENTS

Preface 11

PART I: Planetary Digressions

Chapter One: The Human Situation Redux 25
Chapter Two: Like Vodou; Towards a Dissident Poetics 50
Chapter Three: A Few Notes on Authorial Descent 73

PART II: Writing Ecologies

Chapter Four: Imperceptible Signs; The Art of Invoking Virginia 103
Chapter Five: Diving for Pearls; Riffing Off Others' Words 122
Chapter Six: Writing Contagious Reality 132

PART III: Feminist Bombs/New Maps

Chapter Seven: A Queer Morphology for Germaine Greer 199
Chapter Eight: A Strange Hybridity in Italy; Or a Siren's Interlude 221
Chapter Nine: Re-Mapped in London 239
Chapter Ten: A Daughter of Exile, or A Ghost Flesh Sequence 256
Chapter Eleven: On Becoming the Wave at St Ives 277

Bibliography 294

Preface

Border Crossing Moments

This book redresses the era of identity politics that we find ourselves in. We are continually required in late so-called advanced, more like end-time-capitalism, to perform our identities, to endlessly indicate our positionalities, primarily through various social media platforms. This has in fact been an important phenomenon, even revolutionary, insofar as hitherto a homogenous man-centric, white, heteronormative identity was the main positionality from which all discourse initiated, and via which all marginalised others to varying degrees were colonised. It could be argued that a democratisation of identity has occurred through the internet of things, especially via social media networks. So why does it often feel like false liberation, which has us working harder than ever to keep performing ourselves as a set of identity markers? Of course, we don't choose all of those markers. Some of them are even vital to our very beings. You can't erase race, nor would you want to. It's very hard to change class stratification. It's not possible to change sexual preference. But when these markers of identity become overly fixed and marketable we need to get suspicious about how they're being used to plug us into the matrix—we've become a bunch of algorithms. We are constantly being reduced in this way.

Money is of course a currency. It has no identity in and of itself. Capital requires identity to produce value. We are all constantly colonised by capital, used by it, we're literally a body in which it harvests, and replicates. A literary body—a meaning making machine required to constantly rewrite ourselves as end-time-capitalism's bitch. So shouldn't we aim to get in charge of how we write ourselves? This book is about empowering you to re-write yourself along poetic fault lines. It's about using poetic writing to deal in another valuable currency, and which can bring about an affirmative morphology that favours immersion with others, human and more-than-human alike. For we are after all nervous systems talking to that which is beyond ourselves all the time. That is, in addition to being representational beings, whereby we demarcate specific identity markers, we are also non-representational beings, or perhaps we are extra-representational. We are plugged into a vast nexus of planetary phenomena, of social and environmental ecologies. We are in constant confluence with other humans, nonhuman animal species, plantae species, bacteria, viruses, minerals, data flows, spiritual stuffs, matter, and so on. This is what I mean by planetary—the condition of being terrestrial, an earthling, is to be a relational being.

In this book I argue that poetic writing can most adequately account for living planetary. Poetry, and perhaps poetic prose more so, is deployed as the most adequate not-discourse, but rather writing-of-rift, which can account for the state of being migrated into everything and everyone ongoingly, and which more adequately demonstrates this weaving of invisible and the visible phenomena, of the known and the unknown, the sensuous and the uncomfortable or painful realities. And I resonate strongly with Donna Haraway's notion of embracing our kinship as highly differentiated cohabitors on earth and specifically in terms of sympoiesis, or 'worlding-with, in company.'[1] We are continually merging multifarious beings; caught up, tangled up, in one another's lives for better or for worse. We feel into one another continuously.

In part one of this book I issue a call to re-write ourselves as planetary players along poetic fault lines and pertaining to my own life experience, as well as with regards to inspiring poets, and writers of poetic prose such as Virginia Woolf, as well as key artists who've forged a diversified pathway. In part two I advocate undertaking poetic prose writing experiments as a form of narrative therapy towards a radical shift in how we think and do human at the planetary turn. In part three I demonstrate my own poetic writing experiments and provide some new maps, or ways out of this Anthropocentric mess we're in. I explore lost lineages rediscovered and propose new trajectories for humanity uncovered through wayfaring; deliberately straying from the prescribed patriarchal path. My proposition is that when we drift or even undertake a pre-planned journey we encounter a schooling in diverse social and environmental ecological encodings. When these excursions are recorded in poetic writing they become radical testimonials of our embodied sensuous experience in confluence with external landscapes, urban and rural alike, and towards the precise recording of contemporary ecologies, many of

---

[1] Haraway, Donna. 2016. *Staying with the Trouble: Making Kin in the Chthulucene.* Durham, North Carolina: Duke University Press.

which are tragically under threat. Writing these landscapes becomes a means of political activism, a safeguarding of places, and in pursuit of an affirmative ethics of reciprocal living on planet earth.

I believe that we desperately need a re-schooling in our connectivity; our status as networked beings. I received this schooling back in my late twenties when I was dragged by my partner against my will to a self-help seminar designed to encourage its participants to put the past in the past, with the aim of bringing about a self-revelatory moment. The seminar leader advocated narrative therapy; sought to explain the world in terms of the stories we tell, retell, some helpful, some not so helpful. The seminar leader intended to empower us to dispense with the mythos that we reiterate, so as to recreate ourselves as something more affirmative, more sustainable. We had to go back to ground zero, trace our own labyrinthine genealogies, dispense with them. Well, I did that for the most part, I severed my connection with a law of the father that operates under patriarchy (although it is of course an ongoing project). I sought to rebirth myself as not that. Then something happened to me quite unexpectedly at the end of the seminar series, having 'popped,' as the seminar leaders termed it, or having come to understand that I am free of the family mindset, liberated to tell my own narratives. My heart began to palpitate, to pound in my chest. I thought I was having a heart attack. I straightened my posture, was about to raise my hand to obtain some help, when three successive images flashed above me—entirely enveloped me. It may have been hallucinatory—although it felt very much like a visionary experience.

Preface

The first vision was of a bird soaring over me, its wing span colossal, driving an airshaft, on some higher mission—planetary. The second vision was of a First Nations elder in a hut. She sat on the earth, took up a stick to write something in the dirt. Lastly, I saw myself standing next to my beloved, our two children on either side of us, in front of an A-frame house. I immediately wondered if these were three fates that had flashed before me. Suddenly I was aware of myself again in the auditorium with the speaker out front. I raised my hand so that I could be picked to share with the group, slowly walked to the microphone, told everyone what I'd experienced. As I spoke to the audience I felt an unparalleled acceptance of myself and everyone. As I sat down I felt present as never before. I experienced no separation from any other life form on planet earth. I recognised myself as part of a continuum. The woman who sat next to me touched my thigh gently, comfortingly, so as to reassure me that she understood. Later on, a man randomly approached me to say that he thought I had experienced some kind of enlightenment and set off the experience for others. He too had undergone a spontaneous feeling of no separation after I'd spoken. I somewhat skeptically told him that the awareness lasted approximately around half an hour—dissipated. But, nevertheless I'd experienced it. And that awareness resonates within me now, albeit on a sublimated level. That experience cannot be held wholly within human thought ongoingly because it is beyond. Still, I think it's what we must learn to draw on, to access a principle of connectivity, toward a more sustainable, and affirmative experience on planet earth. I'm definitely not suggesting that we efface difference. I merely hope humans might consider trading their idiosyncratic identities for an infinite identity now and then. To save this earth we need to learn to affirmatively stray *together* from what we've collectively become—and which is after all a non-sustainable planetary system.

I now understand that those three visions that flashed before me at the seminar series were some kind of call to power. Power can be non-despotic. It can be reorchestrated pertaining to an affirmative web of interconnective planetary vitality. I was again alerted to this reality on a holiday up to Mallacoota in Victoria's East Gippsland region several years ago, not long after the death of my brother Simon, also known by his yogic name Shambhu. I was petitioned from the air by a pair of Whistling Kite eagles. The first one ascended from the cliff's edge, populated by charcoaled trunks, burnt in the catastrophic NSW and Victorian fires of 2019/2020 that horrified the world, so severe that plumes of smoke were detected from the international space station. Whistling Kite soared out over the ledge of the charred woodlands that have miraculously regenerated themselves in the region. The new branches having simply grown out of the blackened boughs, looked something like Dr Seuss' Truffula trees (on account of the way the eucalypts sprout out their plumage in tufts). They are of course something that everyone needs *to preserve* over and above endless exploitation of resources in service of capitalist production. The Whistling Kite magisterially rode the current. Its white underling compartment checkered with patches of brown edged by darker feathers was visible from the beach. It attentively coasted along the shore hunting for fish, gliding, riding, playfully putting on a show of agility and auspicious eloquence. Then it effortlessly collapsed its wings, swooped into the woods in pursuit of prey. Of course, the bushfires likely killed off most of its prey, although life has rapidly regenerated in that most wondrously high-spirited place of vast biodiversity.

The Whistling Kite soared up and down the shoreline hunting, but mostly demonstrating its ability to ride the current, to glide along as a kite discoursing with the elements. It kept flying low, closer and closer to me, over my head. What was it trying to draw my attention to? Maybe it was trying to ascertain if I was edible. I suddenly recalled the vision of the prayer bird in the seminar series. For weeks I'd been seeing eagles, albeit different species of eagle. This was my first Whistling Kite. I found myself asking: 'what is a leader?' And turned to my children for an answer. I figured who better to ask than one of the most othered demographics, entirely at the effect of the patriarchal framework that turns so-called individuals into normative subjects, most damagingly through the dysfunctions of the nuclear family model, but also via unprogressive state-run education systems. My children informed me that: 'To be a leader you must listen, learn, and have the courage to fail.' On the hunt for more answers I watched the film *Dead Poet's Society*. I determined that leaders have to continually face off a rigid dominant economy of masculinity—some don't make it. A good leader must not be afraid to journey to the depths—get reborn something else. Leaders dare to walk a new path—strike new ground. They are unapologetically creative. Brene Brown writes in *Dare to Lead* that leadership is getting out of your comfort zone. 'Leadership is not about titles, status and power over people. Leaders are people who hold themselves accountable for recognising the potential in people and ideas, and developing that potential.'[2] This resonated deeply—

---

[2] Brown, Brené. 2018. *Dare to Lead: Brave Work. Tough Conversations. Whole Hearts*. London: Vermilion.

leadership is the ability to connect—to uphold another's potential and capacity to realise it. In his Ted talk, Drew Dudley, petitions us to create 'lolly pop moments', to foster everyday acts of affirmative kinship whereby we do something, or say something, that makes someone's life fundamentally better.[3] For we are powerful agents for affirmative change in each other's lives when we connect—bring a bit of sunshine. In a way we are helping to redefine that person's understanding of who they are as a planetary being—as affirmatively connected—part of a community. I started to piece together the idea that as a leader I must be courageous and vulnerable enough in equal measure to tell a different planetary tale of the human species '... in the dirt with a twig.'[4] The eagle sighting alighted me to this.

As American writer, feminist and activist, Alice Walker reveals in an interview, she was called to writing at an early age: '... My mother used to say she'd look for me when I was crawling and she'd find me writing in the dirt with a twig.'[4] Walker further attests to writing as a form of activism, which for her has gone hand in hand with blogging in her later years, since the internet of things has provided her with an unmediated and immediate means of reaching her audience. It has allowed her to wander the planet whilst continuing to communicate with her audience. Writing, digital nomadism, and planetary activism struck me as central to my own path as I read Walker's interview. And as Adrienne Rich suggests: 'The way to escape such enclosures [as patriarchy, or a rigid dominant economy

---

[3] Dudley, Drew. Oct 8, 2010. TEDxToronto — 'Leading with Lollipops.' https://www.youtube.com/watch?v=hVCBrkrFrBE
[4] Tranter, Kirsten. May 10, 2014. Interview with Alice Walker. "I'm still writing in the Dirt with a Twig." *The Age Good Weekend.*

Preface

of masculinity] is to be an artist: not a woman who sings the words of men but one who composes her own song.'[5]

In the interview, Walker goes on to talk about the death of her sister with whom she was very close. But as she discloses their relationship was not without its challenges. She writes: 'Part of the issue with her and me was that her life was so painful, but it was a pain that she never learnt to reject by learning how to avoid it.'[4] Walker conveys that she was unable to elevate her sister out of a cycle of destruction. She says: 'But when she died, all hell broke loose inside. The grief ... What do you make of a life like that, where there's no consciousness, ever, about how to free yourself? I fell apart from the pain of losing her, and losing the her of her: not the mess, but the her of her that could never bloom as what she was.'[4] I experienced the loss of my brother mid-2020 in this way, insofar as I felt the acute loss of his intelligence—not the mess his life had become. In contrast to Walker's sister, my brother was able to bloom in his earlier years mostly. He had a rhapsodic personality—people were drawn to him. Still, Shambhu was ultimately unable to break loose from a cycle of self-destruction driven by substance abuse. It is important to point out that during an insurmountable number of hospitalisations, over fifty, my brother was continuously overmedicated. Psychiatric institutions in Australia used increasingly high dosages of chemical restraints on him, especially in the later years of his illness, which were torturous. He was severely abused by the so-called 'mental health' system, and he was unable to recover from this terrible harm done to him. Despite my advocacy for my brother, and especially my

---

[5] Doherty, Maggie. 2020. "The Long Awakening of Adrienne Rich." *The New Yorker*, November 23, 2020. https://www.newyorker.com/magazine/2020/11/30/the-long-awakening-of-adrienne-rich

mother's ongoing support, he was ultimately broken down. He fell into the crack irretrievably. He lost his voice.

My brother died aged forty-three, likely overdosed on sleeping pills, although the cause of his death is inconclusive. In the end his life had become too difficult—with no foreseeable solution in sight. In the end he was afraid of homelessness. His drug abuse, particularly his use of methamphetamine, had taken him beyond a psychic border, perhaps he believed from which there was no coming back. Although it is important to point out that he'd managed to stop using methamphetamine in the final months of his life. My brother's death was not heroic, but it was a tenable exit from the reality foisted on him—a pathological straight jacket. He was pathologised by the state, injected by order of the government on a monthly basis with anti-psychotic medication. My brother attempted all his life to embrace a productive life affirming non-pathological ego-loss. I think he achieved that to a large extent in his earlier years through his yoga practice. He shed his identity to mediate channels of the imaginal, like breathing, he understood the complex poetic orchestration of life. He was a wayfarer. Whilst undergoing mania he surfed waves of rhapsodic being. He never wanted to come back from those dérives into the cosmos.

When he died the illusion of separation was again dispelled for me; a kind of psychic replay of the self-help seminar. A veil was temporarily lifted. I was left an amputee longing for that lost part of me. It was a harrowing realisation, which has made its place in me in the shape of a lasting grief. Separation is an illusion. Fascism cultivates separation, it is invested in separatist identity politics rather than collectively embracing difference. Australian culture, and many other western cultures, separate the mentally divergent, place them under a negatively inflected taboo. I have witnessed Victorian psychiatric hospitals treat inpatients in abhorrent ways, specifically by imposing isolation for extended periods, and also by using chemical restraints to the point of torturous overmedication. As I drove away from visiting my brother for the last time I saw an eagle pass over a field beside the road. Perhaps a signal for me to bear witness to the reality of our interconnected lives. As I write this down I feel my writer's twig dragging in the red Australian dirt, which is a vast ancient place, and is tended by First Nations custodians who deserve their sovereignty. My family is my plan A—my good fortune. The three fates have guided me to tell my story. But this book is far more than my own story, it is a call to embrace planetary synthesis by rewriting ourselves as interconnected planetary beings, and specifically through adopting a poetic agency and mobility.

PART I

Planetary Digressions

Chapter One

The Human Situation Redux

A while back I read an article written by Louis Menard in *The New Yorker*, in which he upholds Yoko Ono as one of the first conceptual artists. He also argues that she is a utopian. I disagree. In my view Ono harnesses the power of what critical thinker Adrian Parr calls 'the emancipatory political imaginary.'[6] I'm thinking specifically of her 1964 *Grapefruit* event scores, which are not so much instructions for performances as they are for imaginary acts that might have the capacity to shift consciousness. Although Ono is now considered a key member of Fluxus, she never wanted to be incorporated into an art movement. Fluxus art was never intended for museums or galleries. It was all about de-institutionalised creativity. Surely then 'Imagine,' which Ono co-wrote with John Lennon, is an event score for imagining no separation, an instruction for revolutionary action that eclipses avant-garde pretension, as well as pop, to teach humanity how to comprehend that you are me and I am you. Lennon purportedly publicly apologised for omitting Ono off the album credits—better late than never I suppose. We can still learn a lot from what Ono and Lennon were trying to initiate. At this moment on earth we need to migrate our awareness to become more disposed

---

[6] Parr, Adrian. 2017. *Birth of a New Earth: The Radical Politics of Environmentalism.* New York: Columbia University Press. p. 171.

towards others ongoingly and pertaining to 'planetary thought,' and 'planetary feeling' as Gayatri Chakravorty Spivak eloquently informs us in *Death of a Discipline*.[7] This is our real condition—embracing planetary connectivity against the rhetoric of global apocalypse. We are planetary beings after all and we can learn to navigate this planet and interact with one another ethically—to affirmatively stray together. We are migrated ongoingly toward other humans and more-than-human worlds, and which I'd further suggest is inherently linked to an imaginal impulse, a drive to narrativise, so as to make sense of our lived experience.

But of course many First Nations peoples of the world have long understood non-hierarchical continuum, which assumes a commonality that is vital, albeit through preserving difference.[8] For instance in her article 'The Inward Migration in Apocalyptic Times', Alexis Wright author and land rights activist from the Waanyi Nation tells of an 'inward gaze' linked with ancestral knowledge, as well as with an imaginal turn, which is inseparable from the 'sacred text' of the landscape. She informs us that:

> ... OUR SYSTEM of interconnectedness is kept strong through constant and deep respect for the traditional laws associated with ancient story knowledge. We know that many of these ancient stories, passed down through the ages, have deep associations with events that occurred a very long time ago. This helps us to remember the power of the world we live in, that it can change and will go through cycles of renewal, and that new stories of the land will also be composed. This careful system of story keeping through story practices keeps the stories strong, and it helped

---

[7] Gyatri Spivak. 2003. *Death of a Discipline*. New York: Columbia University Press. p. 73.
[8] Braidotti, Rosi. 2019. *Posthuman Knowledge*. Cambridge: Polity. p. 7.

our people survive long enough to become the oldest living culture in the world. This is the Aboriginal system of enlightenment.⁹

Wright upholds First Nations custodianship of Country, evoked in song, language, ceremonies and ritual practices, and which serves to reiterate interconnectedness; a vital honouring of ancestral beings and a safeguarding of cultural knowledge. Wright also gives special credence to poets, such as Seamus Heaney, who have become mouthpieces for their own specific landscapes, or country.

So too, Donna Haraway innovatively and expansively explores our collective coherence on this complex planetary system beyond Anthropos and the Capitaloscene in her seminal book *Staying with the Trouble: Making Kin in the Chthulucene*.[10] Haraway argues that the Chthulucene is a necessary third story, an alternative narrative that might account for 'staying with the trouble' of multispecies worlding together. She issues a call to 'revolt' through deploying 'tentacular thinking,' which is embracive of our intersecting lives with other humans and the more-than-human world. Haraway writes: 'The unfinished Chthulucene must collect up the trash of the Anthropocene, the exterminism of the Capitalocene, and chipping and shredding and layering like a mad gardener, make a much hotter compost pile for still possible pasts, presents, and futures.'[11] For we are dynamically involved with one another and the present state of our planetary condition calls for radical 'multiplayer, multispecies

---

[9] Wright, Alex. 2022. "The Inward Migration in Apocalyptic Times — Alexis Wright." *Emergence Magazine*. October 26, 2022. https://emergencemagazine.org/essay/the-inward-migration-in-apocalyptic-times/

[10] Haraway, Donna. 2016. *Staying with the Trouble: Making Kin in the Chthulucene*. Durham, North Carolina: Duke University Press. p. 58.

[11] Ibid. p. 71.

thinking and action.'[11] And Haraway further links our planetary connectivity with a poetic agency.

A couple of years back, during the 2022 Rising Festival in Melbourne, I saw a contemporary dance piece called *Multitud* directed by Uruguayan choreographer Tamara Cubas, which speaks directly to Haraway's work. It was the human compost pile—the seething human mass becoming together. In Melbourne Town Hall's grand ballroom the audiences' eyes were pinned to a vast empty square at the centre of the room. Performers started to enter the stage one by one. They stood randomly spaced apart. They were not especially attractive, nor were they well dressed. They were just ordinary citizens. After a while the performers began to augment their bodies, to fall down, rise back up, hold various poses. This went on for quite a while. Bodies wandered about, forged different alliances through looks, holding them like a pact to their dissolution. Bodies continually negotiated, renegotiated different approximations and associations, which were explored, and disengaged from. All the while the soundtrack played; an edgy futuristic, industrial, discordant composition. Then bodies started randomly dropping. I thought they might be perhaps miming contagion. People randomly caught the falling figures, mercifully they were motivated to not let others smash their bodies on the ground.[12] The performers again stood up, started to rotate around the space, formed various clusters, a few disparate lone individuals passed through these clusters, contorted themselves in order to push through a confined gap. A whirlpool of bodies propelled onward until stillness was achieved at the centre. A heaving mass of bodies

---

[12] In the wake of the terrifying recent Hamas attack on civilians at a desert rave this performance takes on an extra dimension.

piled on top of one another. They suddenly erupted into laughter. A mass catharsis got underway. Then they were up again—running. The relentless pursuit. The mob turned on one particular individual, pulled her, contorted her. Demonstrated the force of a crowd to affect someone, to tear off her clothes, push and pull her. An Amber Heard.[13] Then they started screaming, ashamed, having recognised the horror that they just enacted against a sanctioned other. There were many discordant whimpers, an audible cry, a dispersion. Bodies laid down, were strewn across the performance space, they slept, exhausted, then reawakened, scurried around the space bug-like—maybe having undergone some kind of Kafkaesque transformation. The flinging and slinging of people across the space commenced—bodies ricocheted to and fro—thrown into various relations. It looked a bit like the workings of an atomic particle. Then clusters of bodies started moving around the space again. They seemed to be mutating. They started undressing, shedding, casting off the old identity to become something else. They threw off their clothes into the air. Some pulled clothes off others. Everybody wanted everybody else's stuff. Partially and fully naked bodies paraded the space. A gradual symphonic shift occurred in the music; a softening was brought about by an undertone of violin. Bodies splayed across the ground to create a human bridge, so that other bodies could climb across, be propelled along; the infinite identity of a river. Humans merged with one another to create a moving sculpture. One organism—contagious life. A happening for a planetary revolution.

---

[13] Johnny Depp vs Amber Herd trial. *ABC News*. 2022. "'The Whole Thing Has Been Such a Circus': How the Jury Reached Its Verdict in the Johnny Depp-Amber Heard Case," June 1, 2022. https://www.abc.net.au/news/2022-06-02/johnny-depp-amber-heard-verdict-explained/101117404

Surely at this moment of heightened planetary crisis we must expediently recognise that: '... we require each other in unexpected collaborations and combinations, in hot compost piles.'[14] Haraway insightfully advocates the idea of 'companion species,' which rejects 'human exceptionalism.'[15] From this we deduce that '[c]ompanion species infect each other all the time.'[16] Haraway asserts that this is as it should be insofar as '[b]odily ethical and political obligations are infectious.'[17] Contagion is in fact our *lingua franca*: it is our species and interspecies mode of communication on planet earth. Contagion is a demonstration of our viral embodied tractability of the self-becoming other ongoingly. Devastatingly humans have polluted their ecosystems to their own severe detriment, which means that we've polluted ourselves. What we do to the planet we do to ourselves—contagion has revealed this to us. The COVID-19 virus has been a big dose of reality, or indeed what Haraway terms sympoiesis.[18] It is how we approach contagion, which is a quality or influence that spreads like an ecological dialogue via the body that counts. Perhaps, the thing to do is become ethically and politically astute navigators of the embodied networks we engage with ongoingly, and in so doing promote a more affirmative multispecies cohabitation on the earth.[19]

---

[14] Haraway, Donna. 2016. *Staying with the Trouble: Making Kin in the Chthulucene*. Durham, North Carolina: Duke University Press. p. 4.
[15] Ibid. p. 13.
[16] Ibid. p. 29.
[17] Ibid. p. 29.
[18] This term is taken from Donna Haraway's *Staying with the Trouble: Making Kin in the Chthulucene* and is a '... concept that embraces intersubjectivity combined with creative arts-making.' Sympoiesis means 'making with' and infers 'becoming with.' https://www.igi-global.com/dictionary/abra/110063
[19] Haraway, Donna. 2016. *Staying with the Trouble: Making Kin in the Chthulucene*. Durham, North Carolina: Duke University Press. p. 29.

Of course, Haraway informed us back in the 90s that we are all already cyborgs. She defined the cyborg as: '...a hybrid of machine and organism, a creature of social reality as well as a creature of fiction.'[20] Haraway explored a playful iteration of cyborg as a 'socialist-feminist,' 'postmodern,' 'non-naturalist,' non-gender specific 'utopian' imagining, through which we can potentially subvert the apocalypse.[21] She opened up a meaningful space to re-think machine and organism. For the cyborg is 'ether' or 'quintessence,' which human mammals continually mediate. Haraway augured that: 'We can be responsible for machines; they do not dominate or threaten us.'[22] But, to do this we must learn to read the biopsychosocial landscape in sophisticated ways, for as she perceptively pointed out: 'The main trouble with cyborgs, of course, is that they are the illegitimate offspring of militarism and patriarchal capitalism, not to mention state socialism.'[23] And in *The Subject and Power* Michel Foucault famously identifies a multifaceted network of power, which is potentially a mechanism of exploitation and domination harnessed through the category of subjection.[24] Foucault puts into question our freedom as individuals by asking: Are we really free agents? Are we really autonomous or self-ruling selves? Or are we caught in capitalist networks of digital flows for instance? Are we asked ongoingly in end-time-capitalism to enter into the discursive production and reproduction of ourselves via social media platforms in the creation of our identities? Are we continually being expected to rewrite ourselves subjugate

---

[20] Haraway, Donna. 1991. *Simian, Cyborgs, & Women: The Reinvention of Nature.* New York: Routledge. p. 149.
[21] Ibid. p. 150.
[22] Ibid. p. 181.
[23] Ibid. p. 151.
[24] Foucault, Michel. 1982. *The Subject and Power.* Chicago: Chicago University Press. p. 781.

with respect to these endless meaning and knowledge networks, institutional and otherwise, often pertaining to various competing biopolitical interests?

In *The Lonely City: Adventures in the Art of Being Lonely* the British writer Olivia Laing describes a period of her life, in which she lived in New York. In her tiny bedsit off Time Square Laing experienced an intense loneliness, which she attempted to assuage at the time through engaging in digital forays. Her testimony of this period in her life reads as a case study of being techno-digested, which we've all experienced to some extent.

> It was like becoming a teenager again, plunging into pools of obsession, moving on, riding the rocking swells, the changing surf. Reading about hoarding or torture or true crime or the iniquities of the state; reading misspelled chatroom conversations ...
>
> ... The plunge through, the drift, the awful k-hole of recessive links, clicking deeper and deeper into the past, stumbling out into the horrors of the present ...
>
> What did I want? What was I looking for? What was I doing there, hour after hour? Contradictory things. I wanted to know what was going on. I wanted to be stimulated. I wanted to be in contact and I wanted to retain my privacy, my private space. I wanted to click and click and click until my synapses exploded, until I was flooded by superfluity. I wanted to hypnotise myself with data, with coloured pixels, to become vacant, to overwhelm any creeping anxious sense of who I actually was, to annihilate my feelings. At the same time I wanted to wake up, to be politically and

socially engaged. And then again I wanted to declare my presence, to list my interests and objections, to notify the world that I was still there, thinking with my fingers, even if I'd almost lost the art of speech. I wanted to look and I wanted to be seen, and somehow it was easier to do both via the mediating screen.[25]

Laing explores the desire to digitally plug in, to become socially and politically engaged, to gain knowledge, companionship, but also retain privacy. All the while hoping to mainline the present, hook into the zeitgeist, maybe to forget herself temporarily in the lives of others, but also to register her existence—stand up and be counted as a diversified citizen of the world. What Laing makes plain is that through her engagement with the internet of things and via various social media platforms she is demonstrating her lived experience as a networked being. She exposes the drive to continually hook into digital flows in a bid for superfluity. Albeit, whilst simultaneously increasingly subject to so-called 'civilisation ordering' vectors of power and knowledge, which can be extremely alienating. These technological accelerations that we all endlessly navigate are complex. They can also be exhausting—drain us of vitality.

Although I certainly wouldn't want to diminish anyone's capacity to read the digital landscape in critically astute ways, it would be remiss of me not to point out that we are in part indoctrinated by messages and meanings through algorithmic marketing configurations that designate our many fluid mediations. We are subject to endless data flows—contaminated by them. We face the threat of oversaturation from social media platforms like TikTok, which partially puts

---

[25] Laing, Olivia. 2016. *The Lonely City: Adventures in the Art of Being Lonely*. Edinburgh: Canongate. pp. 219-220.

us under surveillance. But whilst TikTok encourages us towards ongoingly producing and reproducing our identity in relation to capitalist and Anthropocentric flows, it also offers us a digital framework to convey our embodied sensorial connectedness on a planetary scale. A 'media-nature-culture continuum' situates humans in relation to 'components of larger ensembles,' which has the potential to facilitate our collective liberation *if* we manage to create an affirmative and ethical cartography.[26] Perhaps the most pressing dilemma that we are now facing is how to liberate ourselves from our autobiographies (that we've been trained into through the patriarchal nuclear family saga, as well as through various institutions and state run organisations that have undoubtedly shaped and made us who we are, and continue to primarily in contemporary society by way of the internet of things, most notably through social media networks). We need to give ourselves a bit of narrative therapy—to actively stray—become something more planetary. We can embrace this someone who is migrated, merging, perpetually becoming a planetary player. We are morphological beings after all. We are not separate. We are continually becoming with other beings, with social and environmental ecologies, and with digital flows alike.

Oscar Wilde famously said: 'Just be yourself, everybody else is taken,' but the reality for most people is that they're indoctrinated by work, by plugging into endless digital flows that sap vitality, by mind-numbing substances, by a plethora of social commitments, and so on. And yet, sometimes we refreshingly encounter an affirmative digital exploration of our shared identity. Musician and writer Nick Cave explains in one memorable *Red Hand Files* blog post that he

---

[26] Braidotti, Rosi. 2019. *Posthuman Knowledge*. Cambridge: Polity. p. 113.

aims to provide a much-needed listening to people, which I'd say exemplifies the great hope of the planetary turn. His project puts me in mind of Pablo Neruda's *The Book of Questions*, which seeks to respond to the complexity of human existence. Cave writes in post #166:

> This practice of reading the questions is, in its way, a form of prayer, because prayer is primarily about listening. It allows the necessary space to experience the subtle intimations of the divine, and to acknowledge God's divine need — what is required of us. In the questions that come into The Red Hand Files I feel this same want echoed in my own need, the speaking of one's pain into the pain of another, the toing and froing of our mutual desire for simple affirmation.[27]

In fact, it seems as though Cave has found a divinity in his fan base or blog reading audience, which is precious. We must give this listening to ourselves—affirm ourselves to ourselves in all of our beauty and distress. And, we must also give this listening to others. At best digital forums can allow such a transfer—a life affirming kinship. Cave's project is affirmative because it addresses, or seeks to rectify, this lack of selfcare and care for others, which is insidiously present in contemporary society. The need to listen to the self, to attend to one's own grief by reaching out to others, and in so doing opening a portal, providing an access point—is a valuable freedom. Fascism is about cultivating the illusion of separation, but life is contagious. Life is viral. We are part of a living network of

---

[27] Cave, Nick. 2021. "Happy Red Hand File Anniversary! Three Years! How Time Flies When You Are Answering Multiple Questions At ..." The Red Hand Files. September 15, 2021. https://www.theredhandfiles.com/happy-anniversary-three-years/

diverse organisms—that's the reality. And we must *involve* ourselves creatively and imaginatively with one another to evolve as a species.

Feminist theorist Rosi Braidotti argues that humans have the opportunity to reinvent themselves if they embrace the 'experimental energy' characteristic of this pivotal location in the human situation, sandwiched between two forms of acceleration: 1). The Fourth Industrial Revolution, which '...involves the convergence of advanced technologies such as robotics, artificial intelligence, nanotechnologies, biotechnology and the Internet of Things' bringing about the intersection of 'digital, physical and biological boundaries.'[28] And 2). The sixth extinction, which 'refers to the dying out of species during the present genealogical era as the result of human activity.'[29] 'Man' and 'Anthropos' are perhaps not a valid point of reference, from which to build sustainable futures.[30] In fact, 'Bios,' which 'refers to life of humans organized in society' as 'regulated by sovereign powers and rules' is potentially not a tenable heterogeneous landscape.[31] On the other hand 'Zoe' is posited by Braidotti (prefaced on the work of Giorgio Agamben) as 'life of all beings,' which relocates humans across a variegation of non-hierarchical 'social and environmental ecologies.'[32] For we are always already mediated through other things and states; part of a

---

[28] Braidotti, Rosi. 2019. *Posthuman Knowledge*. Cambridge: Polity. p. 2.
[29] Ibid. p. 2.
[30] Ibid. p. 8.
[31] Ibid. p. 10.
[32] Ibid. pp. 3-10. Women must remain alert to any attempts to eliminate their embodied difference, which Agamben does through his neglect to incorporate a woman's body into his theoretical framework of 'bare life.' Women remain a threshold body—at the removal of political and cultural life.

Agamben, Giorgio. (1995) 1998. *HomoSacer: Sovereign Power and Bare Life*. Translated by Daniel Heller-Roazen. Stanford, California: Stanford University Press. https://www.thing.net/~rdom/ucsd/biopolitics/HomoSacer.pdf

vast web of life. But, rather than describe this predicament as our posthuman situation Haraway prefers the term 'companion species' to describe this ongoing planetary migration that we undergo when we relate to others by allowing difference to proliferate, and which she points out is an inherently 'sympoetic' process, or 'worlding-with, in company,' as I've already stated.[33] The long and the short of it is that we humans are mammalian beings leaning into each other and everything else continuously—poetically.

And in addition to many First peoples of the world, and philosophers, who have long understood the planetary experience in terms of embodied network, poets have also nurtured this antithetical knowledge. In fact, we can learn a lot by inhabiting the position of the poet. We can learn to become 'nothing but a fine nerve meter' as French poet Antonin Artaud did.[34] For the poet continuously crosses borders—navigates a seamless web of convergences. They demonstrate exceeding subjection ongoingly. The poet 'raids the inarticulate' as T.S Eliot suggested—operates at planetary nexus.[35] A poet deals in contagion. Contagion is a fluid embodied planetary traversal. Poetry, and perhaps poetic prose even more so is the most adequate not-discourse but rather writing-of-rift to adequately capture our contagious reality at the planetary turn.

---

[33] Haraway, Donna. 2016. *Staying with the Trouble: Making Kin in the Chthulucene.* Durham, North Carolina: Duke University Press. p. 58.

[34] Artaud, Antonin, and Susan Sontag. 1988. *Antonin Artaud, Selected Writings.* Berkeley: University Of California Press. p. 36. This term comes from Antonin Artaud's *The Nerve Meter* poetry collection.

[35] Eliot. T.S. 1943. 'Four Quartets.' https://poetryarchive.org/poem/four-quartets-extract/

In Virginia Woolf's essay 'The Narrow Bridge of Art' she argues that poetry when liberated from formal constraints accounts far more accurately for the full gamut of the human experience.

> For the course of poetry has always been overwhelmingly on the side of beauty. She has always insisted on certain rights, such as rhyme, metre, poetic diction. She has never been used for the common purpose of life. Prose has taken all the dirty work on her own shoulders; has answered letters, paid bills, written articles, made speeches, served the needs of businessmen, shopkeepers, lawyers, soldiers, peasants.[36]

When poetry is freed from not just formal constraints, but also content constraints, to marry prose, it can better convey the waves of rhapsodies, 'ideas, dreams and imagination' that humans encounter in relation to the outside world, which are fundamental to who we are, taking in our 'complexities,' our incongruities and contrasts towards all queer morphologies.[37] And in fact, poetic prose is a styling, rather than a formal category like prose poetry is. As Nikki Santilli explains in *Such Rare Citings: The Prose Poem in English Literature* (2002):

> It is precisely this style that cannot be contained inside the severe parameters of the prose poem. Prose enacts a continuum, a process that moves the reader and itself inexorably, onward (not necessarily forward). Poetic prose facilitates this movement by characteristically florid verbosity. The style of

---

[36] Woolf, Virginia. (1927) 1958. 'The Narrow Bridge of Art' collected in *Granite and Rainbow: Essays by Virginia Woolf.* New York: Harcourt, Brace and Company. pp. 11-23. Quote taken from p. 17.
[37] Ibid. pp. 19-20.

the prose poem, on the other hand, is constrained by a relatively unnatural brevity.[38]

However, I have to take issue with Santilli's charge of 'florid verbosity', poetic prose under Woolf's orchestration, and within the modernist novel framework, is an experiment in more accurately conveying the dramatic realities of living.[39] She assigns poetic prose the task of accounting for the human situation of not being separate, but rather of being continuously migrated into everything all the time. Woolf was profoundly inspired by the modernist free verse stylings of Walt Whitman, albeit diversified towards a more prosaic writing style that she achieved most fully in *The Waves* to my mind.

The human tendency toward trying to contain ourselves, putting up walls, separating ourselves from one another in houses and apartments with locks, using bolts and alarm systems, is a ruse, argues Woolf in her essay. We simply can't pull off the charade. Wires and cables connect each home, and in contemporary society digital flows are invisible fonts on the air that encode our lives, intertwine them. Although we are often 'secret' and 'suspicious' animals who keep up a show of politeness, measured, 'tolerant' and 'self-contained' behaviour for the most part (that is unless we're engaging in waring), we are actually seeping out, contaminating each other all the time with thoughts, ideas, bacteria, viruses and emotional ruminations. Woolf gives the example of the way mind wandering takes over when out for a walk, seemingly disparate things are juxtaposed,

---

[38] Santilli, Nikki. 2002. *Such Rare Citings: The Prose Poem in English Literature*. New Jersey: Fairleigh Dickinson University Press.

[39] Woolf, Virginia. (1927) 1958. 'The Narrow Bridge of Art' collected in *Granite and Rainbow: Essays by Virginia Woolf*. New York: Harcourt, Brace and Company. pp. 11-23. Quote taken from. p. 20.

knitted together, and in fact walking becomes central, or pivotal to her modernist experiment. Everything is commingled, imaginal meanderings, feelings, thresholds of pleasure and pain enter the mind indiscriminately with respect to observations in the outside world. 'In the human mind beauty is accompanied not by its shadow but by its opposite ...'[40] And so, Woolf hopes to account for this orchestration of life on the street, the situation of humans merging together, accessed by way of walking, and demonstrated in poetic prose. Woolf advocates deploying poetic prose to better convey variances, as well as the commonalities, of being human. She augurs that this 'new' mode of writing will be dramatic, produce emotional effects, 'draw blood' in the reader.[41]

It is Woolf's project to demonstrate the way that human perception plays out as a multiplicity of highly relational aptitudes, an ongoing entering into 'subtle labyrinths,' like when we are moved by 'the power of music, the stimulus of sight, the effect on us of the shape of trees or the play of color, the emotions bred in us by crowds, the obscure terrors and hatreds which come so irrationally in certain places from certain people, the delight of movement, the intoxication of wine.'[42] In fact, a poet continuously opens to these ongoing heightenings—to multitudinous currents. American poet A.R. Ammons refers to this as 'the becoming thought' in his poem 'Corson's Inlet.' He writes of heading out for a walk to Corson's Inlet and of being liberated by his engagement with the landscape—'released from forms.' He relays:

---

[40] Ibid. p. 16
[41] Ibid. p. 22.
[42] Ibid. p. 23.

> I allow myself eddies of meaning:
> yield to a direction of significance
> running
> like a stream through the geography of my work:
> ... I have reached no conclusions, have erected no boundaries,
> shutting out and shutting in, separating inside
>> from outside: I have
>> drawn no lines:
>> as
> manifold events of sand
> change the dune's shape that will not be the same shape
> tomorrow,
> so I am willing to go along, to accept
> the becoming
> thought, to stake off no beginnings or ends, establish
>> no walls ...[43]

Following Ammon, and I'd argue directly writing under his influence, American poet Jorie Graham augurs this relational principle in her poem 'Some Notes on the Reality of the Self' with respect to a riverscape. She writes:

> Watching the river ...
> ... The long brown throat of it sucking up from some faraway melt ...
> ... Crocus
> appear in the grassy dark leaves. Many
> earth gases, rot gases.
> I take them in, breath at a time, I put my

---

[43] Ammons. A.R. 1988. 'Corson's Inlet' can be read in full on *The Poetry Foundation* website. https://www.poetryfoundation.org/poems/43073/corsons-inlet

> breath back out
> onto the scented immaterial ...[44]

Graham mediates the materiality of her experience with the immaterial reality. Graham tells the *Paris Review*: 'I'd say poetry wants to be contagious, to be a contagion ...' And this too is what Woolf elaborates so beguilingly in *The Waves* ahead of both Ammons and Graham, albeit with the intention of liberating poetry from its formal constraints more so towards prose stylings; deploying stream of consciousness technique. We can learn a lot from Woolf who vies for poetic drama as a cure for the human ailment, a catharsis from the human predicament of enforcing separation—of putting up walls. Time to daydream, to mind wander, to rhapsodise towards another—to consider our planetary kinship.

At this moment on earth we must urgently build bridges between the digital, the vast social and environmental variety of life including the animal, the plant, the mineral, the bacteria, the human, the actual, or perceived reality and the imaginal, and so on, towards a new planetary world view which errs on the side of poetry, or what Haraway terms sympoiesis. Perhaps more accurately we must begin to recognise that these links have always been there, albeit often ignored. Aldous Huxley wrote back in the 1950s in *The Human Situation* about the need for 'a man of letters' to build bridges between disciplines, specifically between science and art. But, it is much broader than that. He calls for the need for a language that can adequately account for 'the human situation.' Huxley draws on

---

[44] Graham, Jorie. 1992. "'Notes on the Reality of the Self,' by Jorie Graham." The New Yorker. August 17, 1992. https://www.newyorker.com/magazine/1992/08/24/jorie-graham-poem-notes-on-the-reality-of-the-self.

Shakespeare to uncover an integrated point of view and of course completely overlooks Woolf. He simply cannot countenance a woman as arbiter of 'a literary, artistic vocabulary' that encompasses: '... the world of abstractions and concepts, the world of immediate experience and objective observation, and the world of spiritual insight—which must, in any integrated point of view, be brought together.'[45]

As I've already mentioned, Woolf works with poetic prose within the frame of the modernist novel most successfully in my view in *The Waves*, which I undertake a close reading of in this book. In fact, there are many artistic inheritors of Woolf's experiment in *The Waves* who articulate the 'married state' of existence in highly poetical writing, and some of whom I'll survey.[46] Woolf accounts for the weave of the inner and the outer, the ceaseless involutions and evolutions that we undergo as humans, and which poetic writing especially taps into and registers (also touching on broader political and spiritual insights). Interestingly, Huxley defines his three-poled personal essay model along these lines. And perhaps even through reading such explorations in poetic prose we can achieve this heightened awareness too, become enlivened, more connected. We have all, at some point, read a book that induced a profound kinship, such that we felt migrated.

In *The Human Situation* Huxley asks some prescient questions in relation to the need for a mode of writing that can adequately account for the human situation as highly relational. He asks: 'What is our relationship to the planet? What are we doing with the world

---

[45] Huxley, Aldous. (1959) 1989. *The Human Situation*. London: Grafton Books. p. 13.
[46] Ibid. p. 17.

on which we are living and how are we treating it? How is it likely to treat us if we go on treating it as we are now?'[47] Huxley muses over the 'geological force' of *man* to destroy the earth at such a rapid rate through deforestation, through the destruction of soil grade, or erosion, as a consequence of agricultural practices, through extinction of species by way of overpopulation. He proffers that the main problem is the way we have perceived our relationality to the planet—by insisting on this false notion that we are somehow separate. Huxley points out that the idea of *man* as apart from 'nature' is a relatively new concept. He echoes that First Nations cultures have always considered themselves imbedded in the 'natural world,' and which Huxley finds evidence for in the concept of totemism, fertility rites that draw parallels between human sexual cycles and the ecosphere, and the cosmos more broadly, as well as in 'polytheism and the divineness of natural objects.'[48] He warned in the late 1950s that: 'We have to treat the planet as though it were a living organism, with all the love and care and understanding which any living organism deserves. If we do not treat it in this way, then we shall destroy the world on which we live, and this destroyed world will in turn destroy us.'[49] Huxley invokes Darwin's 'Origin of the Species' as a counter-revolutionary text to the predominant Judeo-Christian doctrine supporting the patriarchal capitalist imperative. But I'm far more interested in a strain of neo-Darwinian studies in which the volume is turned right down on 'natural selection,' and conversely turned right up on interspecies relationality and communication.

---

[47] Ibid. p. 20.
[48] Ibid. p. 38.
[49] Ibid. p. 37.

The Human Situation Redux

In *Staying with the Trouble* Haraway draws on a paper titled 'Involutionary Momentum' written by Carla Hustak and Natasha Myers, in which they bring Darwin under critical review, specifically pertaining to the sexual life of bees and orchids. Hustack and Myers suggest that: '… "involution" powers the "evolution" of living and dying on earth. Rolling inward enables rolling outward; the shape of life's motion traces a hyperbolic space, swooping and fluting like the folds of a frilled lettuce, coral reef, or a bit of crocheting.'[50] Hustak and Myers paper on involution is critical because it exposes how in neo-Darwinian biology studies: 'The stories of mutation, adaption, and natural selection are not silenced; but they are not turned up so loud as to deafen scientists, as if the evidence demanded it, when increasingly something more complex is audible in research across fields.'[51] Hustak and Myers attest to species involvement and augmentation on planet earth. They call attention to the need to amplify our 'ecological relationality' and highlight the implications of our responsibility to upholding 'species difference' pertaining to 'affect, entanglement, and rupture.'[52] Haraway adds: 'To be an animal is to become-with bacteria (and, no doubt, viruses and many other sorts of critters; a basic aspect of sympoiesis is its expandable set of players).'[53] Humans must necessarily undergo these involutions in order to evolve as a species.[54]

---

[50] Hustak and Myers are cited by Haraway, Donna. 2016. *Staying with the Trouble: Making Kin in the Chthulucene*. Durham, North Carolina: Duke University Press. p. 68.
[51] Ibid. pp. 68-9.
[52] Ibid. p. 68.
[53] Haraway, Donna. 2016. *Staying with the Trouble: Making Kin in the Chthulucene*. Durham, North Carolina: Duke University Press. p. 65.
[54] Ibid. p. 71.

For what else is life but a vast *poetic* orchestration? Perhaps we need to learn to re-write ourselves—poetically—in order to better conceive of what it is to be a planetary relational human. Increasingly, our digitally mediated world makes writers of all of us to some extent, whether it's texting our friends or updating a digital post. As Peters argues in *The Marvellous Clouds: Toward a Philosophy of Elemental Media*:

> Writing provides an excellent way to consider our embedment in matter and media. Speech enables action, the changing of the political world, but writing enables work, the changing of the physical world. Literate humans are amphibians who live both in the fluid of speech and, more rarely, the terra firma of writing ...[55]

It does often seem that we are constantly reporting our ongoing synthesis with a seemingly endless number of people, places and phenomena. As Gilles Deleuze informs us in his essay 'Literature and Life': 'Writing is a question of becoming, always incomplete, always in the midst of being formed, and goes beyond the matter of any liveable or lived experience. It is a process, that is, a passage of life that traverses both the liveable and the lived. Writing is inseparable from becoming: in writing, one becomes-woman, becomes-animal or vegetable, becomes molecular to the point of becoming imperceptible.'[56] Like Woolf, Deleuze privileges the writer as more capable of embracing these ongoing synthesis we encounter as part

---

[55] John Durham Peters. 2015. *The Marvelous Clouds : Toward a Philosophy of Elemental Media*. Chicago ; London: The University Of Chicago Press. p. 263.
[56] Deleuze, Gilles. (1993) 1998. *Essays Critical and Clinical*. Translated by Daniel W. Smith and Michael A. Grew. London: Verso. p. 1.

of living planetary. And I'd argue that the poet rides the pinnacle of these strange copulations.

In 'Someone is Writing a Poem' American poet Adrienne Rich argues that poetry is 'rift,' or a 'lapse,' which she aligns with language and voice, albeit at the remove from the 'commodity fetishism' of capitalism and its technologies of representation.[57] In Rich's view, poetry is preverbal, initiating with the nervous system of the poet, and thereafter brought to language through the body, registered in the material stuff of words and their electric charges; 'a force field,' which gets arranged in the theatre of a poem. A poem has life, which cannot be separated from the body of the poet, although poetry tries to reach further, to overcome its own limitations. Poetry thus becomes a special or privileged space of registering differences—of breaking silences. It is not a spectator sport, it's an ongoing migration undertaken by the poet from the inside to the outside, and vice versa, an evisceration of such borders even, and which resonates in an assemblage of words on the page. There can be no faking it, a poet has to access registers within themselves or the poem doesn't land at the foot of another. It has to come from this deep sounding, this well of the self, albeit which is drained away to other pools, other resonances. Someone reading a poem goes to it to 'receive the experience of the *not me*, enter a field of vision we could not otherwise apprehend.'[58] In fact, a poet makes a cartography of becoming something else for everyone. Nerve meter poetry attempts to bring about such a metamorphosis. When married with prose

---

[57] Adrienne Rich. 2010. "Someone Is Writing a Poem by Adrienne Rich." Poetry Foundation. May 12, 2010. https://www.poetryfoundation.org/articles/69530/someone-is-writing-a-poem
[58] Ibid.

perhaps poetry more flexibly attends to movement, digression, and synthesis.

Even as I write this down I'm plugged in—I'm sitting on a chair in my back garden typing on my laptop as a butterfly touches my skin, momentarily perches atop my nose, flitters away to trace the sunlight. It declares a pathway through ritual movement. It dances on lobes of light. Its hymnal acuity awakens other laws within me. But, I am not just me. I am intermingled with those particles of light in the ether, with encoded language being produced in, and around me through digital flows. I am traversed, cached, sent into space, returned perpetually. I am turned into a writing machine by way of digital flows, but I'm not just that, I'm more than that—I'm a planetary player. And, I'm also a poet—full disclosure. I am entrained to the paths of flight of White Cabbage Butterflies, *Pieris Rapae*, introduced species, laying larvae that feed on the cabbages, cauliflower, broccoli, radishes and rocket in my vegetable garden. As I type they burst into metamorphic flight in vast numbers around me, a cloche of post-larval cerebration, an expansive cloud of terminal transformation. Their becoming, my becoming, is thick in the air. I am being stripped of my many limitations. My new self has the veins showing. I'm all paper-thin wings. I'm not tougher as I age, but rather I'm becoming *more* a fine nerve meter. We are told ongoingly in end-time-capitalism to become more resilient, to toughen up, and which serves a hierarchy species imperative (the school of hard knocks and which takes the heat off institutions to register and respond to difference), but in fact what's urgently required is an enhanced sensitivity. This exposure of my involutions to the outside is what's required. I no longer have the will to rail against metamorphosis. I can feel it overtake me, burning away the ontological dross, delivering everything animated, enlivened. The White Cabbage Butterflies side swipe me in flight, prop on my hand, envelope every pedestrian thought, turn them nodal. I am, we are, constantly navigating a multitude of convergences. We are continually commingling, getting tangled up in one another's lives. We must re-write ourselves planetary—along poetic fault lines. We need to recognise that we are part of a vast planetary system. The reality is contagious.

Chapter Two

Like Vodou; Towards a Dissident Poetics

I used to think that the world was doing it to me and the world owed me something, and that either the conservatives or the socialists or the fascists or the communists or the Christians or the Jews were doing something to me. And when you're a teeny-bopper, that's what you think. But I'm 40 now, and I don't think that anymore, because I found out it doesn't fucking work! The thing goes on anyway, and all you're doing is jacking off, screaming about what your mommy and your daddy did. . . But one has to go through that. For the people who even bother to go through that — most assholes just accept what it is anyway and get on with it, right? — but for the few of us who did question what was going on . . . well, I've found out for me personally — not for the whole world — that I am responsible for me, as well as for them. I am part of them. There's no separation: We're all one, so in that respect I look at it all and think, "Ah, I have to deal with me again in that way. What is real? What is the illusion I'm living or not living?" And I have to deal with it every day. The layers of the onion.

John Lennon.[59]

---

[59] Cott, Jonathan. 2010. "John Lennon: The Last Interview." Rolling Stone. December 23, 2010. https://www.rollingstone.com/feature/john-lennon-the-last-interview-179443/

In her eloquent introduction to French poet Antonin Artaud's collected works Susan Sontag writes: 'Artaud is someone who has made a spiritual trip for us—a shaman. It would be presumptuous to reduce the geography of Artaud's trip to what can be colonized. Its authority lies in the parts that yield nothing for the reader except intense discomfort of the imagination.'[60] Sontag goes on to pronounce that Artaud 'failed.' Perhaps she means that he didn't successfully deliver to us a body of complete works, an oeuvre, but rather a diadem of fragments. For 'What he bequeathed was not achieved works of art but a singular presence, a poetics, an aesthetics of thought, a theology of culture, a phenomenology of suffering.'[61] Artaud demonstrated poet as seer, but with reference to his suffering above all else, a 'microstructure of mental pain,' and pertaining to his contempt for literature.[62] In *The Umbilicus of Limbo*, Artaud informs us that:

> Man must get rid of the Mind, just as we must get rid of literature. I say that the Mind and life communicate on all levels. I would like to write a book which could drive men mad, which would be like an open door leading them where they would never have consented to go, in short, a door that opens onto reality.[63]

To this end he undertakes a spiritual journey to the depths, an underworld of sorts, to retrieve an alternative perspective on human experience for all of us, which is aligned with a wild foray in language—a dissident poetics. In *The Poem of St Francis of Assisi*,

---

[60] Artaud, Antonin, and Susan Sontag. 1988. *Antonin Artaud, Selected Writings*. Berkeley: University Of California Press. p. lxiii.
[61] Ibid. p.xx
[62] Ibid. xxi
[63] Ibid. p. 59

Artaud writes of the saint's path, albeit which we might speculate also pertains to his own story: 'I am he who can dissolve the terror of being a man and going among the dead.'[64] In *The Nerve Meter* Artaud chants 'I am a total abyss.'[65] What can we learn from all of this?

Artaud's project is to remake himself beyond the confines of singularity, which he documents poetically, at times harrowingly. He departs for the 'risky country,' crosses the border, takes us into a psychic terrain of ecological mutations. In his poem *Verlaine Drink's* Artaud weaves a kind of torpor wisdom of man's imperfection, but with a lilt of optimism threaded through: 'As if a spider were weaving her web with the filaments of discovered souls.'[66] And so, he journeys to the *Black Garden*, the abyss 'pounded by the sea.' Where dark flowers bequeath the '[i]llumination of a capsized sun.'[67] Then he wanders back to the world, thoughts flowering, having survived. He courageously tells us: 'What you mistook for my works were merely the waste products of myself, those scrapings of the soul that normal man does not welcome.'[68] I'm interested in these waste scrapings of a soul, the anomalous psychic matter of the human creature, the excess, albeit which is supported by a material structure, because it offers a pathway to stray from normative expectations and concepts societally. Artaud reminds me that I don't have to continue to perform my subjectivity based on a reductive hierarchical species imperative, run globally through the machinations of end-time-capitalism. My project as a human is definitely *not* to become binary opposite of a

---

[64] Ibid. p. 5
[65] Ibid. p. 80
[66] Ibid. p. 3
[67] Ibid. p. 5.
[68] Ibid. p. 83.

universal hu*man* subject in replication. I'd rather mobilise my many poetic morphologies in excess of dominant knowledge and meaning frameworks. 'Virginia Woolf ... made all her life and work a passage, a becoming, all kinds of becomings between ages, sexes, elements, and kingdoms ...'[69] She writes of the self as a 'threshold,' a doorway, which we must pass—into another plausible reality.[70]

Woolf is reported to have had bipolar disorder, historically termed manic depression, just like my brother. I do not want to idealise madness, but rather argue that people like Woolf, like my brother, like Artaud, show us how to avoid becoming fascist by demonstrating that there is no other choice but to *undergo* metamorphosis ongoingly. For we must become something else, which necessarily passes through a testimonial of creatureliness; some kind of re-wombing *not* process, but rather revelation. 'Don't be stupid, don't be dumb vagina's where you're really from' Pussy Riot told us.[71] I urge you now—descend the ladder—enter the womb-like abyss that you are. Get reborn as something else as Artaud suggested. And some women also need to undergo non-pathological ego-loss in order to get reborn beyond universal hu*man* subject replicant. Although many women are already *not that* and are lying underneath the seam, in the crack, diffuse (keeping company with the fellow anomalous), waiting for a moment to sing and be heard. I petition them to return—to sing their becomings Woolfian—at the helm of unindoctrinated knowledge.

---

[69] Deleuze, Gilles and Guattari, Félix. (1980) 1987. *A Thousand Plateaus: Capitalism and Schizophrenia*. Translated and with a foreword by Brian Massumi. Minneapolis: Minnesota Press. p. 252.
[70] Ibid. p. 249.
[71] Pussy Riot. n.d. "Pussy Riot - Straight Outta Vagina (Feat. Desi Mo & Leikeli47). Official Music Video." YouTube. https://www.youtube.com/watch?v=Bp-KeVBNz0A

In my view, Woolf writes closer to musicality—a dissident poetics as Artaud does. In *The Waves* Woolf portrays the lives of six children: Bernard, Susan, Rhoda, Neville, Jinny, and Louis. She charts their augmentation to adulthood by way of a succession of poetic dialogues, through which she seeks to document their involvement with one another, as well as with everything else that they engage with. Woolf writes in her diary, January 7th, 1931, of her desire to '... make prose more — yes I swear — as prose has never moved before; from the chuckle, the babble to the rhapsody.' Her extraordinary tractability in *The Waves* is to demonstrate what is apart from the law of the institution and the discourse that underpins it. As a child Louis sits in the classroom ruminating on what he knows—the fibres of his being entwined in the earth. A radically different kind of schooling. Prior to entering the classroom Louis experiences a profound connectivity with the environmental ecological world.

> I am alone. They have gone into the house for breakfast, and I am left standing by the wall among the flowers. It is very early, before lessons. Flower after flower is speckled on the depths of green. The petals are harlequins. Stalks rise from the black hollows beneath. The flowers swim like fish made of light upon the dark, green waters. I hold a stalk in my hand. I am the stalk. My roots go down to the depths of the world, through earth dry with brick, and damp earth, through veins of lead and silver. I am all fibre. All tremors shake me, and the weight of the earth is pressed to my ribs. Up here my eyes are green leaves, unseeing. I am a boy in grey flannels with a belt fastened by a brass snake up here ...

> ... I am green as a yew tree in the shade of the hedge. My hair is made of leaves. I am rooted to the middle of the earth. My body is a stalk. I press the stalk. A drop oozes from the hole at the mouth and slowly, thickly, grows larger and larger.

> Now something pink passes the eyehole. Now an eye-beam is slid through the chink. Its beam strikes me. I am a boy in a grey flannel suit.[72]

Woolf's poetical writing is closer to the phantasmagorical, to a rebellious flow of speech, albeit aligned with our material beings, and which has the potential to liberate us from the confines of a reductive framework of enclosed and rigid selfhood. She deftly describes in richly sensate language the orchestrations of humans in ceaseless divergent exchange with other humans, animals and various environmental ecological networks.

She petitions us to listen for 'the murmur of the waves in the air.'[73] To return to the wood as children do—an 'unsubstantial territory'. When the children are called into the classroom for the days 'lessons' they are again imposed on by institutional learning. But Louis refuses to conjugate the verb when he can feel his roots like fibres 'round and round about the world.'[74] And so, Woolf reveals a child's imaginal forays as a more tenable learning. She encourages us to re-map our coordinates beyond prescribed ontological frameworks, such as those imposed by institutional education. We share indisputable links with other humans, nonhuman animal species, ecosystems, technology and matter. We are planetary beings becoming everything all the time—that's the reality. Poets and artists demonstrate this, or perhaps more accurately they undergo this learning. And as such, their artworks and writings are testimonies of such planetary mutation.

---

[72] Ibid. p. 12.
[73] Ibid. p. 12.
[74] Ibid. p. 13.

Nothing But a Fine Nerve Meter

I have encountered more than a few of these luminaries on my travels. Avant-garde American filmmaker Stan Brakhage undertakes a journey to the transformative abyss for his audience much like Artaud and Woolf. In my mid-twenties whilst completing my honours thesis, I became intrigued by Brakhage's cinematic poetics. He proffers the notion that film can act as a clairvoyant witness of our many deaths and our perpetual rebirths—a continual approach to life from imaginal realms. Brakhage deals in poetic celluloid flows. In his manifesto text *Metaphors on Vision* he writes: 'Imagine an eye unruled by man-made laws of perspective, an eye unprejudiced by compositional logic, an eye which does not respond to the name of everything but which must know each object encountered in life through an adventure in perception.'[75] He writes about appropriating 'the camera eye' for the expressed purpose of distorting 'classical composition' in his work.[76] It is undoubtedly under the influence of American avant-garde filmmaker Maya Deren that Brakhage utilises his tool bag of cinematic techniques, together with his editing practice of splicing contrasting images to craft a poetic rhythmic structure. Although in my view, Brakhage even more successfully adopts Deren's imagist mode of filmmaking to poetically forge an alternative perspective on human experience.

---

[75] Brakhage, Stan. 1963. *Metaphors on Vision*. U.S.A: Film Culture Inc. p. 17.
[76] Ibid. p. 18.
In his text Film at *Wit's End* Brakhage cites Maya Deren as a major cinematic influence. In his text *Metaphors on Vision* Brakhage discusses his methodology in *Dog Star Man* by theorising the idea of the 'camera eye' and his arsenal of impressionistic visual effects adopted to subvert classical composition.

Like Vodou; Towards a Dissident Poetics

There's this wacky story worth telling, albeit briefly. Apparently Brakhage went to New York sometime in 1959, just prior to the initial filming of his epic *Dog Star Man* (although the film was not completed until 1964). He stayed with Deren in her Greenwich Village apartment for several months. Deren was heavily involved in Vodou ritual and held many ceremonies at her home. During Brakhage's stay with Deren two pivotal events took place. He infers in the film about Deren's life titled *In the Mirror of Deren* (2002) that the events had a major impact on his health.[77] It seems that both occurrences inform his development as a film maker, directly influencing the cinematic technique by which he constructs *Dog Star Man*, and other subsequent works. Deren was asked to be in charge of Vodou wedding rituals at the wedding ceremony of her Haitian dancer friend Jeffrey Holder and requested that Brakhage take photographs at the event. As Brakhage tells it in his book *Film at Wits End*, the Broadway people hosting the event disrespected Deren on the day of the wedding by stopping her from putting up all of the necessary Vodou ritual objects in the room, and this upset her. She became possessed by the God Loco in the kitchen of the house. The possession was so powerful that she lifted a fridge and threw it to the other side of the room. Holder quickly ran into the kitchen to put a protection around Deren and ushered her upstairs, together with other friends at the ceremony, into a private room.

After Deren had calmed down somewhat she summoned Brakhage and spoke to him, still under the influence of the God Loco. Brakhage had witnessed the fridge throwing and the subsequent distortion of

---

[77] The documentary *In the Mirror of Maya Deren* is a film about filmmaker Maya Deren (1917-1961).
Kudláček, Martina, dir. 2002. *In the Mirror of Deren*.

her character and voice during the possession. He was frightened to enter the room. He comments:

> This is the power of Haitian Voodoun: that the voice, the manner, the whole person becomes so different, that you almost see the god that's in possession. At the end of this blood-chilling chant, I was informed that I had been blessed by Papa-Loco for having given homage in my art to the Haitian Voodoun ritual and ritual wedding objects.[78]

There is another vital aspect to the Loco blessing. In the documentary *In the Mirror of Deren* (2002) Brakhage tells the story of Deren putting a curse on him for being late to help her prepare some mail outs, which exposes an extreme aspect of her temperament that was undeniably fierce. Brakhage goes on to comment that he subsequently got very sick and the only way that he survived the curse in his view, and according to a friend well-schooled in Vodou, was because he had previously been blessed by Papa Loco through the medium of Deren. All of this had an impact on Brakhage and his filmmaking practice, which unravels in both *Sirius Remembered* (1959) and *Dog Star Man* (1964).

In his book *Metaphors on Vision*, Brakhage tells how he repeatedly visited his deceased dog's decaying body in the woods and filmed it for *Sirius Remembered*, a film he made prior to *Dog Star Man*. He discusses how the intensive filming of the corpse of the dog effectively undermined his abstract notions of death. He views himself as entering into the 'animal parts' and ascribing that creaturely part of himself. It seems to be Brakhage's intention to get inside, or indeed

---

[78] Brakhage, Stan. 1989. *Film at Witsend*. London: Polygon. pp. 91-112.

within a primal attribute of man, by which he renders the instinctual life visible.[79] Following on from this macabre foray, in *Dog Star Man* Brakhage continues to work through the curse, attempts to cast it off. He documents his journey to the abyss to transform himself and re-emerge renewed. He makes a spiritual journey to retrieve something vital—an alternative poetic perspective on human animal convergence.

I think he achieves this most filmic exposition of animal human convergence most dynamically and poetically in *Window Water Baby* (1959).[80] Brakhage depicts his first wife Jane Brakhage giving birth to their child in this film. We see her full bellied getting into the bath followed by successive snippets of the window, the water, her fecund body and then the baby emerging. It is a poetic cinematic waltz. The abstruse intimacy of the event, the tenderness, the fluids, mucus, blood. The seam of sperm on her vulva as the camera unnervingly returns to her sex repeatedly—the wonder of it. We are heightened to the fact of their love making during labour. Jane's belly is stretched to its limits. Her labia minora, labia majora, clitoris, swollen lips are focal. We feel at our voyeuristic capacity as an audience. The crowning head, again the intervention of the doctor's hand, until Jane pushes out the infant. Her vulva remarkably stretches. More fluids, bloods, juices, membranes—the miraculous birth of the placenta. The handling of the newborn. The business of the umbilicus and the newborn not on its mothers skin immediately, which disturbs. Significantly, Stan emphasises his

---

[79] Brakhage, Stan. 1963. *Metaphors on Vision*. U.S.A: Film Culture Inc. pp. 6-7.
[80] Stan Brakhage's *Window Water Baby* (1959) can be viewed on the following link: https://www.youtube.com/watch?v=-drSrvTtZ1k&list=PLfTaZIagMDn6_SuMT-CzeBBKmOo8KoRCy&index=7

collaboration with Jane in the editing of the film, which heightens me to her complicity in the intimate filmic exposition of the birth. In my view, it is his collaboration in this short film with his wife, which most successfully distorts classical composition in favour of presenting an alternative poetic mode of human experience that is undeniably sensuous. We are made aware of our mammalian status, or our creatureliness, through this most intimate and moving exploration of human beginnings. In part two of *Window, Water, Baby* (1959) Stan utilises his poetic editing technique to emphasise Jane's vulva repeatedly whilst giving birth—it becomes a kind of sensorial eye.[81] The viewer's gaze is aligned with another order of meaning, in which a woman's sexed perspective is paramount. Stan Brakhage seems to get enwombed—accesses planetary rebirth. And in his later film, *Mothlight* (1963), Brakhage edits quick succession clips of moths flitting at close range, their delicate membranes quiver, microscopic patternings of wings and fleshes mesh in a kind of governance of metamorphoses.[82] Flora too emerges, melds with the moth's magnitudes. In this film, Brakhage achieves a remarkable exposition of life, a highly sensuous, and poetic, celebration of human animal plantae convergences. He documents wild forays by way of celluloid poetics.

Back in my twenties I tried to create my own film poetics after viewing Brakhage's work. I attempted to embrace another order of

---

[81] Stan Brakhage's, *Window Water Baby*, part 2, (1959) can be viewed on the following link: https://www.youtube.com/watch?v=Q_MA8h8PXQM
[82] Stan Brakhage's, *Mothlight* (1963) can be viewed on the following link: https://www.youtube.com/watch?v=Yt3nDgnC7M8&list=PLfTaZIagMDn6_SuMT-CzeBBKmOo8KoRCy&index=11

meaning beyond the authority of a canonical mode of perception. I was swimming in a celluloid sea of my own mutability. I experimented with Brakhage's cinematic techniques, as well as Deren's, accompanied by my own song compositions, which I dubbed *The Celluloid Laments*. I co-wrote *Song for the Boatman*, in which I sang of a place of death and becoming.[83] I documented myself making offerings to the sea—ascending a cliff. I overlaid a series of blue ink drawings of tigers, ravens, moths, bats and various plant assemblages. I became subaqueous to write another song titled *The Lamenting Wife,* in which I got my boyfriend to film me through the bottom of a glass whilst submerged under water. My struggle was affected—tensile. I drew a series of self-portraits in blue ink, which I superimposed over my face.[84] I recorded a cover of Anita Lane and Nick Cave's *Stranger than Kindness* and filmed blue ink drawings magnified through a water glass, projected it over an image of my boyfriend's face, as if re-forging myself by way of another. I was attempting to find a way of conveying myself outside of the dominant domain of representation.[85]

But, I'm trying now to think even further back... I'm trying to think when I very first found a rift in hum*an*ity, a way beyond through to poetic thought. Perhaps it was when I first heard John Lennon and Paul McCartney's song *A Day in the Life*—it wasn't off *Sargent Pepper's* though. I'd bought a vinyl copy of *Imagine: John Lennon*, a

---

[83] Natalie Rose Dyer's 'Song for the Boatman,' *The Celluloid Laments,* can be viewed on the following link: https://www.youtube.com/watch?v=TPr6-Zr91Uk
[84] Natalie rose Dyer's 'The Lamenting Wife,' *The Celluloid Laments,* can be viewed on the following link: https://www.youtube.com/watch?v=v21wgz7AJ10
[85] Natalie Rose Dyer's 'Stranger than Kindness' cover, *The Celluloid Laments*, can be viewed on the following link: https://www.youtube.com/watch?v=1NLtc0HZrSE

soundtrack to the 1988 documentary. I might have been eighteen. I found an old record player, resuscitated it, and played the record on steady rotation. It became the soundtrack to my dysphoria. It provided a cathartic tendering of my emotional sortie in a way that The Pixies *Doolittle* didn't, although it definitely did speak rather profoundly to a maniacal urge to 'drive my car into the ocean on a wave of mutilation'—and I loved that album dearly.[86] Clearly, I was passing over from masochistic teenager in my bedroom late at night, undergoing an intimate meditation with Lennon, on my way towards the auspices of radical thinker. Or no, it was more wayward than that—was I becoming some kind of poet or artist? A slit in the protective constricting umbrella of identity that humans equip themselves with developed a little tear to let in a bit of 'windy chaos' as Deleuze would have it.[87] When *A Day in the Life* came on the record player and Lennon sang of reading the news—mused on his lack of interest in 'making the grade'—the orchestral discordance mounted.[88] McCartney's vocal kicked in—he told of the ordinary man's daily malaise. Then that pivotal moment when Lennon lapses into 'Ahhhh ah ah ah, ah ah ahhhhh, ah ah ahhhhhhhhh ...' He signals another direction—a valid beyond. It was by instinct that I sought to untether myself from 'Get up, get out of bed, drag a comb across my head ...' by whatever means necessary. I did not wish to ascribe to these conventions of doing human, prefaced on a *man* construct, nor the binary opposite. I sought to attend to: 'Ahhhh ah ah ah, ah ah ahhhhh, ah ah ahhhhhhhhh ...' And Lennon most

---

[86] The Pixies. 1989. The song 'Wave of Mutilation' is on their album *Doolittle*.
[87] Theoretical Puppets. 2021. "Gilles Deleuze on Chaos and Creativity." YouTube. May 23, 2021. https://www.youtube.com/watch?v=bqV1uXy0Ny8
[88] Lennon. J. and McCartney. P. 1967. 'A Day in the Life' on *Sgt. Pepper's Lonely Heart Club Band*.

certainly underwent ego-loss, coming off drugs for instance. He had to continually reforge himself by way of song strands.

In Lennon's final interview, conducted by Jonathan Cott for *Rolling Stone*, he said that he had dedicated his life to being an artist—to creating an oeuvre. "'I'm a doer, not a voyeur ... And I've got nothing to hide. Remember the song?'" And Cott replies: "'Everybody's Got Something to Hide Except Me and My Monkey." It's one of my favorites: "Your inside is out, and your outside is in/Your outside is in, and your inside is out." Then Lennon retorts: "'Right, but what did the critics say? A bit simplistic, no imagery in it. Perhaps I should have said, your inside is like a whale juice dripping from the fermented foam of the teeny-boppers VD in Times Square as I injected my white clown face with heroin and performed in red-leather knickers. Maybe then they'd like it, right?'"[89] Lennon points to people's perversions. Their desire to rake his soul, like shoot him at point blank range in front of the Dakota building for exposing the stupidity of allowing hierarchical speciesism to proliferate at the expense of embracing difference. Lennon speaks to a crisis in hu*man*ity that pervades, the fact that people go on trying to expose everybody else's monkey—unable to attend to their own. The fact that I've got a monkey and I can see your monkey is something that many people try not to acknowledge. It's a way of shoring up the self *against* another. It's a way of preserving my identity against yours—differentiating myself though not in a productive way. Or perhaps it is the very basis of production in end-time-capitalism.

---

[89] Cott, Jonathan. 2010. "John Lennon: The Last Interview." Rolling Stone. December 23, 2010. https://www.rollingstone.com/feature/john-lennon-the-last-interview-179443/

What I like about Lennon is his frankness, his intelligence, and his playfulness. His ability to cut through the shit—'except for the occasional Walrus bit,' as he quips.[90] Lennon had an aptitude for recognising the part of us that is animal, which is the key to our collective metamorphosis. For if people sought to reconnect with their creaturely aspect in an affirmative sense, attend to their own monkey for instance, they'd surely be following a creative path, down the rabbit hole, through a stream of phantasms. I mean to emphasise that we cannot evolve as a species if we do not embrace our own ongoing need to involute. We must seek to *continually* undergo creative metamorphosis. I want rupture. I want the existing framework destroyed. A revolution. I want 'Ah ah ah ah, ah ah ah, ah ah ahhhhh.' I want 'Ah! Bowakawa, pousse pousse.' For isn't Lennon petitioning us in *Number Nine Dream* to dare to imagine something beyond the self? 'I believe, yes, I believe, what more can I say.'[91] Dare to believe in a human species beyond war—dare to love—dare to chant something nonsensical that means everything. Dare to recognise the other in yourself. Dare to open up a new doorway into the dark, and which is also a doorway into reality. Yeah ok, he was a boomer, but maybe a fairly anomalous one?

Jean Michel Basquiat was undoubtedly another one of these luminaries—an architect of wild forays. He seems to me an artist who passed through many thresholds. He was an expert morphologist, though he fell irretrievably into the crack eventually

---

[90] Ibid.
[91] John Lennon's 'Number Nine Dream' was first issued on his 1974 album *Walls and Bridges*. https://en.wikipedia.org/wiki/Number_9_Dream

through excessive drug use. In my view, he was clearly influenced by Dutch artists Karel Appel, who sought to stray from the prescribed aesthetic codes of the 1950s, 60s and 70s. Appel was represented in the 1970s by Annina Nosei, the same New York art dealer as Basquiat, and both artists would have been familiar with each other's work.[92] Appel refused to mimic the observable world in his artistic practice. Rather, he advocated for a perspective beyond what is known. He responded to Ezra Pound's famous modernist call to 'Make it new!'[93] Appel radically deferred from a maxim of aesthetics—entered into the wild mutinous stream of experimentation over and over again. Appel reputedly said: 'Creativity is very fragile. It's like a leaf in the fall; it hangs and when it drops you don't know where it's drifting. As an artist you have to fight and survive the wilderness to keep your creative freedom.'[94] He thought that children teach us to enter this mutinous wild stream of experimentation—to keep entering it. In her article 'Karel Appel at Amsterdam' Edith Hoffman writes:

> Children and animals, particularly cats, were the most frequent subjects of Appel's early pictures. His emphasis on eyes, teeth, heads, the atrophy of legs and arms, the placing of all figures in the foremost plane, and their simple, thickly drawn outlines show that he was at the time much impressed by the art of children.[95]

---

[92] Karel Appel and Jean Michel Basquiat were both represented in the 1970s by Annina Nosei, the New York art dealer.
Laster, Pail. 2017. "Karel Appel and the Influence of Outsider Art." *Whitehot Magazine of Contemporary Art*. October 2017. https://whitehotmagazine.com/articles/karel-appel-influence-outsider-art/3796.

[93] It has been highly documented that Ezra Pound made this statement with regards to modernist poetry. North, Michael. 2013. "The Making of 'Make It New.'" *Guernica Magazine*. August 15, 2013. https://www.guernicamag.com/the-making-of-making-it-new/

[94] Hoffmann, Edith. 1965. "Karel Appel at Amsterdam." *The Burlington Magazine* 107 (750): 484—482. https://doi.org/10.2307/874653

[95] Ibid. p. 484.

By paying attention to the child's perspective, Appel attempted to show that we can repeatedly challenge dominant patriarchal capitalist imperatives. Perhaps Appel was trying to relearn what he already knew as a child, but had been taught to forget.

Patriarchal capitalist imperatives certainly come under critique ongoingly in Basquiat's work. On attending the opening of *Basquiat Haring Crossing Lines* at The National Gallery of Victoria back in 2019, I was dazzled.[96] Biblical references, beat poetry, and bebop jazz references commingled to forge a kind of psychobabble of 80s cultural phenomena. The man of colour is the central protagonist in Basquiat's works—he looks back at the viewer in order to challenge centuries of racial subjugation. He is crowned. *Masque* (1981) is a study in white man's colonial gaze on 'the black man' and the rage that loaded look provokes. Basquiat brings about a reversal and subverts the troublingly termed *l'art primitive*. In *Untitled* (1982) the hero with the three-pointed crown is depicted with menacing hallowed yellow eyes and gnashing teeth—enraged by the legacy of slavery and oppression. He's ironically holding a bone, again Basquiat critiques damaging colonial discourses of the racialised other throughout history, specifically the abhorrent racist trope that historically held that Africans were on the lower end of the evolutionary scale.[97] Similarly, in the exquisite *Untitled* (Armstrong)

---

[96] The Crossing Lines exhibition was at The National Gallery Victoria, Australia. (1 Dec 2019-15 Mar 2020).

The National Gallery of Victoria. 2019. "Keith Haring | Jean-Michel Basquiat | NGV." The National Gallery of Victoria. December 1, 2019. https://www.ngv.vic.gov.au/exhibition/keith-haring-jean-michel-basquiat/

[97] Alfred Russel Wallace responded in 1864 in his essay "The Origin of Human Races and the Antiquity of Man," to Darwin's evolutionary theory, that stated we are descendent of barbarians, and Africans are on the lower end of the scale, which horrendously became the main view of human social and racial evolution in the nineteenth century. https://people.wku.edu/charles.smith/wallace/S093.htm

mixed media on paper (1985), Basquiat directly challenges the racist discourse on the man of colour's supposed closer ties with the animal, which women have also been aligned with on account of their biological functions, and in terms of a perceived primal regression. Of course, there has also been a long troubling history of biologically determining women under a regressive patriarchal framework, which has held that they need to be *civilised*. And yet, in this fraught space of late capitalism and global environmental devastation, humans must urgently re-imagine their embodiment in radically affirmative connection with other humans, as well as 'nonhuman animal species, ecosystems, technology and matter.'[98] We need to use our imaginations to reclaim our mammalian and indeed our creaturely status as a bridge to an affirmative commune with the planetary.

It seems to me that Basquiat was continuously confronted by the daily nightmare racist realities, with which he battled to the death in his work, insofar as he bequeaths us an oeuvres which challenges the patriarchal capitalist structures of power. The artist, poet, seer or visionary becomes something else to re-imagine humanity, which is challenging, sometimes bloody, and of paramount importance. And so, for all of the artists, poets, and seers who have staged these daring forays, shirking their subjectivities, we too must brave a journey to that risky country, an abyss that is transformative, a wilderness, with the aim of returning renewed. Of course, the binary opposite of hierarchical speciesism is barbarism and primitive regression—it won't do.

---

[98] Parr, Adrian. 2017. *Birth of a New Earth: The Radical Politics of Environmentalism*. New York: Columbia University Press. p. 191.

In more recent times, I have discovered contemporary luminary Brazilian artist Juliana Notari who initiates a wayward creaturely tract. In *Dra.Diva* (2003-2007) Notari drills into the wall and opens up the crack. She attempts to get 'out of the blackhole of subjectivity.'[99] When Notari inserts a speculum in the wall and splashes ox blood over it she exposes the cultural reduction of a womb to a wound in many patriarchal cultures. Of course, a negatively inflected menstrual taboo still exists today despite the free bleeding movement.[100] The faux-penis metal speculum used to forcibly open up a woman's, or a trans man, or non-binary person's vagina is an instrument in part, through which to colonise with a prosthesis—in the name of pathology. In Brazilian Vogue January edition, 2021, Beta Germano writes that with each hole that Notari opens up in the cleansed white walls of the gallery space, over which she smears blood, it is a bid to keep the patriarchal *wound*s inflicted open.[101] Similarly, Julia Kristeva warns against closing over the wound. It is through exposing the colonisation of a woman's womb in her performance that Notari demonstrates a lacunae—a gap, an interstices, a hole in cultural texts, which is after all a woman's sexed perspective.

---

[99] Deleuze, G and Guattari, F. (1980) 1987. *A Thousand Plateaus: Capitalism and Schizophrenia*. Translated and with a foreword by Brian Massumi. Minneapolis: Minnesota Press. p. 188.
[100] Dyer, Natalie. 2020. *The Menstrual Imaginary in Literature: Notes on a Wild Fluidity*. Cham, Switzerland: Palgrave Macmillan. pp. 5-6.
[101] Beta, Germano. 2021. "Os Motivos Que Tornam a Vulva 'Diva' Tão Polêmica." Vogue. January 7, 2021. https://vogue.globo.com/Vogue-Gente/noticia/2021/01/os-motivos-que-tornam-vulva-diva-tao-polemica.html

By following her *Dra.Diva* project with *Diva*, Notari fashions a portal of rebirth through which to get born planetary. Notari's 33-metre long vulva entitled *Diva* (2021) is made from concrete and resin and exhibited in a rural park in Pernambuco, Brazil. The Guardian newspaper reported that the right wing government was highly threatened by Notari's vulva installation.[102] On Facebook, Notari announced that her intentions in making the artwork were centrally to garner a 'female perspective,' specifically as a means of altering the '… perspective of our relationship between humans and humans and nonhumans …'[103] Gender reductive assignations aside, surely Notari demonstrates with her massive vulva sculpture cast into the earth a far more affirmative view of human life on this planet, a valid and relevant beyond late patriarchal capitalist society for instance, which reorchestrates our lives as irrevocably entwined with all planetary phenomena.

After first sighting Basquiat's artworks I decided I would not try to be a visual artist, but merely dapple in making outsider art instead. I turned my attentions to writing in the main, predominantly poetry. I apprehended that I could never be as good as Basquiat and it opened up a pathway to another artform for me. Louise Bourgeois writes in her collected diaries *Deconstruction of the Father, Reconstruction of the Father*, that after viewing a Picasso's exhibition in New York she was unable to create a single work for over a month. All she

---

[102] Phillips, Tom. 2021. "The Vagina Dialogues: 33-Metre Artwork Draws Far Right's Ire in Brazil." The Guardian. January 3, 2021. https://www.theguardian.com/world/2021/jan/03/the-vagina-dialogues-33-metre-artwork-draws-far-rights-ire-in-brazil

[103] Notari, Juliana. 2020. "Julia Notari's Post on Facebook." Facebook. December 31, 2020. https://www.facebook.com/juliana.notari/posts/10219401789651753

could do was humbly clean her brushes and move things around in her studio.[104] Of course, Hannah Gadsby's rant about Picasso in *Nanette* is on point, clearly he engaged in reprehensible sexual misconduct throughout his life.[105] This doesn't alter the fact that Bourgeois perceived in Picasso's work a genius to which she dared not even aspire, psyched out for a time, albeit which she thankfully managed to eclipse. Her *Arch of Hysteria* (1993) is beguiling—a powerful representation of the decentering of man. White golden man bent backwards, as if pre-empting the death of his narcissistic ego. His genitals slightly raised in an insignificant mound—bearing a trace of castration. To reiterate Oprah in her 2018 Golden Globe's speech: '... we all have lived, too many years in a culture broken by brutally powerful men. And for too long, women have not been heard or believed if they dared to speak their truth to the power of those men. But their time is up. Their time is up. Their time is up.'[106] Where to from here? A revolution?

I'm with Lennon. Become an artist, a musician, a poet. It's these brave individuals, alongside the visionaries, who are able to open up a rift in humanity by ongoingly attempting to exceed their positionality, outrunning their identities. Maybe the revolution is about stopping agreeing to perform ourselves, refusing to continually re-write ourselves digitally, to retweet ourselves or post a new Instagram pic. What if you started to show up on the digital maps by way

---

[104] Bourgeois, Louise. 1998. *Deconstruction of the father, reconstruction of the father: writings and interviews, 1923-1997*. London: MIT Press in association with Violette Editions.
[105] Gadsby, Hannah. 2018. "Hannah Gadsby: Nanette (2018)." *IMDB*. https://www.imdb.com/title/tt8465676/
[106] "'Their Time Is Up': Oprah's Inspiring Golden Globes Speech." 2018. The Irish Times. January 8, 2018. https://www.irishtimes.com/culture/film/their-time-is-up-oprah-s-inspiring-golden-globes-speech-1.3348262

of traces, the waste products of your soul, the excess, the spiritual nexus substance, the stuff we imbue into a creative work? Share the artwork. Post the poem instead. In 2023 I saw Tracey Emin in conversation as part of the National Gallery of Victoria Triennial exhibition.[107] She was illuminating. Emin talked about how she'd realised that her 'singularity,' her 'massive ego,' had taken her a certain way, had driven a vision, and was necessary in that sense. But, when she was diagnosed with bladder cancer and had to undergo a seven and a half hour surgery, was subsequently unable to attend her own exhibition alongside the works of her hero Edvard Munch on account of being laid up in bed recovering from surgery, she realised that her art was the transference, the legacy, not her. When staring into the abyss, faced with death, Emin got over herself. She, the vessel, the artist making work 'like a banshee' is coming out of her, 'like being pursued by wolves,' or 'a spiritual ascension.'[107] In her National Gallery of Victoria talk she said: 'It's like an internal thing that connects to everything.'[107] This ceasing to be fixed in oneself in favour of marrying everything indiscriminately when making a work of art. A prolonged creative frisson. Cathartic. Yes. Although she told the audience that she hated to admit this, since in the 80s art was supposedly all about 'masculine control' and confessional was a tag used mainly on women artists as if they'd vomited onto the page. (It's the same with the women so-called confessional poets like Sylvia Plath, Anne Sexton and Sharon Olds). But, being an artist, musician, film maker, or a poet isn't as much about maintaining control over the medium as it is about the medium taking over. A going under. Though you are its conductor—like Vodou. This is not to denigrate the artist's or poet's agency. Rather, it's to shift the

---

[107] "Live and in Conversation After-Hours: Tracey Emin | Triennial | NGV." 2023. Vic.gov.au. 2023. https://www.ngv.vic.gov.au/program/keynote-tracey-emin-in-conversation/

focus to the process of engaging in creativity as the moment we lose subjectivity—cast off that tired performance for something far more expansive. Something infinite. Fervent. Enlivening. Something that opens doorways into reality. The evidence is in the artwork or the poem, or work of poetic prose—does it live? And this was Susan Sontag's point: 'Art is not only about something; it is something.'[108] It is something you, the mammalian being, have given birth to. At the end of the conversation Emin told the audience: 'Art has come to save me, to cradle me, to pick me up.'[109]

It is the philosopher poets, the artists, the mentally divergent, the so-called sensitives, the fine nerve meters, like Artaud, like Woolf, like Brakhage, Lennon, Basquiat, Emin, and many others besides, who have the greatest capacity to bring about a paradigmatic shift in how we think and do human. They refused to perform their subjectivities—or could not. Many have been punished severely for not doing *normal*. Perhaps they discovered that it's possible to refuse to perform variations of the dominant subjectivity without going under entirely. It requires individuals to enter the crack, the transformative abyss as a means of rebirthing into the lacunae and resurfacing beyond. To agree to undertake this process ongoingly is to win one's own access to song—to oracular lineages. It is attunement to planetary nexus. For we can and we must imagine something entirely different, in excess of prescribed codes of meaning—a planetary story of collective human becoming.

---

[108] Sontag, Susan. 1966. *Against Interpretation; And Other Essays*. New York: Farrar, Straus, Giroux. p. 21.
[109] "Live and in Conversation After-Hours: Tracey Emin | Triennial | NGV." 2023. The National Gallery of Victoria. 2023. https://www.ngv.vic.gov.au/program/keynote-tracey-emin-in-conversation/

Chapter Three

A Few Notes on Authorial Descent

'Sometimes we are lucky enough to know that our lives have been changed, to discard the old, embrace the new, and run headlong down an immutable course. It happened to me... when my eyes were opened on the sea.' Jacques Cousteau.[110]

'Women's imaginary is inexhaustible, like music, painting, writing: their stream of phantasms is incredible.' Hélène Cixous.[111]

In order to find my voice in my mid-twenties I had to descend the ladder of writing. I enrolled in Hélène Cixous' school of writing, that is to say that I closely read most of her writings, including *Three Steps on the Ladder of Writing* in which she explores the idea of writing as descent, a commune with the dead: 'To begin (writing, living) we must have death. I like the dead, they are the doorkeepers who while closing one side "give" way to the other.'[112] But it's a rare book that we open to discover we have '... already crossed the border.'[113] Cixous

---

[110] Cousteau, Jacques. Y. 1977. *The Silent World*. New York: Ballantine Books. p. 6.
[111] Cixous, Hélène.'The Laugh of the Medusa' in *Signs*. Volume 1, Number 4 (Summer 1976). Chicago: University of Chicago Press. pp. 875-893.
[112] Cixous, Hélène. 1993. 'The School of the Dead' in *Three Steps on the Ladder of Writing*. New York: University of Columbia Press. p. 7.
[113] Ibid. p. 82.

draws on Franz Kafka to demonstrate the significance of books that confront us like death. In a 1904 letter Kafka wrote to a friend: 'I think we ought to read only the kind of books that wound and stab us. If the book we're reading doesn't wake us up with a blow on the head, what are we reading it for?'[114] That is to say, while some books hold up a mirror to the self, other books are windows, which offer an entirely new view. Whilst we need to read books that affirm us, that speak to our particular set of identity markers, and which help us to firm up a sense of self, we also require books that take us into new terrain. I think Kafkaesque texts act as both mirror and window. They allow us to see ourselves, but they also productively destabilise our identity in favour of embracing a poetics of transformation.

Socrates famously said: 'The unexamined life is not worth living' and gives a definition of literature based on the idea that '... literature is the space in which questions about the nature of personal identity are most provocatively articulated.'[115] Kafkaesque texts contain discussions of what happens when the myth of the so-called stable subject faces its crisis. They touch on the power of art, centrally literature, to transform the self.[116] The writer of these types of books takes a strange journey to a foreign land for the reader over and over again—facing death as a means of purveying a truth.[117] Afterall, writing is a hankering after truth—the truth is 'down

---

[114] Marta Bausells cites Franz Kafka.
Bausells, Marta. 2016. "Why We Read: Authors and Readers on the Power of Literature." *The Guardian*. April 23, 2016. https://www.theguardian.com/books/2016/apr/23/why-we-read-authors-and-readers-on-the-power-of-literature
[115] Bennett, Andrew, and Nicholas Royle. 2004. *An Introduction to Literature, Criticism and Theory*. Longman Publishing Group. p. 104.
[116] Ibid. p. 103.
[117] Cixous, Hélène. 1993. *Three Steps on the Ladder of Writing*. New York: University of Columbia Press. p. 20.

A Few Notes on Authorial Descent

below.'[118] Writing is plunging in, in search of an unerasable truth. But, as Cixous wisely advises her readers: 'The moment I say "truth" I expect people to ask: "What is truth?" "Does truth exist?"'[119] And so, to descend the ladder of writing is to attempt to go in the direction of truth against absolutes, to venture beyond the limited confines of selfhood, to open up to the possibility of undergoing a transmutation.

In *Metamorphosis* Kafka creates a literary device, or apparatus, in which Gregor's becoming bug intervenes on the family drama, acts as a monstrous rupture that produces further transformations. But, does Gregor undergo nervous illness? Or does Kafka bring about his own radical metamorphosis through writing his creatureliness? Does Kafka mobilise a literary machine as a means of becoming something else—becoming-animal? Certainly, Kafka's story highlights the search for agency through creative practice, which may be found elsewhere—beyond the patriarchal capitalist framework. This is illustrated by Kafka when the bug-like Gregor leaves his room in pursuit of music, specifically his sister Grete's violin playing. He seeks a better source of nourishment. Gregor is near death. He ventures to move out of his bedroom-prison and into the livingroom. He is covered in dust, fluff, hair and remnants of food. The rotted apple his father threw at him is decomposing into his broken carapace. He has been abused and is beyond bothering to clean himself. And Grete who had initially cared so deeply for Gregor is by this stage completely repelled by him. In the end it is Grete who refutes that Gregor's spirit inhabits this 'repulsive vermin,' and opts to get rid of *it*. She becomes monstrously inhuman, is indoctrinated by a societal

---
[118] Ibid. p. 6.
[119] Ibid. p. 36.

norm that denigrates others who are ill at ease, or in suffering. She reduces Gregor. Presumably Grete gives up any vocational aspirations of playing violin, gets married, and sets to working for the infernal patriarchal capitalist machine. Kafka demonstrates that Gregor is more human than anyone else in his family on account of his having had the courage to undergo metamorphosis, in an attempt to become something in excess of the Anthropocentric framework, which Kafka seems to preempt.

At this time in my life of reading Cixous and Kafka, I too became creaturely to descend the ladder of writing and retrieve something worthwhile—my voice. I sought after Grete's violin, the sublime unearthly music. But oh how this first abyss was harrowing. It was Kafkaesque. I awoke in terror in the early hours of the morning having undergone a hideously visceral dream. I'd seemingly been dragged into the netherworld through my umbilicus. An unwritten text appeared to be cutting me open from within. I experienced terrible insomnia, which abated after much torment. I wrote an experimental novel titled *Kore's Inferno*, in which I brought Dante's cantos under a feminist treatment—attempting to free myself from a Christian philology. I descended the ladder of writing to chant Sylvia Plath out of the suicide forest. I wrote a whole poetic soliloquy to Plath, following the mad manic music of my own ascent. My entire being seemed to place-hold rift. I managed to hold onto my sanity—by a tenuous thread. I understand now that I was undergoing major ego-loss. Having entered into an abyss of sorts, I had to write my way out of it. To transform myself through writing.

A Few Notes on Authorial Descent

Cixous advises us that: 'There are two ways of clambering downward—by plunging into the earth or going deep into the sea—and neither is easy.'[120] During this period, I was also undertaking the research and writing of my honors thesis on film poetics. And so, I'd ride my bicycle to the Australian Centre for the Moving Image screening room (then housed in South Melbourne) to watch 16mm footage of Jacques Cousteau and his diving team. I revered Cousteau as a man with a singular vision. I liked that he was a wayfarer, or perhaps more specifically a seafarer. I admired that he opined the many wonders of the sea, its various bounty and splendid inscrutability, which he aimed to tell of in order to conserve. In *The Silent World* (1956) Cousteau advises that subsumed in the darkness 'The coral takes on nightmare of shapes.'[121] By day his team aboard the Calypso dive in the Mediterranean sea, the Red sea, and the Indian ocean to discover hitherto undisclosed worlds of brain hemispheres, fanned fungal shapes, coral that looks like skirts of a sail, anemones which dance in the sea current—they witness the marvelous variety of marine life nestled into vast shadowy planes. I immersed myself in Cousteau's labyrinthine filmic peregrinations in the silent world. I registered in Cousteau a kindredness. Perhaps I perceived his exploration of the sea as a spirited radical departure, for Cousteau takes a journey for us as the poet does, as Artaud did, bravely retrieves something vital from imaginal depths—an alternative perspective. His cinematic tractability is hypnotic—a poetics of the silent world.

---

[120] Ibid. p. 5.
[121] Cousteau, Jacques. Y. 1977. *The Silent World*. New York: Ballantine Books.

Shortly after I commenced the writing of my thesis, my supervisor advised me that my writing made no sense. It was overly abstract. In retrospect I comprehend my obsolescence was being overly disposed toward milking the unconscious as Anne Sexton describes it.[122] Or perhaps like Artaud I had an aptitude for entering the abyss, albeit a transformative abyss—a productive abyss. Perhaps this is a poet's true vocation, to undergo authorial descent. It's where interesting and arresting imagery comes from, a sublimated landscape that poets turn their attention to, focus on, and take from as a discipline. The poet perpetually undergoes an archeological dig, searches for buried treasures, fragments and dissolutions of a culture and its peoples, captures that resonance in a carefully crafted assemblage of images—thereafter registers this poetic vision lyrically. The poet attempts to get the feeling that they apprehend in the silent world into words—a unique signature.

For instance, the first poem that Seamus Heaney wrote, in which he thought he'd gotten his feelings into words was a poem called *Digging*.[123] This was his initiation poem. He was able to accurately convey the depths of human experience—to get it true. His poem *Digging* gave him excitement and confidence as a poet. He had found his voice. Heaney explains 'Finding a voice means that you can get your own feeling into your own words and that your words have the feeling of you about them ...'[124] To be able to allow the first

---

[122] Ostriker, Alice. 1988. 'That Story: The Change of Anne Sexton.' *Anne Sexton: Telling the Tale*. Ann Arbour: The University of Michigan. pp. 263-288.
[123] Heaney, Seamus. 1966. "Digging." Poetry Foundation. Poetry Foundation. 1966. https://www.poetryfoundation.org/poems/47555/digging.
[124] Heaney, Seamus's 'Feeling into Words' (1974) is collected in Jahan Ramazani, Richard Ellmann, and Robert O'Clair. 2003. *The Norton Anthology of Modern and Contemporary Poetry*. W W Norton & Company Incorporated. pp. 1097-1109.

'alertness' in its preverbal life and then let flow from the edges of thought, a feeling that rises to meet its correct articulation. A kind of gleaning. He also terms it divination, which may be a bit romantic.

But, what is gleaning without craft? Gleaning without craft is doomed—overly abstract. In my mid-twenties I didn't have much craft. Auden advises in *The Dyer's Hand & other Essays* that apprentice poets must get a literary transference. This is true not just for poetry, but for all forms of writing. When we read another poet or writer and it speaks to something essential in us, which resonates with our own experience—it is gold.

> In imitating his Master, the apprentice acquires a Censor, for he learns that, no matter how he finds it, by inspiration, by potluck or after hours of laborious search, there is only one word or rhythm or form that is the right one. The right one is still not yet the real one, for the apprentice is ventriloquizing, but he has got away from poetry-in-general; he is learning how a poem is written.[125]

Here I ran into serious trouble: a male dominated canon. I'm reminded of American poet Adrienne Rich's recollection of the formative years of her education, exposed to a canon of celebrated writers, almost exclusively men, which could not accurately convey her experience as a woman.[126]

---

[125] Auden, W.H. (1948) 1962. *The Dyers Hand*. London: Faber & Faber. p. 38.
[126] Rich, Adrienne. 1986. *Blood, Bread and Roses*. New York: W. W. Norton & Company.

Roland Barthes proffers in *The Death of the Author* that when '... the voice loses its origin, the author enters his own death, writing.'[127] He argues for the need to topple the empire of the author, for instance a male dominated canon, although he identifies Stéphane Mallarmé as the first to recognise the need to '... substitute[ing] language itself for the man who hitherto was supposed to own it ...'[128] Paul Valéry too 'mocked the Author.'[129] Marcel Proust also engaged in 'blurring' or bringing about a 'radical reversal' by making his life the literary work.[130] Barthes' suggestion is that the author's identity ought to be displaced for the performativity of language. And yet, Barthes' death of the author is still a radical deferral for a man writing. And I was, am still, a woman writing.

Ironically, it was Cousteau who directed me to the idea that Barthes' death of the author is inherently patriarchal, for it always already assumes a man undergoing the loss of his origin, and consequently in search of a portal to get reborn from. Ultimately, Cousteau's team dynamite a coral reef and commit an act of vandalism on *The Silent World*. We might bear in mind that the film was made in the 1950s. Still, whilst Cousteau was a pioneer exploring this subsumed seascape, he unwittingly colonises it. In *The Silent World* we witness his diving team playing about on yellow dick-shaped underwater scooters, disrupting schools of fish, hitching a ride upon a turtle who is clearly infringed on. Perhaps Cousteau continues to return to the sea because it's a kind of maternal haven for him. Suffice to say that in my twenties it became increasingly obvious to me that I needed to

---

[127] Barthes, Roland. (1967) 2006. "The Death of the Author." http://tbook.constantvzw.org/wp-content/death_authorbarthes.pdf
[128] Ibid.
[129] Ibid.
[130] Ibid.

look elsewhere for mentors. I needed to turn to subversive women writers to learn my craft. I discovered the philosophical writings of Luce Irigaray and many others. I continued to defect to Cixous.

Irigaray informs us in *This Sex Which is Not One* that it requires a special aptitude to hear a woman's voice, which arises from the liminal spaces of society. She works off the premise that the central economy of desire of patriarchal societies globally has been a phallic ideal that is mobilised through language, towards the exposition of normative subjectivities, and associative meanings and ideas.[131] Irigaray hit the nail right on the head for me. Quite simply, 'we are born into language,' and more specifically into *the name of the father* under patriarchy (as in our surname).[132] 'We are *subject* to language.'[133] Jacques Derrida, Cixous's mate, terms this predicament 'phallologocentrism,' which refers to the privileging of the masculine in the construction of language and meaning structures.[134] For '... questions of personal or individual identity are indissociably bound up with language' and a masculine point of view historically.[135] Irigaray turned me on to the idea that women have a special capacity to enter into things and states beyond prescribed codes of meaning, on their cusp, at the poetic outer limits of experience. She pointed

---

[131] Irigaray, Luce. (1977) 1985. *This Sex Which is Not One*. Translated by Catherine Porter with Carolyn Burke. Ithaca, New York: Cornell University. p. 110.
[132] Bennett, Andrew, and Nicholas Royle. 2004. *An Introduction to Literature, Criticism and Theory*. London: Longman Publishing Group. p. 105.
[133] Ibid. p. 106.
[134] "Phallogocentrism." 2025. Jacques Derrida. https://derridapresentation.weebly.com/phallogo-centrism.html
[135] Bennett, Andrew, and Nicholas Royle. 2004. *An Introduction to Literature, Criticism and Theory*. London: Longman Publishing Group. p. 105.

out to me that when a woman speaks it is already always from the seam of humanity—they are fluent with epistemological rift on account of the fact that they have been historically marginalised for possessing a reproductive system—for not having a penis.

Of course, this is the aspect of women's material existence, in addition to trans men and non-binary people's existence, that has historically socially been negatively maximised in order to biologically determine them; to define them pertaining to *lack*, as well as cast them as magical mysterious witches to be ritual separated, or tabooed, but also revered. However, we can and must shift our thinking around a woman, trans man, or non-binary person's reproductive capacities at the planetary turn. Irigaray elaborates a mimetic 'mother-matter-nature' category aligned with 'waste' and 'excess' that has marginalised a woman's embodied voice—has made them inaudible in regressive social systems such as patriarchy for instance.[136] But, a woman's embodied voice must be registered—actually listened to. It takes a certain aptitude to register a woman's embodied voice since it is more diffuse. That is to say that on account of their anomalous social status, women have historically spoken in the 'mimetic' underside of masculine desire, embedded in so-called *rational* discourse. Women can subvert this dominant story of hu*man*ity.

Anne Carson reveals in her essay 'The Gender of Sound' that: 'Putting a door onto the female mouth has been the main project of patriarchal culture from antiquity to the present day. Its chief tactic is an ideological association of female sound with monstrosity,

---

[136] Irigaray, Luce. (1977) 1985. *This Sex Which is Not One*. Translated by Catherine Porter with Carolyn Burke. Cornell University: Ithaca, New York. p. 110.

disorder and death.'[137] Women in the archaic and classic periods were not encouraged to 'pour forth unregulated cries' in civic spaces (and which we can also consider canonical space). Not just women, but also '... catamites, eunuchs and androgynes fall into this category. Their sounds are bad to hear and make men uncomfortable.'[138] 'Madness and witchery as well as bestiality are conditions commonly associated with the use of the female voice in public, in ancient as well as modern context.'[139] In antiquity 'Female sound was judged to arise in craziness and to generate craziness.'[140] Carson argues that certain lower pitches associated with manliness are still considered more desirable, healthy, authoritarian, commanding respect, and demonstrate self-control.

And so, rather refreshingly, Carson calls for the need to look more closely at the patriarchal ideology that disdains 'female' sound.[141] To this end she points out that designated gendered celebrities of classic mythology are often aligned with creatureliness pertaining to their voicings.

> For example there is a heart chilling groan of the Gorgon, whose name is derived from the Sanskrit word garg meaning "a guttural animal howl that issues as a great wind from the back of the throat through a hugely distended mouth." There are the Furies whose high pitched and horrendous voices are compared by Aiskhylos to howling dogs or sounds of people tortured in hell (Eusenides). There is the deadly voice of the Sirens and the dangerous ventriloquism of Helen (Odyssey) and the

---

[137] Carson, Anne. (1992) 1995. *The Gender of Sound*. New York: New Directions Books. p. 121.
[138] Ibid. p. 119.
[139] Ibid.
[140] Ibid. p. 126.
[141] Ibid. p. 129.

> incredible babbling of Kassandra (Aiskylos, Agamennon) and the fearsome hullabaloo of Artemis as she charges through the woods (Homeric hymn and Aphrodite) ...[142]

The woods are often the domain of such creaturely women. They preside over the unbounded; the place of transgressions and animal-transitions.

> The wolf is a conventional symbol of marginality in Greek poetry. The wolf is an outlaw. He lives beyond the boundary of usefully cultivated and inhabited space marked off as the polis, in that blank no man's land called to aperion ("the unbounded"). Women, in the ancient view, share this territory spiritually and metaphorically in virtue of a "natural" female affinity for all that is raw, formless and in need of the civilizing hand of man. So for example in the document cited by Aristotle that goes by the name of The Pythagorean Table of Opposites, we find the attributes curving, dark, secret, evil, ever-moving, not self-contained and lacking its own boundaries aligned with Female and set over against straight, light, honest, good, stable, self-contained and firmly bounded on the Male side (Aristotle Metaphysics).[143]

Alkaois tells of the 'otherworldly echo of women shrieking with the wolf-thickets,' women uttering a particular kind of ritual shout called 'ololyga.' These ritual shouts of women occurred at certain 'climactic moments in ritual practice,' such as during sacrifice, childbirth, the registering of intense pleasure or pain, and specifically at women's festivals.[144] When Alkaios found himself surrounded by

---

[142] Ibid. p. 121.
[143] Ibid. p. 124.
[144] Ibid. pp. 124-5.

these particular voices he knew he was out of bounds. We can deduce then that the unregulated sound of women has been historically sanctioned, separated from the polis, from civic space. It has been made liminal. The objective of patriarchy has long been to restrict women's animalistic 'outpourings' to a minimum.'[145]

Since Grecian times, men have been charged with the responsibility of controlling gendered ritual creaturely outcries. For women have been thought to supposedly lack 'sophrosyne,' which bears out in Freud's psychoanalytical framework. 'Verbal continence is an essential feature of the masculine virtue of sophrosyne that organizes most patriarchal thinking on ethical or emotional matters' i.e. self-control and/or moderation of voice.[146] Under patriarchy, the control point of logos, of language, has been owned by men on account of the idea that women have been thought to not be able to control their sign language; the coming through the body of their language (hence the existence of a predominantly male-authored canon historically). Freud registered the consequences of women being shut up, censored, not allowed to orchestrate the productions of their interior life externally, for instance in public life, and which he aligned with pollution. He realised that hysteria, neurosis, tics, and eating disorders were a symptom of not being able to speak, to find a good channel for their libidinal energy. And so, he offered 'the talking cure.' 'Freud conceived his own therapeutic task as the rechannelling of these hysteric signs into rational discourse.'[147] He provided a *patriarchally sanctioned* pathway for a woman's voice to be registered at the level of culture—contained within

---

[145] Ibid. p. 127.
[146] Ibid. p. 126.
[147] Ibid. pp. 128-9.

a psychoanalyst's private rooms. For a woman is a transgressive creature who '... puts the inside on the outside. By projections and leakages of all kinds—somatic, vocal, emotional, sexual—females expose or expend what should be kept in ...'[148]

As Carson reveals, in fact '... Greek myth, literature and cult show traces of cultural anxiety about such female ejaculation.'[149] For there is a correspondence of mouth and genitals in ancient Greece. When both mouths speak it's embarrassing, confusing. Carson gives the example of Baubo whose face is on her torso—in close proximity to her vulva. Consequently, a woman's sounds have historically only been allowed to be enunciated in certain sanctioned controlled situations, such as during funeral rites, processions and laments. Or in the last century within the cloisters of the psycho-analyst rooms. Gendered sound is historically aligned with a source of pollution as well as purification, which engenders a catharsis/katharsis of the body through incantation. The means of liberation from reductive patriarchal frameworks, such as psychoanalysis, for girls, women, nonbinary and trans people is surely to give voice to their embodied experience in the heart of cultural life, to speak their mammalian-ness or creatureliness publicly—and as a means of rupturing social discourse. To be unsanctioned. To speak materially resonant truths out of bounds is to break down patriarchal doors on girls' and women's sexed-hexed-mouths. And we cannot achieve a fully liberated society until such a breaking down of lingering patriarchal constraint is brought about.

---

[148] Ibid. p. 129.
[149] Ibid. p. 132.

A Few Notes on Authorial Descent

Although a woman is certainly not reducible to her womb, let's not pretend it doesn't exist as a portal of birth and rebirth, offering access to extra-being; a wild element. Respect! As for a phallus-logic that has been thrust through women repeatedly—she heals the site of that wound and gives birth to a flow elsewhere—a fountain of 'pure pleasure.'[150] Surely, this reductively gendered *feminine* wound site is man's castration and not a woman proper. So, let's finally get completely outside of the empire of the selfsame, but not in terms of a trace of castration—women are of course not castrated! Women are in excess of prescribed codes of meaning and knowledge networks. They are planetary players. And we can, we must, get our planetary thoughts and feelings into words by drawing on a sensorium of human experience beyond Anthropos. I think this is what Ursula Le Guin is talking about when she says: 'We are volcanoes. When we women offer our experience as our truth, as human truth, all the maps change. There are new mountains.'[151]

Much like Irigaray's 'mother-nature-matter' category, in *Death of a Discipline*, Gyatri Spivak contends that a woman becomes an instrumental player in the 'shifting of the function of discursive systems' pertaining to a 'woman-as-mother-as-vagina' category.[152] Spivak further theorises a figuration of alterity that she terms 'planet-thought,' which engenders a re-imagining of ourselves as 'planetary subjects,' as opposed to 'global agents' or 'entities,' whereby otherness is not conceived of as 'our dialectical negation,'

---

[150] Borges, Jorge Luis. (1967) 1974. *The Book of Imaginary Beings*. Translated by Norman Thomas di Giovanni. New York: Avon. p. 93.
[151] Le, Ursula. 1986. "We Are Volcanoes." Speakola. May 1986. https://speakola.com/grad/ursula-le-guin-we-are-volcanoes-bryn-mawr-1986
[152] Spivak, Gayatri Chakravorty . 2003. *Death of a Discipline*. New York: Columbia University Press. p. 74.

but as a productive transgression.[153] For instance, women who demonstrate their affirmative poetic confluence with others, human and more-than-human worlds alike, forge new sustainable perspectives on human existence. They can make new cartographies by recording these relational experiences textually—poetically. For poetic writing can open up new possibilities of expression when it disrupts the framework through which language is assigned meaning in the world toward a discourse of the limit.[154] Significantly, this refutes the phallocentric hierarchical species stratification of colonial power that seeks to continually replicate itself as dominant heteronormative masculine identity, over-written onto the bodies of the oppressed.

In my mid-twenties I had to descend the ladder of writing, to enter a transformative abyss, in order to liberate all of those women's voices within myself—the ritual shouts of women from wolf-thickets. And when I gave birth to my children all I could hear was their animal howlings petitioning me. In *Women Who Run with the Wolves*, Clarisa Pincola Estes writes compellingly of the wild woman archetype throughout time who she argues is anomalous to *a law of the father*. Estes sutures another order of storytelling beyond patriarchy, which is linked with women, liminality, the animal and ecological worlds.

---

[153] Ibid. p. 73.
[154] Foucault, Michel. (1966) 1970. *The Order of Things: An Archeology of the Human Sciences*. Translated from the French. London: Tavistock Publications.

A Few Notes on Authorial Descent

La Loba, the wolf woman; or La Huesera, the bone woman. She is called in Hungarian "Erddben", She of the Woods, and Rozsomdk, The Wolverine. In Navajo, she is Na'ashje'ii Asdzaa, The Spider Woman, who weaves the fate of humans and animals and plants and rocks. In Guatemala, among many other names, she is Humana del Niebla, The Mist Being, the woman who has lived forever. In Japanese, she is Amaterasu Omikami, The Numina, who brings all light, all consciousness. In Tibet she is called Dakini, the dancing force which produces clearseeing within women. And it goes on. She goes on.[155]

Estes warns against 'separation from the wildish nature [which] causes a woman's personality to become meager, thin, ghostly, spectral.'[156] Estes is a Jungian scholar who favours the notion that when women follow a faultline at the edge of discursive networks they access a different kind of storytelling that she associates with folklore and fairytale, and which I would argue is antithetical to mythos, but rather aligned with the phantasmagorical, as well as poetical rift. And critically, women orators of these stories must return to register culturally what they have encountered in the unbounded abyssal realms, or forest-like spaces. Significantly, Estes mobilises a concept of womanhood that draws on her Indigenous lineage.

Let me state now once and for all, at the very heart of cultural life, that the category *woman* under patriarchal rule is a thoroughly colonial affair. If I am liminal, society has made me so (on account of having reproductive organs and sharing alignment with mammals

---

[155] Estes, C.P. 1992. *Women Who Run With the Wolves: Myths and Stories of the Wild Woman Archetype.* New York: Ballantine Books. p. 14.
[156] Ibid. p. 16

and other creatures that are linked with my voicings). We all know that the human species has historically been framed reductively in terms of 'Man-humanity, the one who makes decisions in the family ...'[157] But, there is another story that breaks the surface of a reductive western subjectivity for instance—like a blow to the head. A mammalian and/or creaturely woman singing, writing, creating. As Cixous advises in *Three Steps on the Ladder of Writing* there is a need to convey '[a] "tangling" in us all—The dark, wild, good-part in us; the beast part in human beings.'[158] This embodied woman's voice must be registered—listened to. It is a howling voice petitioning from the depths. A woman poet/writer must gain a platform culturally, and this has frequently required that a certain modus operandi is observed; a sanctioned way of articulating meaning. So how do you get society to listen to a language that it doesn't yet speak, or once did but has forgotten on account of a patriarchal program to perform a mass erasure? Cixous has a few answers, of course.

In 'Three Steps on the Ladder to Writing' she enthuses: 'I am interested in a chain of associations and signifiers composed of birds, women, and writing,' which may at first seem out of the ordinary—peculiar even.[159] Cixous is referring to the religious taboos that outlaw the consumption of birds, which are deemed unclean in the Bible. It is considered an abomination to eat birds in *Leviticus* for instance. She turns to Clarice Lispector, specifically her novel *The Passion According to G.H.*, to illustrate an example in which a woman

---

[157] Cixous, Hélène. 1993. *Three Steps on the Ladder of Writing*. New York: University of Columbia Press. p. 43.
[158] Ibid. p. 43.
[159] Ibid. p. 111-112.

A Few Notes on Authorial Descent

encounters her creatureliness through a poetic mode of fictional writing.

> In The Passion According to G. H., G. H., a woman reduced to her initials, encounters in complete solitude, face to face-even eye to eye a cockroach, an abominable cockroach. In Brazilian the word for cockroach is barata, and it is feminine. So a woman meets a barata, and it becomes the focus for a type of fantastic, total, emotional, spiritual, and intellectual revolution, which, in short, is a crime. The revolution leads G. H. to completely revise her clichéd way-our clichéd way-of thinking: our relations to the world in general and to living things in particular. She must deal with the phobia, with the horror we have of so-called abominable beings. I will now quote from a chapter in the middle of the book, after G. H. has had an initially ordinary reaction to the barata: that is, she has almost "killed" it by crushing it. A kind of white paste spurts out of the barata, which is nonetheless immortal. G. H. comes into contact with this paste; she starts thinking about what the white paste is and how to relate to it.[160]

G.H. comes into contact with something *impure*. 'In Brazilian "impure" is *immundo*.'[161] Cixous corrects the American translation of Lispector's text, in which G.H. refers to the Bible and the impurity of birds. Cixous retranslates the passage more accurately to reveal that Lispector intentionally emphasises that the Bible is aligned with the masculine. Lispector infers that the 'He-Bible' tells us what is supposedly 'unclean and abominable,' birds, alongside women and writing, who are banished to the outside.[162] 'Outside we shall find all those precious people who have not worried about respecting the

---

[160] Ibid. p. 111.
[161] Ibid. p. 112.
[162] Ibid. p. 113.

law that separates what is and is not abominable according to Those Bible.'[163] And so, Cixous affirms that Lispector is among other 'netherworld' writers, the ones that undergo a descent on behalf of the reader to retrieve a truth, albeit which is not absolute, but rather relative to circumstances—like the reductive historical circumstances for women under Judo-Christian morality for instance. Lispector reads a textual gap. And that's the only way for a woman poet/writer to learn her craft—by learning to read textual gaps—detecting what is forbidden or hidden. Performing a 'writing back' to a woman's embodiment. A woman poet/writer has to enter the crack and return with her own creaturely-tongue in-tact. A foreign tongue.

Lispector reveals that women alongside birds and writing are aligned with the forbidden. Although Lispector's G.H. experiences the terror of being impure she thereafter discovers the joy of being 'out of the world.'[164]

> That is my theme for today: to be "imund," to be unclean with joy. Immonde, that is, out of the mundus (the world). The monde, the world, that is so-called clean. The world that is on the good side of the law that is "proper," the world of order. The moment you cross the line the law has drawn by wording, verb(aliz)ing, you are supposed to be out of the world. You no longer belong to the world.'[165]

Surely with Lispector we are approaching a secret other world of women's writing and artistic capacity aligned with their creaturely embodiment, with the poetical and phantasmagorical, drawn into

---

[163] Ibid.
[164] Ibid. p. 117.
[165] Ibid.

A Few Notes on Authorial Descent

the *real*—intervening. Cixous conducts an experiment in exceeding subjection and aesthetic models of representation through giving voice to this creaturely tract, which has been sent underground, or liminalised, and therefore must be retrieved, brought out into the light of day.

Cixous courageously considers a mode of writing that is conducted by women, which attempts to re-access a wilderness component. She draws on something pre-linguistic 'beneath the earth' and 'in zones where music is spoken.'[166] She encounters Kafka's dreamscape there: 'It so happens that Kafka ... wrote in a phantasmic rather than poetic way. His apprenticeship was as a guest of the dead, which is what enabled him to write an authorless dream. Nobody knows.'[167] Here she syphons off the poetic from the phantasmagorical. But, they cannot be separated—one is the other. This 'risky country,' close to the unconscious, can only be reached 'through the back door of thought.'[168] A woman poet/writer continually crosses this border. And the woman poet/writer is not a man poet/writer—she must return from these sojourns, she must orate another not-history, inscribe the unwritten volume of the new. Overly abstract? Perhaps with an excess of phantasm hewn into it. But don't expect a woman poet/writer to learn her craft groveling at the ankles of a canon that does not know her name.

---

[166] Ibid. p. 104.
[167] Ibid. p. 106.
[168] Ibid. p. 114.

Nothing But a Fine Nerve Meter

In my mid-twenties I came to inscribe myself in these terms, with regards to a creaturely part of human experience '... deep in my body, further down, behind thought. Thought comes in front of it and it closes like a door. This does not mean that it does not think, but it thinks differently from our thinking and speech. Somewhere in the depths of my heart, which is deeper than I think. Somewhere in my stomach, my womb, and if you have not got a womb-then it is somewhere "else."'[169] I wrote of the dream door opening—of something ceremonial springing out of me. I mused on a life entrusted to ravens and owls to barter over, to prize out the head, bring out the body, its scrawly legs, its fierce claws, until another species of bird emerged, less scavenger than raven, more fuelled by daylight than owl. It seems owl partially won, somehow a woman-bird-thing emerged no longer human bound, rather guided by her own principals of stealth, no surrender, equipoise in flight and voice, not shouting, rather gathering steads of emptied out sun, tying them back together in an apprenticeship of letters. I gained a currency with which to speak. Poetry became my currency. But, it's not just the currency of women of course. It is also the currency of any person who has been marginalised. Nerve meter poetry puts the abyssal into language. It speaks of all queer morphologies. It is highly relational writing. It is Kafkaesque, for it opens up a window and wanders outside, finds new pathways, a new age at the planetary turn, but only after having recomposed the self out of depth. No more performing man-canon speech acts (that can be traced back

---

[169] Ibid. p. 118.

A Few Notes on Authorial Descent

to Plato's Cave and a designated man-philosopher-authored-reality) just so we can pass, be heard in the straight world.

In a strange way during my poet/writer apprenticeship in my mid-twenties, whilst I was engaged in learning my craft, searching for women mentors beyond the canon, I keenly identified with Helen Keller. I wanted to break into meaning from an outer limit. I was not deaf or blind which makes the comparison redundant to a large extent. And yet, I seemed to approach meaning from a sphere of exile—from subaqueous depths. It's just that when I read Keller's story, it opened a portal in me. I thought, here's a woman who feels the world and recites it from the nerve ends. Here's a woman who articulates another story. There is so much we can learn from Keller—a woman who has inhabited the silent world and returned in writing perpetually to expose a valuable other perspective on the human condition. She has something original to write about because she draws from another not-logic based in the sensual world, which denounces the primacy of vision pertaining to the way perception works. In her book *The World I Live In*, Keller writes:

> In any case, it is pleasant to have something to talk about that no one else has monopolized; it is like making a new path in the trackless woods, blazing the trail where no foot has pressed before. I am glad to take you by the hand and lead you along an untrodden way into a world where the hand is supreme. But at the very outset we encounter a difficulty. You are so accustomed to light, I fear you will stumble when I try to guide you through the land of darkness and silence. The blind are not supposed to be the best of guides. Still, though I cannot warrant not to lose you, I promise that you shall not be led into fire or water, or fall into a deep pit. If you will

follow me patiently, you will find that "there's a sound so fine, nothing lives 'twixt it and silence," and that there is more meant in things than meets the eye.'[170]

We must take our cues from Keller, an expert on the silent dark world, and the emancipatory potential of harnessing the miraculous imagination. Blind and deaf, Keller more fully apprehends the world with wondrous acuity. Keller writes: 'To the blind child the dark is kindly.'[171] And I would add that it is a wilderness that we wander into—feel for as 'fine Nerve Meter[s].'[172] But we must return to speak the truth about our experience. That is to say that, we might take on poetic sensibilities to better negotiate writing our reality.

In the absence of in-person mentors to teach me how to harness my aptitude for accessing this wilderness in me, which was framed societally as vulnerability, disorder, or in terms of being 'difficult,' uncategorical, I found Keller. I read Cixous, Irigaray, Artaud and Woolf. I identify as 'Nothing but a fine Nerve Meter': 'A kind of incomprehensible stopping place in the mind, right in the middle of everything.'[173] A deferred to transformative abyss—a darkness. Not a 'total abyss' as with Artaud.[174] I do not let it swallow me. I do not idealise my pain, or make it into an abortive reality to which I defer. Rather, the transformative abyss is where I go to draw on the imaginal, return, forge new exchanges in the ecosphere. I am not 'lost in the shadows of man,' not anymore since I learnt how

---

[170] Keller, Helen. 1908. *The World I Live In*. London: Hodder & Stoughton. p. 3.
[171] Ibid.
[172] Artaud, Antonin, and Susan Sontag. 1988. *Antonin Artaud, Selected Writings*. Berkeley: University Of California Press.
[173] Ibid. p. 86.
[174] Ibid. p. 80.

to sing my creatureliness—become something else.[175] To be a 'Fine Nerve Meter' is a poet's vocation—to engender a plausible valuable other reality, which links us to an entire phantasmagorical ecological cornucopia.[176]

To deal in poetic forays. A lifetime of gleaning the transformative abyss. I have lived on these borders, these outer limits of human as sorceress, creature, hysteric, menstruant—dealing in contagion.[177] As Albert Camus writes: 'But, what does it mean, the plague? It's life, that's all.'[178] We must rethink contagion in terms of an influence or a quality that is transmitted or communicated, an intrinsic part of being a human mammal or creature, although we've damaged the ecological environment on which we rely and so we've effectively poisoned ourselves. The poet/writer deals in this transmittable flow of vitality and death. But, this requires great courage and responsibility. It requires many life affirming deaths. Perhaps that's why it so moved me when I first read Cixous in my mid-twenties—here was a woman writer who dealt in poetic rebirth. Here was a woman who spoke my language, or perhaps more aptly who sang and seemed to expansively redefine writing in terms of poetical rift. Here was a woman thinker poet who accounted for her many

---

[175] Ibid.
[176] Ibid. p. 86.
[177] Dyer, Natalie Rose. 2020. *The Menstrual Imaginary in Literature: Notes on a Wild Fluidity*. Cham Switzerland: Palgrave Macmillan.
In my book *The Menstrual Imaginary in Literature: Notes on a Wild Fluidity* I argue that French anthropologist Marcel Mauss's '…work establishes the fact that menstruation has historically been considered an aspect of women's 'nature' that challenges religious systems and the dominant masculine hierarchy on account of its association with magic, mana, contagion and taboo' (Dyer, 2020). Menstruation's historical links with magic, mana, contagion and taboo further connects it to the sorceress and liminal space. This sphere of women's experience has been negatively pathologised in Western culture.
[178] Camus, Albert. (1947) 2015. *The Plague*. London: Penguin.

creaturely divergences in affirmative planetary terms. She helped me to understand that I am becoming this constant negotiation of borders—a perpetual mutation—a vector of contagion.

PART II

Writing Ecologies

Chapter Four

Imperceptible Signs; The Art of Invoking Virginia

"Those who dream by day are cognizant of many things which escape those who dream only by night."
                                                        Edgar Allan Poe.

One day whilst living in Amsterdam and during high summer, I wrote in my journal of a homesick longing for the dark: 'This northern land is enveloped in daylight, bathed in a sea balm of phosphorescence. It grows hotter as the cut rasp of energy blasts. I pine for the dark—its chloroform drenches. I want to feel the dark enclose me; a metier of silent velvet pulled over the length of my corpus. I want to undergo the full evacuation of the light—the weight of my heart staring down entropy as we rotate away from sun's emblematic furnace. Instead, energy constricts in my chest, it cannot sink. I've never-before known summer as this handle of endless light. I've mostly known empyrean skies, a milky way of flashy opals spread out across the vastness: Orion, Sirius, Canopus. Down south the open bowl of dark pours in through the arterial valve, sets in the veins, and the blood runs night. So, I visit the Planetarium just to sit in dimness a while. I look up hungrily at the milky dome—silently wait on the repose of the dark.' But beyond homesickness my longing for the dark perhaps signalled something like a desire to enter into uncharted time and space—to undergo reveries.

In her diary, dated Thursday June 30th 1927, Virginia Woolf records the eclipse. She tells of plunging through the midlands in a train with Vita Sackville-West and their coterie. Woolf writes: 'How can I express the darkness? It was a sudden plunge, when one did not expect it; being at the mercy of the sky; our own nobility; the druids, Stonehenge; and the racing red dogs; all that was in one's mind.'[179] Woolf gives wonderful fluency to the ruminations of her mind. The dark draws Woolf toward her many divergent phantasmagorical thoughts. In Rebecca Solnit's essay 'Woolf's Darkness' she calls attention to Woolf's accessions to the dark, which she claims is a declaration of the importance of confronting the unknown.[180]

In Woolf's essay 'Street Haunting: A London Adventure', also written in 1927, she transcribes a walk across London in the early evening, which gives rise to immersive thinking and an enlivened experience in the city more broadly. Solnit surmises that: 'Woolf is celebrating getting lost, not literally lost as in not knowing how to find your way, but lost as in open to the unknown, and the way that physical space can provide psychic space'—the latitude to mind-wander.[181] I've always been disposed to daydreaming. I do it best while walking in the woods near my house—or further afield.

---

[179] Woolf, Virginia. 1980. *The Diary of Virginia Woolf; Volume 3, 1925-1930*. Editor Anne Olivier Bell. Assisted by Andrew McNeillie. New York: Harcourt. p. 144.
[180] Solnit, Rebecca. 2014. *Men Explain Things to Me and Other Essays*. London: Granta. p. 86.
[181] Ibid. pp. 98-9.

And Woolf clearly mind-wandered whilst walking too. Whilst living in Amsterdam, my son was told at his newcomer's language class that he too was a serial daydreamer—he was reprimanded for it. As if it isn't a valuable part of human experience to feel one's fluid fibres entwine everything. To veer closer to the phantasmagorical, to make accessions to the dark, on a regular basis liberates us.

Neurologist Marcus Raichle states that: 'When we daydream, we're at the centre of the universe.'[182] Here we are set drift in a fluid, non-linear, meandering of free associations and 'intuitive leaps,' which can lead to extraordinary insights. In *The Wandering Mind: What the Brain Does When You're Not Looking*, Michael Corballis writes:

> ... mind-wandering has many constructive and adaptive features—indeed, we probably couldn't do without it. It includes time travel—the wandering back and forth through time, not only to plan our futures based on past experiences, but also to generate a continuous sense of who we are. Mind-wandering allows us to inhabit the minds of others, increasing empathy and social understanding. Through mind-wandering, we invent, tell stories, expand our mental horizons. Mind-wandering underwrites creativity, whether as a Wordsworth wandering lonely as a cloud or an Einstein imagining himself travelling on a beam of sunlight.[183]

Mind-wandering is closely linked with identity formation, as well as identity de-formation. We tell stories to ourselves about who

---

[182] Marcus Raichle cited by Josie Glausiusz. 2013. "Living in an Imaginary World." *Scientific American* 23 (1s): 70—77. https://doi.org/10.1038/scientificamericancreativity1213-70
[183] Corbalis, Michael. 2015. *The Wandering Mind: What the Brain Does When You're Not Looking*. New York: The University of Chicago Press. p. 10.

we are in the world with respect to other beings and phenomena through mind-wandering—we firm up a sense of self this way. And yet, mind-wandering goes against-the-grain of societal expectation. It brings about the possibility of potentially straddling a border of sanity. As Woolf points out it has historically been considered a regressive enterprise. She writes in her essay 'Street Haunting': 'The good citizen when he opens his door in the evening must be a banker, golfer, husband, father; not a nomad wandering the desert, a mystic staring at the sky …'[184] The fact that Woolf assumes a man is indicative of the patriarchal landscape in which her essay was written, although Woolf was clearly a ground breaking feminist writer. To do as Lily, an artist, does in *To the Lighthouse*: 'Certainly she was losing consciousness of outer things. And as she lost consciousness of outer things … her mind kept throwing up from its depths, scenes, and names, and sayings, and memories and ideas, like a fountain spurting …'[185] But, according to Gilles Deleuze and Felix Guattari it is most frequently the writer who experiences this principle of uprooting their humanity in favour of involuting.

In *A Thousand Plateaus* they propose that: 'If the writer is a sorcerer, it is because writing is a becoming, writing is traversed by strange becomings that are not becoming-writer, but becomings-rat, becomings-insect, becomings-wolf, etc.'[186] Or indeed, becomings Woolfian, especially as Deleuze and Guattari certainly have Woolf in mind when concocting their take on metamorphosis. They argue

---

[184] Woolf, Virginia. (1942) 1961. *The Death of the Moth and Other Essays*. Middlesex: Penguin Books.
[185] Lehrer, Jonah. 2012. "The Virtues of Daydreaming." The New Yorker. June 5, 2012. https://www.newyorker.com/tech/frontal-cortex/the-virtues-of-daydreaming
[186] Deleuze, Gilles and Guattari, Félix. (1980) 1987. *A Thousand Plateaus: Capitalism and Schizophrenia*. Translated and with a foreword by Brian Massumi. Minneapolis: Minnesota Press. p. 265.

that Woolf: '... experiences herself not as a monkey or a fish but as a troop of monkeys, a school of fish, according to her variable relations of becoming with the people she approaches.'[187] Woolf demonstrates repeatedly in her writing the need to kill off singular identity—the idea of a woman as 'Angel of the House' for instance. She orchestrates this liberation principle most overtly and eruditely in *The Waves*.

On June 18th 1927, Woolf recorded her wish to write 'a continuous stream, not solely of human thought, but of The Waves of the ship, the night etc., all flowing together: intersected by the arrival of the bright moths.'[188] This rumination in her journal pertaining to *The Waves*, which was originally to be titled *The Moths*, is 'a completely new attempt.' On November 7th, 1928 Woolf writes: 'Yes, but The Moths? That was to be an abstract mystical eyeless book: a playpoem.'[189] Occulocentric perception is de-hierarchised in *The Waves* in favour of a more sensuous terrain. Woolf closely registers the awareness of six key players: Bernard, Susan, Rhoda, Neville, Jinny and Louis over the course of their lives, commencing in childhood, as they continue to elaborate their existence in poetic soliloquies. The characters of *The Waves* establish themselves through 'thought patterns' or mind-wanderings, which are conveyed in surges of poetic vernacular.[190] Woolf's novel, if it can be called a novel at all, more poetic rumination, attempts to trace what has been unnamable, undefined, formless, or fluid in human experience. She highlights the failure of discourse, its limited capacity to convey the

---

[187] Ibid. p. 264.
[188] Woolf, Virginia. 1980. *The Diary of Virginia Woolf; Volume 3, 1925-1930*. Editor Anne Olivier Bell. Assisted by Andrew McNeillie. New York: Harcourt. p. 139.
[189] Ibid. p. 203.
[190] Woolf, Virginia. (1931) 1992. *The Waves*. Introduction by Kate Flint. London: Penguin. p. xiv.

gamut of rolling inward, feeling things deeply, at the nexus of human experience, and the subsequent rolling outwards with respect to many varied others and planetary phenomena that we undergo.

For as Foucault tells us, poetic writing can open up new possibilities of expression when it disrupts the framework, through which language is assigning meaning in the world, towards the potential rupturing of normative identity and/or subjectivity. That is, if we accept the idea that identity is primarily constructed 'through an individual's deployment of language' and the stories we tell ourselves and others.[191] Certainly Woolf highlights the 'inadequacy of language' to convey the full gamut of human experience in *The Waves*, our aptitudes and insights, our wild musings, which 'disrupts material experience.'[192] She explores the possibility of wandering through a rift in language beyond that which is named. As Solnit surmises:

> It is difficult, sometimes even impossible, to value what cannot be named or described, and so the task of naming and describing is an essential one in any revolt against the status quo of capitalism and consumerism. Ultimately the destruction of the Earth is due in part, perhaps in large part, to a failure of the imagination or to its eclipse by systems of accounting that can't count what matters. The revolt against this destruction is a revolt of the imagination, in favour of subtleties, of pleasures money can't buy and corporations can't command, of being producers rather than consumers of meaning, of the slow, the meandering, the digressive, the exploratory, the numinous, the uncertain.'[193]

---

[191] Ibid. p. x.
[192] Ibid. p. xxxii.
[193] Solnit, Rebecca. 2014. *Men Explain Things to Me and Other Essays*. London: Granta. p. 105.

Woolf asserts that *The Waves* must take up the liberation stratagem begun in *Orlando; A Biography*, albeit ride it somewhere new, to convey a greater breadth of human experience. The minds-wanderings arrive like conscious flows and counterflows of the central protagonists in *The Waves*—fathomed as 'the phantom waves.'[194] Woolf ruminates in her diary that there must be 'freedom from "reality,"' and yet it must be 'relevant,' in this ceaseless navigation between reality and the imaginary experience, which is the phantasmagorical poetical terrain.[195] She seeks to account for the imaginal diversions that mediates our actual material existence. The waves are of course a metaphor for the mind's many forays, wondrous departures, harrowing staggering losses, and continual returns.

Woolf writes in her diary 23rd June, 1929: 'Everything becomes green and vivified in me when I begin to think of *The Moths*. Also, I think, one is much better able to enter into others—'[196] For instance, on graduating from secondary school and riding a train headed toward his next phase of institutional learning, Bernard articulates his active involvement with others, specifically his interest in a traveler on the train.

> I do not believe in separation. We are not single. Also I wish to add to my collection of valuable observations upon the true nature of human life. My book will certainly run to many volumes, embracing every known variety of man and woman. I fill my mind with whatever happens to be

---

[194] Woolf, Virginia. 1980. *The Diary of Virginia Woolf; Volume 3, 1925-1930*. Editor Anne Olivier Bell. Assisted by Andrew McNeillie. New York: Harcourt. p. 236.
[195] Ibid. p. 236.
[196] Woolf, Virginia. 1980. *The Diary of Virginia Woolf; Volume 3, 1925-1930*. Editor Anne Olivier Bell. Assisted by Andrew McNeillie. New York: Harcourt. p. 236.

the contents of a room or a railway carriage as one fills a fountain-pen in an inkpot. I have a steady unquenchable thirst. Now I feel imperceptible signs, which I cannot now interpret but will later ...'[197]

Bernard perceives the thawing of the prickly man on the train as he extends himself, or rather effaces the illusion of separation through attempting to relate to another. He apprehends that we are not singular beings, but rather part of a continuum. We exist in this amorphous space of exchange—between real and imaginary—in constant phantasmagorical flux. We are uncategorical, hybrid, creaturely beings becoming everything all the time. Take Neville who considers: 'I am a poet, yes. Surely I am a great poet.'[198] Neville comes to this realisation on account of the fact that he perceives all that remains unnamed. For he apprehends the wayward decidua of life—the endless rebirthing of phenomena around him, or rather within him. Neville perceives himself awake to all phenomena. He is able to see things, or no, rather he senses things. And he is not merely Neville, but also Bernard. Neville articulates the feeling of being migrated when his friend appears: '... to have one's self adulterated, mixed up, become part of another. As he approaches I become not myself but Neville mixed with somebody — with whom? — with Bernard?'[199]

In *The Order of Things: An Archeology of the Human Sciences*, Foucault ruminates over a passage in Jorge Louis Borges *The Book of Imaginary Beings* describing a taxonomy of animals found in a

---

[197] Woolf, Virginia. (1931) 1992. *The Waves*. Introduction by Kate Flint. London: Penguin. pp. 49-50.
[198] Ibid. p. 61.
[199] Ibid. pp. 61-62.

Chinese encyclopedia, which breaks down 'the age-old distinction between the Same and the Other.'[200] Foucault apprehends in Borges' taxonomy of animals another system of thought that exposes the 'limitations of our own.'[201] He surmises that this 'strange' categorisation that attempts to 'distinguish' animals between the 'real' and the imaginary, also disbands the possibility of 'dangerous mixtures.'[202] Foucault identifies in Borges' passage a 'rift,' an 'instability' or 'flaw' in this ordering of things—a space in which knowledge diversifies.[203] He advises that in this 'bestiary of the imaginary' the monstrous materialises in 'the interstitial blanks *separating* all these entities from one another.'[204] Foucault proposes that the contrasting disparate categories of a, b, c, d, in fact creates a new hybrid, which is made up of the fruitful 'possibility of juxtaposition,' towards 'the non-place of language,' or the supposition of 'unthinkable space' linked with the poetic.[205] Foucault identifies a space of deviation, or disbanding the 'primary codes,' with which humans engage with.[206] He exposes a middle region that 'liberates order itself,' and which is necessarily poetic.[207]

Woolf's central protagonists in *The Waves* reinforce this notion that we are exotic mixtures of human, animal, ecologies, phenomena, matter and so on. We are continuously in the process of leaning into something else, that which exceeds ourselves. Woolf's key players

---

[200] Foucault, Michel. (1966) 1970. *The Order of Things: An Archeology of the Human Sciences.* Translated from the French. London: Tavistock Publications.
[201] Ibid.
[202] Ibid. p. xv.
[203] Ibid. pp. xxi-xxii.
[204] Ibid: p. xvi.
[205] Ibid. p. xvii.
[206] Ibid. p. xx.
[207] Ibid. p. xxi.

articulate multiple moments of rupture. Perhaps they convey the minutiae of becoming a 'Fine Nerve Meter' as Antonin Artaud had it, of touching on a source at the nexus of experience, circuited to the nervous system, which engenders a tractability to otherness. As an adult Louis tells us: 'My roots go down through veins of lead silver, though damp, marshy places that exhale odours, to the knot made of oak roots bound together in the centre. Sealed and blind, with earth ...'[208] When Susan goes out walking early in the morning she considers: 'I think I am the field, I am the barn, I am the trees ... the flocks of birds, the cow ... I cannot be divided, or kept apart.'[209] And so, what is real, or what is imaginary, becomes entirely reductive, a mere binary that cannot account for the enormity of our multidimensional poetical and phantasmagorical human experience.

In one of the italics sections in *The Waves*, Woolf writes of a girl playing in the waves. She swiftly proceeds to the garden to entertain the consciousness of birds and their appetites. The reader is coerced into speculating whether the birds attentions are focused on a snail shell, the flowers or the 'bright apple leaves' before entering the decomposing soil.[210] We come to inhabit the birds awareness:

> Now glancing this side, that side, they looked deeper, beneath the flowers, down the dark avenues into the unlit world where the leaf rots and the flower has fallen. Then one of them, beautifully darting, accurately alighting, spiked the soft, monstrous body of the defenceless worm, pecked again and yet again, and left it to fester. Down there among the roots where the flowers decay, gusts of dead smells were wafted; drops formed on the

---

[208] Woolf, Virginia. (1931) 1992. *The Waves*. Introduction by Kate Flint. London: Penguin. p. 71.
[209] Ibid. p. 72.
[210] Ibid. pp. 54-55.

bloated sides of swollen things. The skin of rotten fruit broke, a matter oozed too thick to run. Yellow excretions were exuded by slugs, and now and again an amorphous body with a head at either end swayed slowly from side to side. The gold-eyed birds darting in between the leaves observed that purulence, that wetness, quizzically. Now and then they plunged the tips of their beaks savagely into the sticky mixture.'[211]

By describing in minutiae detail the birds' perspective entrained to living matter decomposing, Woolf invites her reader to enter into a strange mixture of mineral, vegetal and animal realms. Thereafter she describes a room: 'The real flower on the window-sill was attended by a phantom flower. Yet the phantom was part of the flower, for when a bud broke free the paler flower in the glass opened a bud too.'[212] Woolf writes about the flower's reflection in the mirror. She points out that imaginary experience is a vital part of *real* experience, delicately interwoven, continually, irrevocably.

To return briefly to Borges, Deleuze and Guattari argue in *A Thousand Plateaus* that he 'botched' *Manual de Zoología Fantástica* because he utilises a 'bland image of myth,' and does not fathom 'the corresponding becoming-animal of the human being.'[213] But surely this is what Woolf upholds in her writing, particularly in *The Waves*, the transformations of the human being. In Deleuze and Guattari's view myth is incapable of registering 'correspondence between relations.'[214] They argue that *becoming* engenders a more

---

[211] Ibid. p. 55.
[212] Ibid.
[213] Deleuze, Gilles and Guattari, Félix. (1980) 1987. *A Thousand Plateaus: Capitalism and Schizophrenia*. Translated and with a foreword by Brian Massumi. Minneapolis: Minnesota Press. p. 266.
[214] Ibid. p. 262.

dynamic and creative mode of expression beyond mythos '... more like fragments of tales,' which are 'secret,' 'subterranean,' an entering into the dark.[215] It is the *phantasm* that supersedes myth—as a de-institutionalised foray into the unknown. This is what Woolf demonstrates for all of us, a phantasmagorical planetary flow, especially in *The Waves*. Woolf delivers poetic fragments that exceed discourse and prescribed rational codes of meaning and being. But, she also manages to thereafter unify these poetic fragments, so as to 'make the blood run from end to end' of the text like a 'currency.'[216] Woolf molds something fluent that honours who we are as mammals or creatures beyond a reductive framework of phallocentric hierarchical speciesism in *The Waves*. It is an unparalleled triumph of poetic prose because it explicates what it truly is to be a human on planet earth.

In *Logic of Sense*, Deleuze proposes 'destroying' as a means of subverting the established order of 'representations, models and copies,' thereby bringing about chaos, which gives birth to a 'simulacra function'—raising a phantasm.[217] This sounds a lot like imagining a wild tract of meaning that refutes empirical knowledge, which is a relation 'essential to language,' as well as ego-loss.[218] Isn't this mind-wandering stuffs? The font of creative works? When we mind-wander we temporarily lose ourselves to become something

---

[215] Ibid.
[216] Woolf, Virginia. 1980. *The Diary of Virginia Woolf; Volume 3, 1925-1930*. Editor Anne Olivier Bell. Assisted by Andrew McNeillie. New York: Harcourt.
[217] Deleuze, Gilles. (1969) 1990. *Logic of Sense*. Translated by Mark Lester with Charles Stivale. Edited by Constantine V. Boundas. London: The Athlone Press. p. 266.
[218] Ibid. p. 1-2. To this end Deleuze reflects on Platonian subterranean dualism that corresponds firstly with 'Ideas and matter' in terms of a 'limited' or 'fixed' measure of 'things' and 'qualities' and 'pauses and rests' in the forging of a subject, and secondly with respect to pure-becoming, when there is no measure, no 'rests,' but in its stead a multidirectional 'mad element' that 'eludes' to the present in the causation of past and future; a flow of 'rebellious matter.'

else—we demonstrate our ongoing metamorphosis. We give birth to a rebellious flow that is paradoxical and troubles fixed identities in the promotion of 'infinite identity.'[219] And when we draw on this subversive phantasmagorical stuffs of the mind's many divergences, to create subversive artistic articulations, we can bring about a revolution in poetic language based in multiplicity and relationality—another kind of poetic catharsis.

In *The Waves* Bernard, Susan, Rhoda, Neville, Jinny and Louis continually proclaim as Walt Whitman does in *Song of Myself*: 'I am multitudes.' Whitman sings of becoming with the ecosphere—'I will go to the bank by the wood and become undisguised and naked/ I am mad for it to be in contact with me.'[220] He enquires: '... have you reckon'd the earth much?/ Have you practis'd so long to learn to read?'[221] To involute is to learn to read the earth and the plenitude of earthly things. To have things through planetary experience—an inception. To be naked in the grass by the river—nearby the woods. To allow ourselves to encounter the exchange of bodies and matter with the atmosphere of trees. To feel the sun's spectral heat on the skin. To have this rebirth of the self in fluid commune, allowing ourselves to practice mind-wandering on a regular basis, becoming with everything, and for the betterment of humankind. To demand a space to discharge thoughts of our own accord—not in accordance with someone else's agenda. To *not* be imposed on, but rather de-institutionalised. To be free to become with everything at will. To evolve.

---

[219] Ibid. pp. 2-3.
[220] Whitman, Walt. (1892) 1979. *Leaves of Grass*. Pennsylvania: The Franklin Library. p. 28.
[221] Ibid. p. 29.

Percival is one of King Arthur's Knights of the Round Table and the original hero in the quest for the grail. He represents humanity's search for self-knowledge. It is as if Percival acts as a kind of principle in *The Waves*, something like the prospect of being a creator on the earth, perhaps mostly specifically a poet. The 'something that is made,' and which is 'globed … together'—a relational principle is apparently orchestrated by Percival.[222] It might be Percival who is articulated in the italics sections of *The Waves*—closest to the tidal rift of becomings. In fact, the death of Percival coincides with the birth of Bernard's child and his entrance into a reductive patriarchal story. Susan tells that Percival falls in India.[223] Where else but the scene of Britain's empirical conquest? Percival's death stands for the renewal of the imperialist ego (aka Trump imperative) in the modernist age against the human capacity for multiplicity and creativity. But, as Bernard warns: 'We are creators' not slaves.[224] And this is what we must collectively alight to.

In *The Waves*, Percival's death marks the severing of human awareness of their connection to others, human and more-than-human alike. 'Percival was flowering with green leaves and was laid in the earth with all his branches still sighing in the summer wind.'[225] The death of Percival is a mournful event indeed, the birth of a capitalist trajectory devoid of embodied imaginal agency. Henceforth there are only exceptions, artists, seers, writers and poets who are sanctioned to orchestrate this creative capacity and with the weight of all humanity on their shoulders. With Percival's passing, humans

---

[222] Woolf, Virginia. (1931) 1992. *The Waves*. Introduction by Kate Flint. London: Penguin. p. 109.
[223] Ibid. p. 147.
[224] Ibid. p. 110.
[225] Ibid. p. 155.

forget that their life is threaded through others in favour of directing attention toward industry and/or commerce.

I am certain that it is because Woolf strayed so close to the border—went *mad* so to speak—that she was capable of bequeathing to us such a sustained exploration of something else beyond this limited framework. This damned patriarchy. I'm forever indebted to her and to Artaud. I'm not advocating madness as a methodology. I am marking out a space of rupture in discourse, in which to argue for multitudinous being—not a single stable unitary self but many. I'm arguing for deformation of singularity. This is the fluency of poetic phantasmagorical planetary reality. For Deleuze the phantasm does not necessitate a distinction between imaginary and real, but rather is distinguished by a 'pure event,' by which he perhaps means to liberate a cosmological thread of knowledge that corresponds with ego-loss, and which is also embodied.[226] In *Anti-Oedipus: Capitalism and Schizophrenia*, Deleuze and Guattari draw on the work of R.D. Laing to expose the notion that: '... ego-loss is in fact the experience of *mankind*, which highlights a primal strain of desire and indeed fluidity associated with the animal and ecological world that cannot be accounted for in psychoanalysis.'[227] But Woolf certainly didn't defer to Freud. She did not undergo analysis. Rather, she diffused herself—continued to become something else. She underwent non-pathological ego-loss and poetical rebirth by way of her work ongoingly. Woolf cast herself out of the empire of the self-same toward all mutations, that which exceeds prescribed meaning

---

[226] Deleuze, Gilles. (1969) 1990. *Logic of Sense*. Translated by Mark Lester with Charles Stivale. Edited by Constantine V. Boundas. London: The Athlone Press. p. 211.

[227] Dyer, Natalie Rose. 2020. *The Menstrual Imaginary in Literature : Notes on a Wild Fluidity*. Cham, Switzerland: Palgrave Macmillan. p. 171.

through undertaking mind wandering and poetic writing, and with respect to her status as a woman. How so?

In her introduction to *The Waves* Kate Flint writes that: 'In its early stages, Woolf conceived of her book as the representation of "A mind thinking"; not a sexless, nor androgynous mind, but the mind, specifically of a woman: But who is she? I am very anxious that she should have no name. I don't want a Lavinia or a Penelope: I want "she."'[228] And yet, as Flint points out, Woolf abhorred gender essentialism. In her essay 'Women and Fiction', Woolf disapproved the idea of any special pleading for either sex. As Flint reveals, Woolf submerges any allusions to autobiography or maternity in *The Waves*. Certainly, *The Waves* is not autobiography in the sense of a life history, but far more expansive than that, rather it might be considered an exploration of thresholds—passages out of patriarchy toward everything else. In *A Room of One's Own*, Woolf gives us a hint when she advises us 'to think back through our mothers.'[229]

In *The Waves*, Neville, the poet, says: 'We are infinitely abject ...'[230] In *Powers of Horror: An Essay on Abjection*, Kristeva argues that the: '... struggle to break away from the maternal influence "fashions the human being" and is thereafter drawn upon through jouissance, that is, when repression is relaxed.'[234] Kristeva's semiotic chora is a compelling theory of human identity formation '... aligned with rhythms, cadences and movements of the maternal body closely

---

[228] Flint and Flint cites Virginia Woolf. Woolf, Virginia. (1931) 1992. *The Waves*. Introduction by Kate Flint. London: Penguin. p. xix.
[229] Ibid. p. xix.
[230] Ibid. p. 114.

related to prosodic formulations of language.'[231] It is reductive to pretend that a mother's endless love of the other and her ongoing nurturing of that bond doesn't impact our development as human beings. It is also reductive to assume that it is always affirmative. And yet, it seems to me downright insulting to erase the influence of the mother. For we can trace the maternal influence to the womb—our first haven. This experience imprints onto the developing fetus. And the kinship forged there surely informs future mediations, albeit in part. Before the breast gave us nourishment the womb did. As Adrienne Rich writes in her seminal book *Of Woman Born: Motherhood as Experience and Intuition*, 'We carry the imprint of this experience for life, even into our dying.'[232] And so, humans who demonstrate their mammalian embodiment in confluence with social and environmental ecologies *think back through their mothers* metaphorically—they're Woolfian.

To further reiterate this point, Woolf tells Ethel Smyth in a letter dated 28th August, 1930, that she wrote *The Waves* '... to a rhythm not a plot.' 'She listened to late Beethoven sonatas when she was first contemplating the form which the novel should take.'[233] Flint asks: 'But what kind of rhythms do the waves beat out?[234] She uncovers that: '... the waves of feeling were, right at the beginning of her draft, something else. They were linked, quite explicitly, to the rhythms

---

[231] Dyer, Natalie Rose. 2020. *The Menstrual Imaginary in Literature : Notes on a Wild Fluidity*. Cham, Switzerland: Palgrave Macmillan. p. 130.
[232] Rich, Adrienne. (1976) 1995. *Of Woman Born: Motherhood as Experience and Institution*. New York: W.W. Norton & Co. p. 11.
[233] Woolf, Virginia. (1931) 1992. *The Waves*. Introduction by Kate Flint. London: Penguin. p. xxi.
[234] Ibid. p. xxi.

of a woman's body as she gives birth.'[235] Flint quotes from Woolf's early draft of *The Waves*:

> "Many mothers, and before them many mothers, and again many mothers," she wrote: "have groaned, and fallen. Like one wave, succeeding another. Wave after wave, endlessly sinking and falling as far as the eye can stretch. And all these waves have been the prostrate forms of mothers, in their night-gowns, with the tumbled sheets around them holding up, with a groan, as they sink back into the sea.[236]

On reading this excerpt, I immediately recalled the final contractions when giving birth to my first child as a series of massive body pounding waves, such as those that take you under into a vortex of immeasurable energy, almost overwhelming with their strength and veracity. It was very soon after these contractions that I gave birth. The rhythmic acuity that the mother undergoes, and which a child's body remembers, is a mammalian or creaturely song thereafter drawn on, redrawn on, in the forging of our planetary flows of conscious awareness. It is imprinted into our bodies and mediates our thinking. The mind-wanderings of Woolf's central protagonists in *The Waves* reflect these many excursions into doing poetic thought, which we all undertake, and that have the capacity to liberate a creaturely planetary anti-logic of being human. We ought to restore social agency to the dreamer, the wayfarer, the stray who sojourns psychically, puts themselves in the place of others, and returns to tell a new tale beyond reductive hierarchy speciesism. It is this poetical phantasmagorical mammalian or creaturely strain of infinite being

---

[235] Ibid. p. xxii.
[236] Flint quotes Woolf from the draft of her manuscript in Woolf, Virginia. (1931) 1992. *The Waves*. Introduction by Kate Flint. London: Penguin. p. xxii.

orchestrated by Woolf in *The Waves*, which demonstrates how to find our way forward *together*, that is, not at the expense of another.

Chapter Five

Diving for Pearls; Riffing Off Others' Words

Doing poetic writing can allow us to cross borders into new ecological frontiers of connectivity. We can give ourselves a bit of narrative therapy, or planetary catharsis, by way of poetic writing. For we must not let the apocalyptic political imaginary shut down our capacity for imaginal flight. The poetic especially can offer an 'exhilarating' space of 'anarchic openness,' and imaginative transformative capacity when we pay attention to what is other-most.[237] To take Walt Whitman's advice as Virginia Woolf did: 'My knowledge my live parts, is keeping tally with the meaning of all things.'[238] And in these terms learning to think and feel our planetary reality or predicament.

We can use poetic writing as a tool to de-form the identity and thereafter to reform it in terms of planetary multiplicity. Walter Benjamin's notion of the imagination as a 'de-forming agent' is critical to this process of fostering the productive de-stabilisation of

---

[237] Bennett, Andrew, and Nicholas Royle. 2004. *An Introduction to Literature, Criticism and Theory*. London: Longman Publishing Group. p. 108.
[238] Whitman, Walt. (1892) 1979. *Leaves of Grass*. Pennsylvania: The Franklin Library.

the ego towards the creation of a more outward perspective.[239] In my book *Notes on a Wild Fluidity* I argued that:

> This political act of de-forming identity by way of the imagination in order to affirmatively rebuild it is a critical work needed to facilitate an outward perspective, which embraces difference. For an ethics of alterity, in Lithuanian-born philosopher Emmanuel Levinas's terms for instance, deliberately brings about a destabilisation of the subject as a means of facilitating self-critique, calling the ego into question, so that the self may come to embrace the possibility of another perspective, which provides an outward orientation. Levinas focuses on our responsibility to the Other. He asserts that: 'The Other as Other is not only an alter ego: the Other is what I myself am not' (Levinas 1989, 48). And, although Levinas problematically conflates the 'feminine' Other with a 'mystery' of 'not myself' he also opens up a space for a de-hierarchised concept of alterity based on love, or Eros, which is potentially emancipatory.[240]

Staying with Benjamin's modus operandi a while longer, straying with Levinas, to find another perspective of not myself, but rather an affirmative notion of another informed by love. We can learn to inhabit another perspective by diving for pearls—riffing off others' words to affirmatively reform the self, and which might be a very necessary initiative at the planetary turn.

---

[239] Walter Benjamin cited in Parr, Adrian. 2017. *Rebirth of a New Earth: The Radical Politics of Environmentalism*. New York: Columbia University Press. p. 170.
[240] Dyer, Natalie Rose. 2020. *The Menstrual Imaginary in Literature: Notes on a Wild Fluidity*. Cham, Switzerland: Palgrave Macmillan. p. 18.

Nothing But a Fine Nerve Meter

In her introduction to *Illuminations*, Hannah Arendt reflects on Walter Benjamin as a '...*flâneur* in his thinking, of the way his mind worked, when he, like the *flaneur* in the city, entrusted himself to chance as a guide on his intellectual journeys of exploration.'[241] Arendt discusses this tendency pertaining to Benjamin's habit of collecting books for his library, albeit not for their market value, rather for their strange and alluring contents. At some point, Benjamin transitioned from book collecting to collecting quotations—literary pearls.

> ... nothing was more characteristic of him [Benjamin] in the thirties than the little notebooks with black covers which he always carried with him and in which he tirelessly entered in the form of quotations what daily living and reading netted him in the way of 'pearls' and 'coral.' On occasion he read them out loud, showed them around like items from a choice and precious collection.[242]

Benjamin recorded quotations from varying sources, such that their juxtaposition forged something of a surrealistic poetic pastiche. Arendt argues that quotations are central to Benjamin's work. She explores this notion with respect to Benjamin's writing on German tragedy:

> The main work consisted in tearing fragments out of their context and arranging them afresh in such a way that they illustrated one another and were able to prove their raison d'être in a free-floating state, as it were. It definitely was a sort of surrealistic montage. Benjamin's ideal of producing a work consisting entirely of quotations, one that was mounted so

---

[241] Benjamin, Walter. 1968. *Walter Benjamin: Essays and Reflections*. With introduction by Hannah Arendt. Translated by Harry Zohn. New York: Schocken Books. p. 43.
[242] Ibid. p. 45.

masterfully that it could dispense with any accompanying text, may strike one as whimsical in the extreme and self-destructive to boot, but it was not, any more than were the contemporaneous surrealistic experiments which arose from similar impulses. To the extent that an accompanying text by the author proved unavoidable, it was a matter of fashioning it in such a way as to preserve 'the intention of such investigations,' namely, 'to plumb the depths of language and thought ... by drilling rather than excavating'[243]

The idea of drilling into literature for 'thought things,' which are re-imagined, put to new use, made to bring about new insight through strange copulations is suggested by Arendt pertaining to Benjamin's work.[244] Benjamin drew on quotations to anarchically refashion the future. He embraced poetic writing as prophecy. 'This method is like the modern equivalent of ritual invocations, and the spirits that now arise invariably are those spiritual essences from the past that have suffered the Shakespearean "sea-change" from living eyes to pearls, from living bones to coral' writes Arendt.[245] The poet/writer is a translator of these literary frequencies and musings.

> Like a pearl diver who descends to the bottom of the sea, not to excavate the bottom and bring it to the light but to pry loose the rich and the strange, the pearls and the corals in the depths, and to carry them to the surface, this thinking delves into the depths of the past—but not in order to resuscitate it the way it was and to contribute to the renewal of extinct ages. What guides this thinking is the conviction that although the living

---

[243] Arendt and Arendt cite Benjamin, Walter. 1968. *Walter Benjamin: Essays and Reflections*. With introduction by Hannah Arendt. Translated by Harry Zohn. New York: Schocken Books. pp. 47-48.
[244] Benjamin, Walter. 1968. *Walter Benjamin: Essays and Reflections*. With introduction by Hannah Arendt. Translated by Harry Zohn. New York: Schocken Books. p. 48.
[245] Ibid. pp. 48-49.

> is subject to the ruin of the time, the process of decay is at the same time a process of crystallization, that in the depth of the sea, into which sinks and is dissolved what once was alive, some things 'suffer a sea-change' and survive in new crystallized forms and shapes that remain immune to the elements, as though they waited only for the pearl diver who one day will come down to them and bring them up into the world of the living—as 'thought fragments,' as something 'rich and strange,' and perhaps even as everlasting Urphänomene.[246]

But what if humans must suffer a 'sea-change' (or a tree change) by undergoing a literary descent; by drawing back to others literary words and launching new poetic epiphanies? To plumb the depths for insight with special attention to the forging of new fusions, or indeed diffusions, as the case may be. The notion that the process of writing is akin to diving for ruins, entering the decay of culture, is simultaneously a process of crystallisation, since the diver finds strange treasure, returns it to the living world—delivers a diadem of poetic thought fragments. Descending to tell new tales about planetary alterity; convergent with a plethora of 'nonhuman animal species, ecosystems, technology and matter.'[247] Benjamin's methodology of refashioning poetic fragments seems to me a kind of template for transformation. He inaugurates a type of play that is steeped in the materiality of language and human metamorphosis. It is challenging the power dynamic by redeploying a quotation to deliver entirely new configurations of human experience, a chance to re-figure the strange and mysterious against-the-grain of patriarchal interpretation (and which may potentially inaugurate a poetical

---

[246] Ibid. pp. 50-51.
[247] Parr, Adrian. 2017. *Rebirth of a New Earth: The Radical Politics of Environmentalism*. New York: Columbia University Press. p. 191.

trajectory to productively re-imagining the self in commune with others).

In an interview, Kenneth Goldsmith, first poet laureate of MOMA, entitled *Plagiarism: Maybe It's Not so Bad*, argues that writers ought to move past these stagnant ideas of originality (as artists already have). 'Visual art has been able to take a different turn' than literature because of the invention of the camera, which 'forced painting to go abstract' to push the boundaries of representation.[248] Goldsmith points out that transcription and juxtaposition, essentially re-mixing, re-imagines and re-envisages what being creative can be. He gives the example of James Joyce's *Ulysses,* whereby the entire Ithaca chapter is patch-writing. Goldsmith points out that: 'Patch writing is what students do all the time, taking several sources and bringing them together, adding a few connecting words to make it all seem unique. My students are so good at patchwork and plagiarism, but it's not done on the down low. The question in my classes is how we can make your technique a bit better.'[249] We might perhaps consider then that it is possible to gain access to poetic rupture by way of Goldsmith's methodological approach.

In 'The Ecstasy of Influence; A Plagiarism,' an essay constructed entirely of citations, Jonathan Lethem echoes W.H. Auden in pointing out that: 'Most artists are brought to their vocation when

---

[248] Goldsmith, Kenneth. 2013. "Plagiarism: Maybe It's Not so Bad | on the Media | WNYC Studios." WNYC Studios. 2013. https://www.wnycstudios.org/podcasts/otm/segments/plagiarism-maybe-its-not-so-bad
[249] Ibid.

their own nascent gifts are awakened by the work of a master.'[250] Lethem writes:

> Finding one's voice isn't just an emptying and purifying oneself of the words of others but an adopting and embracing of filiations, communities, and discourses. Inspiration could be called inhaling the memory of an act never experienced. Invention, it must be humbly admitted, does not consist in creating out of void but out of chaos. Any artist knows these truths, no matter how deeply he or she submerges that knowing.[251]

Lethem gives the example of the contemporary condition of being surrounded by signs, which we ingest, metabolise and spew out. He hypothesises that to ignore this state of affairs, or to label it plagiarism, is to put oneself into some kind of ivory tower or monastic cell. He argues that the world makes room for the second use—it is expansive enough. Patch writing is about demonstrating influences, which is critical work. But, is it *really* possible to stage the revolution in this way? Can we *truly* learn to become something else through copying and remixing the creative practices of talented others? Aren't we still approaching a performance of ourselves cleverly discursively reformulated? Do we still remain somewhat indoctrinated?

Caroline Bergvall's project *48 Dante Variations* is a variation on patch writing, since it is more veering towards transcription, albeit still working with juxtaposition and re-styling existing literature in order to bring about an entirely new configuration. She explains: '… I decided to collate the opening lines of the Inferno translations

---

[250] Lethem, Jonathan. 2007. "The Ecstasy of Influence | Harper's Magazine." *Harper's Magazine*. February 2007. https://harpers.org/archive/2007/02/the-ecstasy-of-influence/
[251] Ibid.

as archived by the British Library up until May 2000.'[252] There have been 200 translations of Dante in less than two hundred years. Bergvall writes illuminatingly about the process of collating the translations:

> The minutiae of writing, of copying out, of shadowing the translators' voicing of the medieval text, favoured an eery intimacy as much as a welcome distance. My task was mostly and rather simply, or so it seemed at first, to copy each first tercet as it appeared in each published version of the Inferno. To copy it accurately. Surprisingly, more than once, I had to go back to the books to double-check and amend an entry, a publication date, a spelling. Checking each line, each variation, once, twice. Increasingly, the project was about keeping count and making sure. That what I was copying was what was there. Not to inadvertently change what had been printed. To reproduce each translative gesture. To add my voice to this chorus, to this recitation, only by way of this task. Making copy explicitly as an act of copy. Understanding translation in its erratic seriality.
>
> There are ways of acknowledging influence and models, by ingestion, by assimilation, by one's total absorption in the material. To come to an understanding of it by standing in it, by becoming it. Very gradually, this transforms a shoe into a foot, extends copyism into writing, and perhaps writing into being. This whole copying business was turning out to be a hands-down affair. This was an illuminating, if disturbing, development.[253]

Bergvall reports that the act of transcribing Dante's work brought about a transformation in her. She enters Dante's abyss and re-emerges with

---

[252] Bergvall, Caroline . 2004. "Via 48 Dante Variations." http://carolinebergvall.com/wp-content/uploads/2018/08/VIA.pdf
[253] Ibid.

treasure. Bergvall successfully re-contextualises Dante's *Inferno*—she brings something new to the original work. The repetition has an hypnotic effect, each translation is varied, sometimes quite strikingly different to the previous translation. The reiteration of different translations of Dante's *The Divine Comedy, Part 1, Inferno, Canto 1*, specifically the opening lines, acts like a charm which brings about a kind of transmutation of the creative process—an entering into the woods. Through copying and juxtaposing the many translations Bergvall gives Dante's *Inferno* another life. In his essay 'Re-typing on the Road' Goldsmith proposes that it is possible to challenge the power dynamic through 'mimesis and replication instead of disjunction and deconstruction' as with the language poets.[254] Bergville's *48 Dante Variations* brings about a kind of de-forming and re-forming of a Dantesque aesthetic, which is quite spectacularly hypnotic, and brings about unexpected affiliations.

By contrast, to reiterate Gilles Deleuze who writes in his essay 'Literature and Life': 'To write is certainly not to impose a form (of expression) on the matter of lived experience. Literature rather moves in the direction of the ill-formed or incomplete ... Writing is a question of becoming ...'[255] Like passing through 'doorways, thresholds, and zones that make up the entire universe.'[256] Deleuze clarifies that: 'To become is not to attain a form (identification, imitation, mimesis) but to find the zone of proximity, indiscernibility, or indifferentiation where one can no longer be distinguishable from

---

[254] Goldsmith, Kenneth. 2011. 'Chapter 7: Retyping on the Road' in *Uncreative Writing: Managing Language in the Digital Age*. New York: Columbia University. pp. 150-157.
[255] Deleuze, Gilles. (1993) 1998. *Essays Critical and Clinical*. Translated by Daniel W. Smith and Michael A. Grew. London: Verso. p. 1.
[256] Ibid.

a woman, *an* animal, or *a* molecule—'[257] He contends that writing is *not* about copying and remixing, but rather it is about rupture. What he means by this perhaps is that writing, and I would further clarify poetic writing, is potentially a way of encountering ongoing thresholds of others and thereby undergoing transformations.

To my mind, poetic writing has the potential to hook into a network of energy flows, circuited to the nervous system, an illogical element 'on the other side of order,' which is a relation 'essential to language.'[258] And I think this is what T.S Eliot meant when he talked of 'raiding the inarticulate' as a means of accessing the poetic register—a unique musical signature. However, I certainly wouldn't want to underplay Bergville's capacity to encounter personal transformation through copying another's literary words and remixing them. Because Bergville does clearly demonstrate the move to inhabit another's consciousness, to embrace that which is not herself by refashioning Dante's literary words. Reading and rewriting selected literary works can clearly engender an inward exploration, an involution, or productive de-stabilisation of the self, a conscious deformation, and a subsequent reformation of the self poetically, intertextually, which may help to bring us closer toward affirmative planetary kinship.

---

[257] Ibid.
[258] Deleuze, Gilles. (1969) 1990. *Logic of Sense*. Translated by Mark Lester with Charles Stivale. Edited by Constantine V. Boundas. London: The Athlone Press. pp. 2-6.

Chapter Six
Writing Contagious Reality

Walking can be a radical approach to doing writing, often veering into uncharted poetical terrain. Walking can facilitate the casting off of old notions of the self in favour of wedding landscapes traversed, and which often brings about restoration through transmutation. That is to say that walking is a fruitful access to mind wandering, which can disrupt fixed notions of identity through fostering affirmative migration to the outside, and which can be further worked through in a writing of these transitions. When we bear witness to a variegation of non-hierarchical social and environmental ecologies through walking, we experience a schooling or reschooling. And yet, clearly roaming, wayfaring, or wandering is a privileged thing to seek out, which requires a certain physical capability, free time, as well as a level of financial security, unless it is a confirmed and critical part of one's lifestyle outside of working hours for instance. It is important to point out that when a person is forced from their home, sent into exile, made a refugee, the circumstances of becoming nomadic veer from potentially liberating towards a matter of survival. Also, it's important to point out that women have long braved the threat of predation to walk alone in both urban and rural spaces, against the sanctioning of their presence to domestic spheres. More than ever we need to register attempts to orchestrate planetary mobilities against fascisms that would confine and diminish a diversity of embodied sensorial voices, especially those coming from the periphery. In order to oppose the trauma of capitalist deterritorialisations we need to recast the ethical subject by demonstrating imaginary digressions in relation to the terrain we are traversing. Or as Joan Didion had it in *The White Album*, we must articulate 'the shifting phantasmagoria which is our actual experience.'[259] I don't want to be deliberately ableist here, and so I'd like to point out that riding a bike, or taking a bus, driving (an electric car preferably), or using a wheelchair, to name just a few alternative modes of transportation, are also excellent modes of access to wandering writing.

I'd like to firstly establish a rich tradition of place-based knowledge in acknowledgement and celebration of First Peoples, with a focus on Australia since it's the place I live and work, before elaborating critical radical and restorative interventions in rural and urban walking writing, and mostly from European and American traditions, albeit with an emphasis on women's voices. For if we think that women's walking writing is now firmly on the map then we might consider for a moment a celebrated contemporary author like Robert Macfarlane writing of a tradition of walking writing, of 'pilgrimage,' and 'trespass' alike, undertaken by almost exclusively men in *The Old Ways: A Journey on Foot*.[260] In his book, Macfarlane claims to have read all of the 'old-way wanderers' who according to him are mostly white men. He tells us that: 'John Clare was fond of footpaths because they were "rich and joyful to the mind": ways of walking that were also ways of thinking.'[263] He refers to William

---

[259] Didion, Joan. (1979) 2009. *The White Album*. New York: Farrar, Straus and Giroux. p. 11.
[260] Macfarlane, Robert. 2015. *Landmarks*. London: Penguin Books.

Hazlitt, but not his wife Sarah Stoddart Hazlitt. He mentions Dorothy Wordsworth's journals in passing without engaging with them. However, he beautifully appraises the work of Nan Shepherd. Still, hereafter it's a firm man-footed path. He possesses a confidence and lyrical flair that's hard to argue with, his is a secured-voice which I enjoy spending time with. However, he doesn't make enough space for women's walking writings, nor for First Nations accounts of enumerating connection with Country. (I do note that in his most recent book *Is a River Alive?* Macfarlane seems to have addressed his omission of First Nations accounts of commune with sacred places in his writing). Clearly, I am not a mouthpiece for First Nations experience, nor would I seek to be, since that would be highly unethical. I do think it's important that I preface an exploration of walking writing by surveying First Nations custodians place-based writing, and with a spotlight on post-pastoral iterations (specifically in the context of Australia).

i) First Peoples Place-Based Narratives & Knowledges/Against Pastoral Iterations

Although Macfarlane doesn't focus on First Nations and women's accounts of place-based wandering writing in his book *The Old Ways: A Journey on Foot* he points out that: 'We inhabit a post-pastoral terrain, full of modifications and compromise.'[261] He subsequently promotes the need for recultivating a 'prosperity of place-language,' specifically in the British Isles.[262] In Australia we clearly require the elevation of First Nations ancestral knowledge and place-names pertaining to Country against pastoral iterations,

---

[261] Ibid. p. 7.
[262] Ibid. p. 8.

which have violently attempted to usurp First Nations memory of Country (often asserting a misplaced romantic idealism regarding the landscape). Alexis Wright, author and land rights activist from the Waanyi Nation, petitions in her article 'The Inward Migration in Apocalyptic Times' for the need to uphold Country as evoked by First Nations custodians through song, language, ceremonies and ritual practices, and which is vital as a means of honouring ancestral beings, and giving back to the landscape, regarding it, holding it in esteem. Macfarlane draws insightfully albeit briefly on Keith Basso's *Wisdom Sits in Places*, in which he writes about the Apache of Western Arizona in The United States of America: 'Words act as compass; place-speech serves literally to enchant the land—to sing it back into being, and to sing one's being back into it.'[263] To charge the landscape with exactitudes, precise descriptions, renews it, re-invokes it, goes some way towards safeguarding it.

In an article titled 'Walking Many Worlds: Aboriginal Storytelling and Writing for the Young' author Ambelin Kwaymullina of the Palyku people, quotes Arrente elder Margaret Kemarre Turner who states that: 'The Land must have people through whom it can talk'. In her poem 'Ngurambang yali — Country speaks' Wirudjuri writer Jeanine Leane issues such a call:

> It's been too long since I sat on granite in my
> Country and thought
>
> Too many years since I breathed this air—
> Bunyi-ng—ganha

[263] Ibid. p. 22.

Felt this dirt—Ngamanhi Dhaagun
Smelt this dust—Budha—nhi Bunan

Listened for the sounds of her words that say
'Balandha—dhuraay Bumal-ayi-nya Wumbay
abuny (yaboing)'—History does not have the
first claim. Nor the last word.
Nghindhi yarra dhalanbul ngiyanhi gin gu
'You can speak us now!'[264]

Leane is referring here to the historical prohibition against First Nations people speaking their own languages in Australia, and specifically with regards to voicing their connection with their Country. As Alexis Wright elucidates in her article 'Telling the Untold Stories:'

> There is a long, deep-rooted vein of history that runs throughout the country where Aboriginal people remember how their families were actively silenced and banned from practising their culture or speaking their languages, or from telling the stories about who they are, or how they felt. This practice of censorship worked through silencing Aboriginal people by state laws and official narratives.[265]

And in Wright's article 'The Inward Migration in Apocalyptic Times' she further elaborates an 'inward migration,' a return to Country, to 'the dwelling place of stories' in the mind, which can be

---

[264] Leane, Jeanine. 2023. "Ngurambang Yali — Country Speaks." Red Room Poetry. 2023. https://redroompoetry.org/poets/jeanine-leane/ngurambang-yali-country-speaks/
[265] Wright, Alexis. 2019a. "Telling the Untold Stories: Alexis Wright on Censorship." Overland Literary Journal. February 8, 2019. https://overland.org.au/2019/02/telling-the-untold-stories-alexis-wright-on-censorship/

invoked through writing, and which is a vital means of commune for First Peoples, against the linguicide of the past. This might perhaps be considered to be a vital protest against past and ongoing attempts to erase First Nations placed-based knowledges and stories.[266]

> The inward migration is most often a solitary journey, a turning away from the bombarding speed of reality hitting your very sense of being and destroying your soul. Returning to the place of country held in the mind is a way of figuring out how to deal with the powerlessness we sometimes feel from having to continually hold back the end-of-the-world times and confront ongoing realities. It's where we go to slowly pick things apart, to reimagine our world in new ways, and sometimes we come out the other side with a map of how to make some sense of our world.[267]

Wright's 'inward gaze' is aligned with an imaginal turn that is further linked with ancestral knowledge, Country, and custodianship. This 'inward gaze' is simultaneously an outward gaze that cannot be separated from the 'sacred text' of the landscape. Wright informs us that the First Nations 'system of interconnectedness is kept strong through constant and deep respect for the traditional laws associated with ancient story knowledge.'[268] Wright draws on Seamus Heaney to make a critical point about Country which is that it 'already exists,' and in fact Heaney suggests that poets become a mouth-piece for landscape imbued with story, which is a 'country of the mind.'[269] By drawing on Heaney, Wright reiterates the notion that poets too are

---

[266] Wright, Alexis. 2022. "The Inward Migration in Apocalyptic Times — Alexis Wright." Emergence Magazine. October 26, 2022. https://emergencemagazine.org/essay/the-inward-migration-in-apocalyptic-times/
[267] Ibid.
[268] Ibid.
[269] Ibid.

capable of reading landscape in nuanced ways. And it is this notion of interconnectedness, of becoming with the landscape as a living entity that many poets grasp, and engage with in their evocation of place, albeit in differentiated ways.

I'd like to now survey some significant First Nations writers that dismantle the pastoral in order to open up a literary space to tell their own narratives in relation to Country, frequently through accessing poetic registers. Tony Birch is a highly celebrated First Nations author who grew up on Wurundjeri lands (in Naarm/Melbourne). In his lecture for The Wheeler Centre 'Indigenous Place' (2014) he speaks specifically of Birrarung Mar (the Yarra River), as 'the central place' of Wurundjeri 'being,' a meeting place with which he has a profound connection.[270] Birch tells of Birrarung Mar as critical with regards to his formation as a person. He iterates that First Nations people have always told stories in relation to geographical place, which he refers to as 'mapping stories.'[271] In addition to his extensive oeuvres, Birch has written three short stories on Birrarung Mar. 'The Sea of Tranquility,' 'The Chocolate Empire,' and 'The Toe Cutters,' a novel titled *Ghost River*, as well as several poems which function as critical counternarratives of settlement, and are also a means of reclaiming that place through narrative, of reimbuing the social and environmental ecology with wonderment and joy against the threat of infringement.

Alison Whittaker's poem 'a love like Dorothea's' is a critical response to Dorothea Mackellar's canonical pastoral poem 'My Country.'

---

[270] Birch, Tony. 2022. "Indigenous Places (Video)." Writers Victoria. February 21, 2022. https://writersvictoria.org.au/resources/writing-tips-and-tools/indigenous-places-video/
[271] Ibid.

Whittaker is a Gomeroi poet and prose writer from Gunnedah and Tamworth in north-western New South Wales who rejects the pastoral lyric form. Whittaker exposes Mackellar's pastoral as 'fetish verse,' a bid for 'white nativity.'[272] She 'writes back' to the so-called 'sun burnt' Country, which was brutally taken, or stolen from First Nations inhabitants.

> I loved a sunburnt country, dislodged in a memory
> I never lived in time to love a love like Dorothea's.
> We're cannibals of other kinds; the white woman has eat the sky
> so where does that leave girls like I? — lost creatures chewing o'er the night.[273]

She redresses the pastoral conflation of First Nations people with the land and its fauna in an offensively regressive move to align them with a primitivism. Whittaker unsettles the white settler gaze and petitions for First Nations sovereignty and custodianship. This is a protest poetry.

Ellen van Neerven, an author of Mununjali and Dutch heritage, further unsettles colonial authority/authorship in speaking back to the genocide and violence committed against First Nations custodians, and which has attempted to erase First Nations connection to Country. Van Neervan's second poetry collection *Throat* is confronting, at times scathing, albeit a moving and erudite bid to write their embodied connection to Country, including

---

[272] Whittaker, Alison's 'a love like Dorothea's' is collected in *Australian Poetry Chapbook Transforming My Country*. 2021. Edited by Toby Fitch. https://emergingwritersfestival.org.au/wp-content/uploads/2021/06/Transforming-My-Country_AP2021.pdf
[273] Ibid.

exploring queer identity. Van Neervan critically dismantles colonial claims, which they further link to climate destruction, but which also must surely be related to late capitalism. In their poem 'Paper ships' van Neerven writes:

I know what you're thinking
    how can we save the world?
        when we have barely
           just survived it

when we have been disposed of
    raped and murdered
        erased and orphaned
           and lost 90% or more of our kin

when we are just getting to our feet
    when we are hurt
    and barely breathing
        from the impact ...[274]

Van Neerven reclaims agency as a First Nations custodian to care for their Country as a means of protest and environmental activism against the colonial 'endeavour' to obliterate an entire peoples, and brutally remove them from their own land, as depicted in the image of tall ships sailing into the harbor.

Similarly, as Nadia Rhook elucidates in her review: 'In *Dropbear*, Evelyn Araluen—poet, editor and descendant of the Bundjalung

---

[274] Van Neervan, Ellen. 2020. *Throat*. Brisbane: University of Queensland Press. pp. 126-128.

nation, asks readers to listen closer to the stories that underwrite the project of settler colonialism in the place many call "Australia".'[275] For instance, a poem in the collection titled 'To the Poets' is addressed to Australian pastoral poets of yesteryear. Araluen confronts idealised colonial settler perspectives. The pastoral is critiqued as a mode of white endeavour that objectifies and exoticises the landscape. Araluen commences her poem by speaking back to the pastoral poets that wrote of the Australian bush as forbidding—a haunted topography. She signposts the spinning of a white imaginary that disacknowledges Aboriginals off in the 'fringes' and 'reserves.' And moreover, which appropriates First Nations epistemological knowledge for its own uses/mis-uses. Araluen chides: 'You ferment myth into the bush and the billabong to give yourself history...'[276] This line makes me think of Les Murray's 'Buladelah-Taree Holiday Song Cycle,' in which he appropriates First Nations song. Araluen exposes pastoral poetry as 'puppeteer poetry.'[277] She argues that the pastoral mode is irredeemable.

Jazz Money, a Wiradjuri poet and artist, relays the struggle for First Nations sovereignty and custodianship in her collection *How to Make a Basket*. In the title poem she sets about relaying the importance of caring for and singing up her Country:

> my Country is beyond the horizon
>
> all plains all river
>
> the edges can be crossed with care

---

[275] Rhook, Nadia. 2021. "Review of 'Dropbear' by Evelyn Araluen." Westerly Magazine. August 12, 2021. https://westerlymag.com.au/dropbear/
[276] Araluen, Evelyn. 2021. *Dropbear*. Brisbane: University of Queensland Press. pp. 37-38.
[277] Ibid.

> you might say the language is
> harsh
> but it is an ancient beauty
> a life that rolls and sings
> and we're singing we're singing ...[278]

So too Kirli Saunders, a Gunai poet, explores returning to the land and at the remove from digital indoctrination in her poem 'Go Rogue.' Saunders issues a call to go off-grid, back to bird watching and swimming in salt water, and specifically as a cure for a broken heart. Her poem iterates the importance of restorative planetary connection through mobilising, which is aligned with her First Nations heritage. She writes:

> ... go rogue
> go smoke signals forged in a fire boiling yabbies we caught in the creek
>
> go clouds of white in blue wren open sky backdropping scribbly gums and their scribbly gum moths frilly wings enchanting ...[279]

Clearly traversing landscape provides an access to reading it, an embodied decoding, towards the promotion of a reciprocity with place, which many First Nations custodians have long understood and practiced.

---

[278] Jazz Money. 2021. *How to Make a Basket*. Brisbane: University of Queensland Press.
[279] Saunders, Kirli. 2023. "'Go Rogue', a New Poem by Kirli Saunders." Australian Book Review. September 23, 2023. https://www.australianbookreview.com.au/abr-online/current-issue/994-october-2023-no-458/11085-go-rogue-a-new-poem-by-kirli-saunders

In Tony Birch's lecture 'Indigenous Place,' he petitions non-Aboriginal people to avoid asking the question: 'How can I understand Aboriginal Country the way Aboriginal people can?' Because it's not possible. But rather to ask instead: 'How can you know this Country in your own way?'[280] He encourages non-Aboriginal writers to consider places that have been pivotal to their own formation. However, in addition to finding and elaborating their own connection to place Birch encourages non-Aboriginal people to speak with First Nations people to educate themselves about First Nations connection with place. In his essay 'There is No Axe': Identity, Story and a Sombrero' Birch writes: 'In colonial societies such as Australia, the work of justice must include not only the right of Aboriginal people to control and speak our own stories, but also the beginnings of a genuinely postcolonial dialogue with non-Aboriginal people, the forging of new and productive narratives.' To open up this space of genuinely decolonial dialogue we must seek to acknowledge the ongoing impacts of colonisation on First Nations people, in addition to upholding First Nations custodianship, and place-based knowledge.

In Tom Bristow's *The Anthropocene Lyric: An Affective Geography of Poetry, Person, Place*, he interviews John Kinsella who explicates his decolonial self-reflexive approach to writing anti-pastoral poetry, which explores place, and from the perspective of a non-Aboriginal person. Kinsella provides some useful pointers for non-Aboriginal writers negotiating ways to approach place-based writing. He states:

---

[280] 2022. "Indigenous Places (Video)." Writers Victoria. February 21, 2022. https://writersvictoria.org.au/resources/writing-tips-and-tools/indigenous-places-video/

> I never overwrite to delete, but to respect. I am even hesitant about my 'right' to dialogue with such traces. But I do, and do so by trying to allow those traces their own speaking space within my 'voice'. I see writing and certainly my presence in 'wheatbelt Western Australia' as deeply problematical. Stolen land. Fact. I don't believe in land ownership per se, and I don't believe in 'title', but I do believe in custodianship, and I do believe in knowledge of place/s (a 'deeper' focus of one's polysituatedness within a particular zone), and through this I acknowledge the Ballardong, Whadjuk, Yamaji, and other peoples of the land I write. My knowledge in terms of that 'place' (large or small) is less than minimal, and my poems can but enter into a conversation with a little of this knowledge. However, I do know what life is, and I do know ecologies through my own interaction with them, and I do always respect the non-human and human alike. This gives me some access, to my mind, to write this/that place. But I have to scrutinise myself—not only because of inevitable complacency, but because I am who I am. I cannot undo the colonial past of family, I cannot undo my presence in the place, but I can challenge its constituent parts.[281]

Kinsella's remarks open up a place for respectful acknowledgement of First Nations connection with Country. He protests past and ongoing atrocities connected with colonisation before seeking to uphold his own embodied connection with environmental ecologies that have been formative to him. In so doing he seeks to do his own part as a poet to safeguard place.

In her article 'Talking to a Stranger: Decolonising the Australian "Landscape" Poem', Bonny Cassidy surveys settler poets' writing

---

[281] Bristow, Tom. 2015. *The Anthropocentric Lyric; An Affective Geography of Poetry, Person, Place*. London: Palgrave. https://link.springer.com/book/10.1057/9781137364753

landscape towards 'a decolonised geopoethics' in Australia, and which has been hitherto addressed by Peter Minter. She tells:

> In such a field of poetry and poetics, writes Minter, 'everyone needs to take responsibility for imagining their own unique kind of transformation. In poetry and poetics, we have to think about how non-Indigenous form, western form, romantic form, lyrical form, white form, have a responsibility to current and future cultural conditions.' This, he suggests, is how the non-Indigenous or settler imaginary can reach 'an existential common ground' with colonised Indigenous lives and expression.[282]

And Cassidy also draws on Stuart Cooke and his theory of 'nomadic poetics,' which is distinctive from the desire to 'become native.' Cooke highlights the need to avoid romantic interpretations of place, or a gaze of ownership, but rather to enact 'light footedness' in the landscape, towards the navigation of a different ontological perspective. As Cassidy points out: 'This poetics invokes a suspension of permanent or continuous, place-based identity; it imagines the settler habitus with a community of others.'[283] And so, a decolonised settler poetics of place might attempt to enact a kind of 'statelessness' that draws attention to the act of 'beinghereness.'[284] But, I'd like to move away from ontological frameworks altogether—they no longer serve—they are overly bound to the Anthropocene in my view. We need a new/ancient way. We can embrace this modality through walking, and which gives rise to poetic, as well as artistic exploration.

---

[282] Cassidy, Bonny. 2017. 'Talking to a Stranger: Decolonising the Australian "Landscape" Poem.' Plumwood Mountain Journal. https://plumwoodmountain.com/essays-interviews/talking-to-a-stranger-decolonising-the-australian-landscape-poem/
[283] Ibid.
[284] Ibid.

I would like to propose that non-Aboriginal poets and writers might navigate writing place through engaging their multisensorial embodied apprehension of landscapes, and which is a First Nations approach that promotes ecological awareness and connectivity. This is not a desire to 'become-native' as such, but rather to learn from First Nations practices. It is a desire to uphold one's own valued and valid embodied connection with environmental ecologies towards a shared goal of affirmative commune, and as a move to safeguard, nurture, and protect the planet. Surely this is part of the decolonial future, narratively nourishing landscapes with which we are connected through listening—translating—entering into sympoetic community. This engagement may engender transformation in awareness, and mutation of consciousness, facilitated through experiencing kinship with landscapes that are animated by a life principle, or force, i.e. that are both physical and spiritual entities. To reiterate Rosi Braidotti and Donna Haraway's assertions, we are always already mediated through other things and states—part of a vast web of life. And so, it follows that treating the landscape as a living entity is the right way to approach it.

These sensory phenomenological perspectives pertaining to place have been cultivated by First Nations custodians for some 65,000 years in Australia. As Dharug artist, academic, and author Liz Cameron explains in her article 'Indigenous Ecological Knowledge Systems-Exploring Sensory Narratives':

> Embodied knowledge is the sensory information built upon repeated observation (Turner & Ignace 2000) through an immersion of self within a cultural place—that serves as the foundations to belonging. It

includes narrative platforms that offer increased comprehension, interest, and engagement with Country. Such narratives speak of a socially connected world with empathy and moral integrity that is essential for pro-environmental behaviours. Light (2010) further identifies narrative as a valuable tool for orienting our ethical commitments to place through knowing the histories connected with a particular geographic area. Our storied world is an interactive engagement that utilises place-based knowing and multisensorial lived experiences to connect with Country in a meaningful way. These cultural stories project the importance of place by engaging and attracting multisensory learning experiences to maintain the social memories of Country.[285]

The cultivation of ecological knowledge based in a sensory phenomenological perspective, and specifically pertaining to 'caring for country,' is a vital safeguarding for many First Peoples, and which is further connected with kinship structures. I would not want to insinuate here that First Nations kinship laws can be learned or entered into by non-Aboriginal poets and writers. Non-Aboriginal poets and writers may however seek to cultivate their own differentiated and nuanced relationship to landscapes through traversing them, and embracing their own embodied sensuous experience. The human cast as agential subject in an Anthropocentric landscape—separate to an objectified planet just isn't the truth—and never was.

---

[285] Cameron, Liz. 2022. "Indigenous Ecological Knowledge Systems — Exploring Sensory Narratives." *Ecological Management & Restoration* 23 (S1): 27—32. https://doi.org/10.1111/emr.12534.

Our rivers, oceans, deserts, mountains, and forests are alive—they have rights and voices. But how can we translate them? Perhaps the answer is to learn to coexist with them harmoniously, to sync up with them through commune over time, and so to sensorially enter into a communication, an embodied reciprocity, and which First Peoples, and poets too have long understood. In his book *Is a River Alive?* Robert Macfarlane points out that: 'Over the past twenty years, energized by ecological emergency, the young Rights of Nature movement has repeatedly inspired new forms of future dreaming, and unsettled long-held orthodoxies by appealing to the imagination as much as to law.'[286] Macfarlane encourages this re-comprehension and re-imagining of environmental ecologies, specifically with regards to riverscapes, as valid, valued, and enlivened other, with which we are in reciprocal relationship, and have a duty of care towards. It is in fact part of us, and we are part of it.

To return to elaborating sensory phenomenological perspectives, Cameron advises that for many First Nations custodians smelling is a navigation tool, so is listening for and examining sounds in ecological landscapes, as is active exploration of Country through touch, tactile signing, and taste. Intuitive guidance or 'insight thinking' is also critical.

> Insight thinking allows us to absorb information from our senses and make connections to the broader world. It is most valuable when tasks cannot be performed through analytical measures (De Vries & Holland 2008) or insufficient data is available to solve a problem. Insight thinking also allows us to screen out the often distracting nuances to focus on the

---

[286] Macfarlane, Robert. 2025. *Is a River Alive?* London: Hamish Hamilton, Penguin Books. p.29.

underlying pattern recognitions and environmental cues. This form of thinking applies abstract skills to look at whole systems through a web of relationships that support interconnectedness and interrelationships.[287]

Cameron adds that the promotion of imaginative process gives rise to thinking embodied network for some First Nations custodians, which encourages human entanglement, or reciprocity, with nonhuman others and environmental ecologies. 'This includes dreams, visions and intuitions that are an integral part of our reality—they break away from our fantasy life to stir true visionary knowledges.'[288] And non-Aboriginal people too might hopefully be prompted to use their imaginations and intuitions to enter into place beyond the limitations of ontological knowledge systems gifted to them through Anthropocentric thought, albeit in differentiated ways. For we must surely cast off the Anthropocentric straight jacket and learn to operate from the present—not from the future. We must kill off the past modus operandi—modernity and its scientific and technical *progress* have gifted new modes of production, and the exponential multiplication of consumer desire for more and more stuff, which has translated into colonial horror, human exceptionalism, extractivism, pollution and waste on a grand scale. Perhaps sensuous embodied reciprocity with place as recorded through artistic practice which gets written, sung, drawn, or painted, is the radical reconfiguration beyond any geo-philosophical apparatus. I'd like to now turn my attention to the creative metamorphosis of some American and European walker writers for further potential planetary pathways.

---

[287] Cameron, Liz. 2022. "Indigenous Ecological Knowledge Systems — Exploring Sensory Narratives." *Ecological Management & Restoration* 23 (S1): 27—32. https://doi.org/10.1111/emr.12534. p. 31.
[288] Ibid.

However, I will just briefly point out here other ways that we might acknowledge and uphold First Nations custodianship of Country. I'm drawn to Stephen Muecke's article '"What country have you walked?" Why all Australians should walk a First Nations heritage trail,' which is written with Goolarabooloo elder Philip Roe's contribution. In this article, Muecke and Roe explore the importance of preserving and promoting First Nations led walking trails as a radical and reparative move towards elevating ancestral knowledge and storytelling practices, as well as granting land rights to First Nations custodians.

> The Goolarabooloo community in Broome has been running the Lurujarri Heritage Trail for over 30 years … On trail, the colonial power dynamic between settler and Indigenous communities is turned on its head. The Goolarabooloo express their sovereignty (never ceded) by welcoming visitors onto their Country … This kind of tourism is a rare, life-changing experience. What is special about the Lurujarri Trail is the participation of the Roe family …

> … There are dozens of Aboriginal walking tracks across Australia: well-known are the Larapinta in Central Australia, the Bundian Way between Targangal (Kosciuszko) and Bilgalera on the coast near Eden, and Mungo Aboriginal Discovery Tours.

> More Indigenous-led walking tracks could trace storied landmarks.

> There is increasing awareness of how Indigenous knowledges are relevant to caring for Country.
>
> Walking tracks can teach what each territory is capable of sustaining. The people further down the track know their Country is that little bit different and what it is capable of. These pathways connect up, and knowledge transforms along the way.[289]

Walking First Nations heritage trails might potentially be considered an act of reconciliation that pays homage to First Nations ways of knowing and understanding landscape encapsulated in the concept of Country, and which safeguards ancestral lineages. It might be an affirmative way to open up a decolonial dialogue.

Following Muecke's call, I recently walked Tony Birch's favourite trail along Birrarung Mar, from Collingwood Children's Farm to the Fairfield Pipe Bridge whilst listening to Birch speak of the significance of this landscape to First Nations custodians, and thereafter relay some of his own attempts to reimbue this place with story.[290] I enjoyed Birch's readings as I walked along the bank, especially an excerpt from his novel *Ghost River*. In *Ghost River*, Birch tells the story of an unlikely friendship between two working class kids, Sonny and Ren, aged thirteen and twelve respectively. He engagingly narrates their adventures down on the Birrarung Mar in the 1970s. Birch evokes the river terrain sensuously as when Sonny and Ren enjoy a first swim. Ren notices the way that the current feels

---

[289] Muecke, Stephen. 2021. "'What Country Have You Walked?' Why All Australians Should Walk an Indigenous Heritage Trail." The Conversation. July 2021. https://theconversation.com/what-country-have-you-walked-why-all-australians-should-walk-an-indigenous-heritage-trail-162519
[290] Birch, Tony. 2020. "Six Walks Episode One: Tony Birch on the Birrarung." ACCA. 2020. https://acca.melbourne/whos-afraid-of-public-space/offsite/six-walks/six-walks-episode-one-tony-birch/

against his body, the shift in temperature, whilst Sonny apprehends the rich mineral scent of the river. Both boys become *of* the river, wear it on their bodies, the dirt 'fine as baby powder,' the scent in their hair when they settle for sleep at night.[291] Birch tells: 'In the days after their first swim the boys couldn't stay out of the water. They explored the banks both upstream and downstream, trying out every swimming hole and increasingly testing their courage, jumping from rocks, out of the trees, and eventually off the bridges that crossed the river.'[292] Birch poetically evokes the river as a storied place, which becomes sacred to Sonny and Ren. And in his poem 'Swimming Hole' Birch relays the first day of summer during his upbringing, of visiting Birrarung Mar, which he addresses as his 'salvation.'[293] It seems to me an important initiative for non-Aboriginal writers to seek out an understanding of the First Nations heritage of a place, and possibly even by seeking to walk First Nations trails, towards fostering further decolonial perspectives.

We must regard the extraordinary wealth of First Nations knowledge pertaining to place towards the fosterage of reconciliation, custodianship, and also affirmative activism. We must intentionally dismantle taking pastoral comfort in place, but rather foster a more self-reflexive mode of being here and writing. We can write towards exploring our own nomadic poetic entanglement with places of significance to us, access the life of place sensuously, and in precise terms, such that we attempt to safeguard landscapes. We can walk light-footed on the precious earth in reciprocity with all humans

---

[291] Birch, Tony. 2015. *Ghost River*. Brisbane: University of Queensland Press. p. 66.
[292] Ibid.
[293] Birch, Tony. 2020. "Six Walks Episode One: Tony Birch on the Birrarung." ACCA. 2020. https://acca.melbourne/whos-afraid-of-public-space/offsite/six-walks/six-walks-episode-one-tony-birch/

and more-than-human others. We will transform along the way as we pay increased attention to precisely apprehending the landscape in highly nuanced and unique poetical terms. Not turning away from the horror of the genocide of the past, but rather exposing it, entering into truth-telling, and towards an understanding of ongoing impacts experienced by First Nations Australians. We must make healing our priority. On the ground socio-economic change—real empowerment—must come for Australia's First Peoples. And that means a platform to speak culturally, politically, and creatively. To reinvoke Donna Haraway here, perhaps what is required is to *stay with the trouble*—to not to try to deny it—but rather to make plain our predicament which is planetary entanglement.

Some European & American Rural Legacies

In *Wanderlust: A History of Walking*, Rebecca Solnit writes eloquently against-the-grain of the historical idea of walking as a wholesome or virtuous undertaking, which has often been preached by predominantly European canonical male-authors; the daily constitutional. Instead she considers that 'walkers are true radicals out to undermine the laws and authorities that stifle others as well as themselves.'[294] She argues that walking in general terms can facilitate rumination and free-thought, potentially bringing about a revolution in the imagination. Whilst walking 'the mind wanders from plans to recollections to observation.'[295]

> The rhythm of walking generates a kind of rhythm of thinking, and the passage through a landscape echoes or stimulates the passage through a

---

[294] Solnit, Rebecca. 2001. *Wanderlust: A History of Walking*. London: Granta. p. 125.
[295] Ibid. p. 5.

series of thoughts. This creates an odd consonance between internal and external passage, one that suggests that the mind is also a landscape of sorts and that walking is one way to traverse it. A new thought often seems like a feature of the landscape that was there all along, as though thinking were traversing rather than making.[296]

Psychological states arise when walking, which can be explored pertaining to varying geographical environments, a kind of knitting together of mindscape and embodied consciousness with landscape, and which can be elaborated and worked through in writing. And so, walking can become a mode for exploring 'the unpredictable and the incalculable' in the self, pertaining to place, as unpacked in writing.[297] Solnit further surmises:

> As a literary structure, the recounted walk encourages digression and association, in contrast to the stricter form of discourse or the chronological progression of a biological or historical narrative. A century and a half later [after Rousseau], James Joyce and Virginia Woolf would, in trying to describe the workings of the mind, develop the style called stream of consciousness. In their novels Ulysses and Mrs Dalloway, the jumble thoughts and recollections of their protagonists unfold best during walks. This kind of unstructured, associated thinking is the kind often connected to walking, and it suggests walking as not an analytical but an improvisational act. Rousseau's Reveries is one of the first portraits of this relationship between thinking and walking.[298]

---

[296] Ibid. p. 6.
[297] Ibid. p. 10.
[298] Ibid. p. 21.

Both Rousseau and Kierkegaard wrote about walking in 'personal, descriptive, and specific work,' that is, in the form of journals and essays.[304] Solnit considers: 'Perhaps it is because walking is itself a way of grounding one's thoughts in a personal and embodied experience of the world that it lends itself to this kind of writing. This is why the meaning of walking is mostly discussed elsewhere than philosophy: in poetry, novels, letters, diaries, travelers' accounts, and first-person essays.'[299] And so, Solnit makes explicit a connection between walking and these non-philosophical, and I'd add digressive, forms of writing which often veer into poetical registers.

In *Reveries of a Solitary Walker*, Jean-Jacques Rousseau (1712-1778) writes of the condition of being 'dragged out of the order of things' by way of walking.[300] Walking and recording one's ruminations in relation to rural landscapes traversed potentially brings about a radical reconfiguration of the self in relation to environmental ecologies. It is as if walking functions for Rousseau as a curative for the human race, whereby he comes to reconcile himself to exile. He writes: 'People can no longer do good or evil to me here. I have nothing more to hope for or to fear in this world; and here I am, tranquil at the bottom of the abyss, a poor unfortunate mortal, but unperturbed, like God Himself.'[301] Rousseau is undoubtedly here referring to being made adversary in relation to his Bildungsroman *Emile, Or on Education,* which was banned in Paris and Geneva, and publicly burned in 1762.[302] He consequently experienced exile and underwent some kind of personal revolution through solo walking

---

[299] Ibid. p. 26.
[300] Rousseau, Jean-Jacques. [1782] 1992. *The Reveries of a Solitary Walker*. Translation by Charles E. Butterworth. Indianapolis/ Cambridge: Hackett Publishing Company. p. 1.
[301] Ibid. p. 5.
[302] Ibid. p. 36.

and daydreaming, which served to free him from the suffering caused by the judgements of the society he formerly kept. He turned to 'conversing' with his 'soul' and documenting it (with no thought for the readership for his writings).[303] What he achieved is moving—there's a lack of artifice in his writing. A transparency is conveyed. His *Reveries of a Solitary Walker* demonstrates that perhaps we can gain something by leaning into exile—deliberately going apart from society. Though this activity also poses the risk of entering into a terrain of despair. However, it potentially also provides an access to unparalleled hope for a wiser reformation of the self in relation to others, and the planet more broadly. Although it's important to note that Rousseau demonstrates a distinct lack of regard for women's authorship. They are apparently not to be included in this revolution in consciousness pertaining to walking. And it seems poignant to note that several of the following men who walked in rural environments and wrote about it also had sisters and wives who often walked right beside them, and who thereafter wrote about it in their journals, although they have only somewhat recently been given sufficient recognition for this undertaking.

For instance, William Wordsworth (1770—1850) made walking central to his life, such that it featured as a methodological approach to writing, and which Solnit argues is unparalleled in any other writer before or after. He seems to have walked nearly every day of his life. Walking was his access to composing poetry. Leslie Stephen, Woolf's father writes:

---

[303] Rousseau, Jean-Jacques. (1782) 1992. *The Reveries of a Solitary Walker.* Translation by Charles E. Butterworth. Indianapolis/ Cambridge: Hackett Publishing Company. p. 5.

> Wordsworth's poetical autobiography shows how every stage in his early mental development was connected with some walk in the Lakes. The sunrise which startled him on a walk after a night spent in dancing first set him apart as a 'dedicated spirit.' His walking tour in the Alps—then a novel performance—roused him to his first considerable poem. His chief performance is the record of an excursion on foot.[304]

Clearly for Wordsworth walking the Lakes District was highly formative, and which cultivated his poetry practice. He also pioneered the idea of trying to understand an event by revisiting a place in order to access its resonance. For instance, Wordsworth attempted to comprehend the French Revolution by walking the streets of Paris and visiting places of significance. However, he mostly valued rural wandering. He 'linked walking with nature, poetry, poverty, and vagrancy in a wholly new and compelling way which entirely sets him apart.'[305] Significantly, he walked frequently in the countryside with his sister who purportedly helped him compose poetry, although she was not formally credited.

Dorothy Wordsworth (1771-1855) was a diarist, writer, and a prolific walker whose work was not published in her lifetime. For her, walking explicitly meant liberation from patriarchal constraint, freedom from prohibitions placed on women's mobility, and in these terms it was a radical act. Having been orphaned at twelve Wordsworth was beholden to relatives taking her in until she moved to Dove Cottage in Grasmere, Lakes District, with her brother whom she loved dearly, and with whom she walked extensively in

---

[304] Stephen, Leslie. (1898) 2012. *Studies of a Biographer*. Cambridge: Cambridge University Press. pp. 254-285.
[305] Solnit, Rebecca. 2001. *Wanderlust: A History of Walking*. London: Granta. p. 105.

the area. She kept a daily journal from the first spring she arrived in the Lakes District relaying in it her many walks with her brother, in addition to her extensive solo jaunts. In *The Alfoxden Journal 1798* (published posthumously), it is clear that Wordsworth is a keen apprehender of place and people alike, taking in the social and environmental ecological landscape with precision and poetic flourish. On January 20th, 1798, Wordsworth writes of the 'green paths down the hillsides,' which become 'channels for streams,' and of the countryside peopled by sunlight after rain. She compares the oak trunks in the wood to 'columns of ruin.'[306] In a later entry, Wordsworth comments on '[t]he ivy twisting around the oaks like bristled serpents'.[311] She eloquently paints a full sensorial picture of hilltop scene on 26th January, 1798:

> ... following the sheep tracks till we over looked the larger coombe. Sat in the sunshine. The distant sheep-bells, the sound of the stream; the woodsman winding along the half-marked road with his laden pony; locks of wool still spangled with the dewdrops; the blue-grey sea, shaded with immense masses of cloud, not streaked; the sheep guttering in the sunshine. Returned through the wood.[307]

On one occasion Wordsworth's party seeks shelter in the wood from a storm and she reports that the trees almost seem to 'roar' and the 'multitude of dancing leaves' have their own distinctive soundings.[308]

---

[306] Wordsworth, Dorothy. 1971. *Journals of Dorothy Wordsworth. The Alfoxden Journal 1798 and The Grasmere Journals 1800-1803*. 2nd Edition. With an introduction by Helen Darbishire. Oxford: The Oxford University Press. p. 1.
[307] Ibid. p. 2.
[308] Ibid. p. 4.

On 4th February, 1798, Wordsworth describes various people she encounters, the 'young lasses seen on the hill-tops,' mothers holding babies, which are contrasted with the 'midges' or 'flies spinning in the sunshine,' and 'the songs of the lark and redbreast,' as well as with local flora such as 'hazels in bloom' and honeysuckles budding.'[309] The 'frisking' of children and the quietude of the elderly in their habitats are noticed by Wordsworth. In one entry she writes of discovering a 'delicious pathway' that takes her up to the Coombe:

> Sat a considerable time upon the heath. Its surface restless and glistening with the motion of the scattered piles of withered grass, and the waving of spiders' threads. On our return the mist still hanging over the sea, but the opposite coast clear, and the rocky cliffs distinguishable. In the deep Coombe, as we stood upon the sunless hill we saw miles of grass, light and glittering, and the insects passing.[310]

Clearly, Wordsworth recorded her sojourns in her journals with a great attention to relaying the intricacies and unexpected marvels of the landscape she traversed.

Whilst Wordsworth reportedly sought a publisher for her travel writing *Recollections of a Tour Made in Scotland* (1803), and was unsuccessful, it was eventually published much later in 1874. In this book, Wordsworth reports that walking gives her access to wellbeing on account of promoting commune with the ecology of the Scottish moor, but also because of the excellent company she keeps by her own estimation, specifically her brother's, and Samuel Taylor Coleridge's on occasion. Walking together with her brother

---

[309] Ibid: p. 5.
[310] Ibid. p. 6.

was clearly reparative, a means of making memories denied them through separation after the death of their parents.[311] And yet, whilst Wordsworth walked prolifically with her brother she also walked alone in and beyond the woods, into the heath, and along coastal pathways.

William Hazlitt's essay 'On Going a Journey,' over a century after Rousseau's *Reveries of a Solitary Walker*, became the formative foundational essay for the genre of walking writing. Hazlitt is preoccupied with the 'musings of the mind' pertaining to walking and writing.[312] I find it inspiring that Hazlitt inaugurates the need to 'vegetate like the country' while out for a walk.[313] 'Solitude' facilitates a deliberate and affirmative shirking off of the self, as well as an escape from people, and their demands. Solitude affords oneself 'breathing space' to enter into 'contemplation.'[318] Hazlitt has no desire to talk, but rather wishes to enter into this community of vegetal life, which gets translated into a text later on.

> You cannot read the book of nature without being perpetually put to the trouble of translating it for the benefit of others. I am for the synthetical method on a journey, in preference to the analytical. I am content to lay in a stock of ideas then, and to examine and anatomise them afterwards. I want to see my vague notions float like the down of the thistle before the breeze, and not to have them entangled in the briars and thorns of controversy. For

---

[311] Andrews, Kerri. 2020. *Wanderer: A History of Women Walking*. London: Reaktion Books. p. 83.
[312] Solnit, Rebecca. 2001. *Wanderlust: A History of Walking*. London: Granta. p. 120.
[313] Hazlitt, William. (1821) 1918. *Twenty-Two Essays of William Hazlitt*. Selected and Edited by Arthur Beatty. Boston, New York, Chicago: University of Wisconsin. D.C. Heath & Company Publisher. P. 87.

once, I like to have it all my own way; and this is impossible unless you are alone, or in such company as I do not covet.[314]

Hazlitt's daydreaming gets intermingled, or migrated, into the rural environment in which he walks. However, he finds it best to simply enter into the exchange, to be present to it, and not try to make sense of things in the act of journeying, but to translate his ruminations later on. Hazlitt augurs that: '... the poet somewhat quaintly sings, "Out of my country and myself I go."'[315] He walks to escape the limitations of his worldly identity, an overly fixed notion of who he is, to open out to the rural landscapes.

By contrast, walking was a means of recovering from divorce and the ensuing legal drama for his former wife, Sarah Stoddart Hazlitt. As Chelsea Kidd of the Sarah Stoddart Hazlitt Project informs us during their marriage William Hazlitt:

> ... had become infatuated with the teenage daughter of the landlady of his lodging house in London. Lacking the financial resources or social influence to obtain a divorce by Act of Parliament, Hazlitt hatched a plan to be 'caught' by his wife in the arms of a prostitute in Edinburgh, where their marriage might be dissolved under Scottish law much more quickly, and more affordably, than in England.[316]

---

[314] Ibid. p. 89.
[315] Ibid. p. 97.
[316] Hazlitt, Sarah Stoddart. 2022. "The Sarah Stoddart Hazlitt Project | about SSH." The Sarah Stoddart Hazlitt Project. https://sarahstoddarthazlitt.wixsite.com/theproject/about-ssh

Over three months Sarah was bullied by William's friends and drawn into her husband's 'degrading schemes' in Scotland.[317] Walking became a means of escaping this oppressive environment—restoring herself from the debilitating emotional and physical impact of her circumstances. Hazlitt walked the Scottish Highlands over the course of a week-long tour, clocking up 180 miles. She walked to the Trossach Hills, through Lochs, negotiated boggy moors with extraordinary determination and fortitude. On glimpsing and exploring Loch Katrine on 15th May, 1822, Hazlitt writes:

> ... There can scarcely be anything more sublime than those masses in which Ben-venue appears to tumble in upon the view at the entrance of Loch Katrine. The first look of the lake itself appears to promise little of the wide and varied expanse to which it stretches out as we proceed... The view of the lake is lost for a few minutes, only to enjoy it again opening with increasing grandeur, and presenting new and picturesque views upon the left, of Benvenue ... More than six miles of water in length, by two in breadth, are under the eye, the remaining four miles to which the lake extends being lost in a turn amongst the mountains to the right ...[318]

Hazlitt traversed both lowland and highland Scotland, enduring and overcoming intense physical discomfort and danger, although overridingly experiencing great pleasure which she compares to a religious experience.[319] Hazlitt acquired self-knowledge and displayed bravery through walking solo, since she wandered in the

---

[317] Andrews, Kerri. 2020. *Wanderer: A History of Women Walking*. London: Reaktion Books. pp. 108-109.
[318] Ibid.
[319] Ibid. pp. 118-120.

country despite the threat of 'molestation or insult' as she pens in her diary.[320]

In Henry David Thoreau's essay 'Walking,' the activity is celebrated as an elevated spiritual practice, albeit which is 'outside of Church and State and People.'[321] He raises the point that walking is a privileged pursuit that requires access to leisure time; the capacity to free oneself from worldly engagements. And he poignantly questions how 'womankind' stand their domestication, as if there were not an entire patriarchal framework to keep women in this situation, such as has been historically ordained and orchestrated by church, state, and people, and which in fact still persists. Thoreau's acknowledgment points to the fact that when women like Dorothy Wordsworth and Sarah Stoddart Hazlitt wandered out alone into the wilderness, they radically altered their circumstances in a bid to obtain freedom and restoration of the spirit. Still, despite his blithe disacknowledgement of the historical, albeit ongoing circumstances of man's elevation over a woman's, Thoreau writes engagingly of fully inhabiting his senses in the woods, and so becoming of the woods. He is interested in an increasing submission to the wilderness, which he upholds as a principle. And yet, although Thoreau calls for the need to conserve the woods, there's an underlying colonial discourse present in this essay-come-lecture that veers at times towards a pioneering western nationalistic impulse. He does elevate First Nations custodians of America to some extent to his credit, aligning them with possessing special knowledge and aptitude pertaining to the wilderness, but also problematically against which he positions so-called civilisation, and also to some extent citizenship.

---

[320] Ibid. p. 118.
[321] Thoreau, Henry David. (1851) 1994. *Walking*. San Francisco: Harper San Francisco. p. 4.

Thoreau is enthusiastically moved and invigorated by wild places and calls for their preservation. 'I believe in the forest, and in the meadow, and in the night in which the corn grows. We require an infusion of hemlock spruce or arbor-vitae in our tea ... There are some intervals which border the strain of the wood through, to which I would migrate, —wild lands where no settler has squatted; to which, methinks, I am already acclimated.'[322] The forest provides sanctuary and the ongoing reformation of his self.

> When I would recreate myself, I seek the darkest wood, the thickest and most interminable and, to the citizen, most dismal, swamp. I enter a swamp as a sacred place, a sanctum sanctorum. There is the strength, the marrow, of Nature. The wildwood covers the virgin mould, and the same soil is good for men and for trees ... To preserve wild animal implies generally the creation of a forest for them to dwell in or resort to. So it is with Man.[323]

And Thoreau adds: '[L]ittle is to be expected of a nation when the vegetable mould is exhausted, and it is compelled to make manure of the bones of its fathers. There the poet sustains himself merely by his own superfluous fat, and the philosopher comes down on his marrow-bones.'[324] He calls for a literature, specifically poetry, that expresses 'Nature,' capital N. 'He would be a poet who could impress the winds and streams into his service, to speak for him; who nailed words to their primitive senses ...'[325] There is still this sense of bending Nature to the will of man and his meaning to some extent, rather than entering into an exchange, or reciprocity, with it.

---

[322] Ibid. p. 20.
[323] Ibid. p. 27.
[324] Ibid. p. 29.
[325] Ibid. p. 30.

Thoreau's desire to see reflected in poetry man's experience and his commune with the wilderness does not necessarily account for a woman's entering into the woods, and which is perhaps more likely to account for shared commune, rather than domination over environmental ecologies. And yet, Thoreau poetically conjures up his wilderness, akin to a holy land, and towards the founding of a divine order outside of the church. He writes of nature against obedience to the laws of so-called civilisation, which surely has a 'speedy limit.'[326] Thoreau comprehends the recklessness of this drive to civilisation. The state and its institutions are identified by Thoreau as fostering a precociousness with their claims to a cultivated knowledge that has nothing to do with the intelligence of nature. He therefore asks 'men' to temper their allegiance to state and nationalisms by wandering into the wilderness, undergoing a border crossing into the untamable woods.

In addition to Virginia Woolf's many London jaunts, she also loved rural walking. Which I'd argue she undertook as a radical and restorative approach to doing writing that veered towards the poetical, and through which she garnered a highly nuanced perspective regarding the human condition. As a young woman, in a letter to Violette Dickinson dated 4th August, 1906, Woolf refers to herself as a 'tramp,' specifically pertaining to her capacity for storytelling.[327] It is with reference to her beloved sister Vanessa Bell, as well as exploring wild unkempt spaces that Woolf tells Violette in an earlier letter dated 16th April, 1906: 'Nessa paints windmills in the afternoon, and I tramp the country for miles with a map, leap

---

[326] Ibid. p. 37.
[327] Andrews, Kerri. 2020. *Wanderer: A History of Women Walking*. London: Reaktion Books. p. 159.

ditches, scale walls and desecrate churches, making out beautiful brilliant stories every step of the way.'[328] It is poignant that Woolf signposts her walking storytelling activities in the rural landscape as a vagrant activity 'outside of the ordinary bounds of settled society,' and especially against the domain of the church.[329] A connection between walking, entering wild spaces, and literary activity is forged, considered a radical act, albeit austere, and Brontë-like (and deployed as a means of transgressing the clean and ordered embodied self for a strain of digressive wilderness). In another letter written to Violette in 1919, Woolf states:

> There is a Greek austerity about my life which is beautiful and might go straight into a bas relief. You can imagine that I never wash, or do my hair; but stride with gigantic strides over the wild moorside, shouting odes of Pindar, as I leap from crag to crag, and exulting in the air that buffets me, and caresses me, like a stern but affectionate parent. That is Stephen Brontëized; almost as good as the real thing.[330]

Woolf intends to lean into latitudes and uncanny aspects in her writing by way of wandering astray. During the period whilst composing her first novel *The Voyage Out*, published 1915 Woolf writes to her brother-in-law Clive Bell 19th August, 1908:

> I think a great deal of my future, and settle what book I am to write — how I shall reform the novel and capture multitudes of things at present fugitive, enclose the whole, and shape infinite strange things. I take a good

---

[328] Ibid.
[329] Ibid. p. 160.
[330] Kerri Andrews cites Virginia Woolf, in *Wanderer: A History of Women Walking*. London: Reaktion Books. p. 160.

look at woods in the sunset, and fix men who are breaking stones with an intense gaze, meant to sever them from the past and the future — all these excitements last out my walks, but tomorrow I know, I shall be sitting down to the intimate old phrases ... I am going to contrive a scheme as I walk.'[331]

Here she conceives of her walking as an access to divergent writing that seeks to account for the embodied ruminations, or mind wanderings, experienced whilst mediating the multiplicity of phenomena encountered beyond the self, bearing witness to her planetary experience, and with special attention to describing in detail the strange and various aspects of the outside world. And in these terms Woolf's letters, but more so her diaries, were a 'literary laboratory' in which she recorded thoughts, observations, meanderings and so on, towards the creation of her main works of literature.[332]

Scottish modernist writer and poet Nan Shepherd (1893-1981) is highly celebrated for her memoir *The Living Mountain*, written mostly in the final years of WWII, not published until 1977. In *The Living Mountain*, Shepherd records her observations and ruminations pertaining to hikes on: 'The Cairngorm Mountains ... a mass of granite thrust up through the schist and the gneiss that form the lower surrounding hills, planed down by the ice cap, and split, shattered and scooped by frost, glaciers and the strength of running water.'[333] Shepherd writes of the granite and glacier landscape,

---

[331] Ibid. p. 161.
[332] Andrews, Kerri. 2020. *Wanderer: A History of Women Walking*. London: Reaktion Books. p. 168.
[333] Shepherd, Nan. (1977) 2014. *The Living Mountain*. With an introduction by Brian McFarlane and a prologue by Jeanette Winterson. Edinburgh: Canongate. p. 1.

which she knows intimately having traversed it frequently solo, as well as with fellow hikers. Her account conveys the learning of a place through revisiting, which veers toward the poetic in seeking to register elemental life in highly nuanced terms. Shepherd writes of the light on the Cairngorm, which is unique, 'penetrating,' and 'luminous without being fierce.'[334] She tells of returning to the source of the river Dee, Avon, the Derry, the Bennie and the Allt Druie to learn the particularity of water, which is 'ungovernable.'[335] Shepherd gives an account of the river Dee as 'frightening' in its simplicity. 'It does nothing, absolutely nothing but be itself.'[336] She adds: 'I love its flash and gleam, its music, its pliancy and grace, its slap against the body; but I fear its strength.[337]

> The young Dee, as it flows out of Garbh Choire and joins the water from the Lairing Pools, has the same astounding transparency. Water so clear cannot be imagined, but must be seen. One must go back, and back again, to look at it, for in the interval memory refuses to re-create its brightness. This is one of the reasons why the high plateau where these streams begin, the streams themselves, their cataracts and rocky beds, the corries, the whole wild enchantment, like a work of art is perpetually new when one returns to it.[338]

She learns to read the Cairngorm through continually returning to climb it, engaging in intensive and precise observation, whereby 'a change of focus' is achieved, and '... static things may be caught

---

[334] Ibid. p. 2.
[335] Ibid. p. 4.
[336] Ibid. p. 23.
[337] Ibid. p. 27.
[338] Ibid. p. 3.

in the very act of becoming.'[339] Shepherd records being enveloped in cloud formations: 'To walk out through the top of a cloud is good. Once or twice I have had the luck to stand on a tip of ground and see a pearled and lustrous plain stretch out to the horizons. Far off, another peak lifts like a small island from the smother. It is like the morning of creation.[340] She returns continually to learn the landscape of the Cairngorm, which is reparative, it nourishes. Shepherd experiences an allegiance to the mountain: 'So I am on the plateau again, having gone round it like a dog in circles to see if it is a good place.'[341]

Shepherd uses the term 'fey' to explain '… that joyous release of body that is engendered by climbing the mountain,' which is itself alive.[342] She associates 'feyness' with taking height, or being at altitude where the air is more rarified, as well as with encountering a 'liberation of space,' and yet the whole enterprise is about commune with this special ecological system, not merely about reaching the summit.[343] This 'feyness' exceeds physiology to engender a reciprocity with the living mountain, which embraces the spiritual, and renders Shepherd speechless at times.[344] For the mountain is a vast and complex network of interrelated and interdependent life.

> The disintegrating rock, the nurturing rain, the quickening sun, the seed, the root, the bird — all are one. Eagles and alpine veronica are part of the mountains wholeness. Saxifrage — the 'rock breaker' — in some of its

---

[339] Ibid. p. 10.
[340] Ibid. p. 18.
[341] Ibid. p. 22.
[342] Ibid. p. 6.
[343] Ibid. p. 8.
[344] Ibid. pp. 12-13.

loveliest forms. Stelloris, the stars with its single blossoms the high rocky corrie burns, and Azoides, that clusters like soft sunshine in their lower reaches, cannot love apart from the mountain.'[345]

Shepherd goes on to describe the life of plants integral to the mountain in vivid and seasonal detail. The feeling of heather underfoot is recorded as a great joy.[346] The smell of pine yields to the sun's heat. The fragrance of bog Myrtle is in its leaf.[347] Shepherd describes the birds, animals and insects on the mountain too. She writes of being charged by a swift flying with 'mad, joyous abandon.'[348] Hiking the mountain gives access to observing eagles in flight: '… if less immediately exciting than that of the swifts, is more profoundly satisfying. The great spiral of his ascent, rising coil over coil in slow symmetry, has in its movement all the amplitude of space. And when he has soared to the top of his bent, there comes the level flight as far as the eye can follow, straight, clean and effortless as breathing …' and she goes on to give a full appraisal of the eagle's hunt.[349]

Whilst Shepherd makes plain that 'man' has polluted and marked the mountain in multiple ways she notes too that it is mountain folk who have instructed her on 'the living mountain.'[350] 'These people are bone of the mountain.'[351] Shepherd tells of sleeping on the mountain as a cultivation of intimacy with it, and which augurs a kind of inactive perception. She writes of sensuous interaction

---

[345] Ibid. p. 48.
[346] Ibid. p. 51.
[347] Ibid. p. 52.
[348] Ibid. p. 60.
[349] Ibid. p. 61.
[350] Ibid. pp. 88-9.
[351] Ibid. p. 89.

through smell, sight, taste, hearing and touch with the mountain—her mode of accessing it. And this clearly resonates in part with First Nations kinship with country outlined by Liz Cameron. Shepherd augurs the full embodied sensuous experience, a profound reciprocity with the mountain, achieved through walking. I cannot imagine that Shepherd did not take a notebook on these sojourns for the exquisite detail of her observations. 'Walking thus, hour after hour, the sense keyed, one walks the flesh transparent. But no metaphor, *transparent*, or *light* as *air*, is adequate. The body is not made negligible, but paramount. Flesh is not annihilated but fulfilled. One is not bodiless, but essentially body.'[352] Shepherd sees the mountain in tandem with her body.[353] It is a pilgrimage to the mountain that Shepherd continually makes, 'a journey into Being,' and which is akin to experiencing pure love.[354] A radical embodied act of love. Shepherd becomes the mountain when she traverses it.

Almost three decades later in *A Fieldguide to Getting Lost*, Rebecca Solnit charts a few of her own maps through walking in an attempt to find out something essential about her own identity beyond fixedness.[355] Solnit deploys the 'blue of the distance' as a metaphor for getting lost, but also with regards to encountering 'melancholy,' 'loss' and 'longing,' as sighted in fifteenth century European painters art works, and especially in the work of Yves Klein, among others. Solnit sets off to walk into that blue of the distance in a physical sense. 'One year of drought the Great Salt Lake fell so low that much of what was ordinarily sea became land, and I went out walking

---

[352] Ibid. p. 106.
[353] Macfarlane, Robert. 2015. *Landmarks*. London: Penguin Books. p. 72.
[354] Shepherd, Nan. (1977) 2014. *The Living Mountain*. With an introduction by Brian McFarlane and a prologue by Jeanette Winterson. Edinburgh: Canongate. pp. 106-8.
[355] Solnit, Rebecca. (2005) 2017. *A Field Guide to Getting Lost*. Edinburgh: Canongate. p. 39.

on it toward Antelope Island, which floated above its reflection, a symmetrical solid object like a precious stone, floating in that blue.'[356] Whilst walking, she mentally wanders into this metaphorical blue of the distance. And as such, Solnit contemplates exploring the abstraction of the self as a necessary and instructive undertaking, which is facilitated by walking without a destination in mind, and recording it in a poetic memoir style of writing.

Kathleen Jamie's *Findings* refutes anger and apocalypticism, instead carrying out a nuanced exploration of the interweaving of human and more-than-human worlds. For instance, she focuses on the 'things' that litter the landscapes of the Monach Islands, Scotland, in the title chapter 'Findings.' Jamie writes of sailing in a yacht to the Monach Islands with two sound recordists. She writes: 'I grew to appreciate the company of people who listen to the world. They don't feel the need to talk all the while. They were alert to bird-cries, waves sucking on rocks, a rope frittering against a mast.'[357] And this too is Jamie's approach, vision is just one embodied sensuous response to recording her surroundings. She takes up listening and touch as equally critical modes of apprehending landscapes and surveying findings on the beachscape, and specifically here in relation to discovering a whale's carcass.

> Walking in this way in the rain [up the beach, along the tideline], head down into the rain and wind, I didn't see the whale until I was next to it. It didn't startle me — it was too big and too dead to be startling ... It must have been on the shore a month or two, the whale, because it was half-blanketed in the orange-coloured weed. Half sinking or half emerging

---

[356] Ibid. p. 35.
[357] Jamie, Kathleen. 2005. *Findings*. London: Sort of Books. p. 54.

> out of a bed of sand and weed. The body was rolled in the motion of a wave, and there was one dark orifice, like a cave, in its mouldering head, perhaps an eyes socket. It was the heaviest creature I had ever seen, dead and out of water's buoyancy, a massive failure. I thought about touching it, with just one finger, furtively, the way a gull pecks, and I wish now I had, because I've never touched a whale and probably won't get the chance again. I should have touched the skin because it looked almost like black leatherette.[358]

Jamie demonstrates a unique deployment of poetic language which elicits the thing's status, in this case a whale carcass, as 'vibrant matter' even as it rots away.[359] This mode of logging environmental ecologies is an important medium for registering the impact of human predation. It responds to the need to provide deeply personal accounts of changing landscapes and the destruction of biodiversity. As Pippa Marland explains in her essay on Jamie, she discusses and surveys ecologies that exist in a 'permanently disfigured state,' and as such her field notes offer 'no pastoral comfort,' and serve as a radical reappraisal of our planetary predicament.[360]

In another later chapter of *Findings*, Jamie writes of visiting Stornoway, Scotland, on the Sabbath. She's there specifically to restore herself prior to re-commencing her university teaching post at the beginning of semester. Jamie infers she's in a difficult place mentally and emotionally on account of the demands of her life in

---

[358] Ibid. pp. 57-8.
[359] Bennet, Jane. 2010. *Vibrant Matter: A Political Ecology of Things*. Durham: Duke University Press.
[360] Marland, Pippa. 2015. "The Gannet's Skull versus the Plastic Doll's Head: Material 'Value' in Kathleen Jamie's 'Findings.'" *Green Letters* 19 (2): 121–31. https://doi.org/10.1080/14688417.2015.1024156

her middle age years, charged with the care of elderly parents and young children, responsible for the education of budding young writers, burdened with the pressures of earning and so on. It is in these terms that Jamie feels she's come to the end of the road, or the cliff's edge. She deploys a self-reflexive mode of writing, pausing to take notes whilst out for a walk. 'I made notes, but the reason I'd come to the end of the road to walk along the cliff is because language fails me there. If we work always in words, sometimes we need to recuperate in a place where language doesn't join up, where we're thrown back on a few elementary nouns. Sea. Bird. Sky.'[361] She walks northwards with the sea at her left, describing the landscape in vivid poetic detail.

> The clifftop land dipped into damp troughs and then rose onto promontories where bedrock broke through thin earth. There were pools of peaty water between rocks, and foraging parties of golden plover. You might call it a wild place, what with the Atlantic to one hand and peat bog to the other, but in each saddle between the headlands was evidence of some human intervention, an enclosure or a wall.[362]

Jamie introduces into her piece this commentary regarding human intervention in the landscape whereby bearing witness becomes a mode of activism. She continues to muse about the need for respite, time out from her overly busy life to feel as she walks. Suddenly she sights a 'monastic cell structure' in the rock face with the aid of her binoculars. She considers that it seems like an appealing place to shelter, so as to feel 'less imperilled.'[363] And although walking

---

[361] Jamie, Kathleen. 2005. *Findings*. London: Sort of Books. p. 164.
[362] Ibid. p. 165.
[363] Ibid. p. 178.

provides access to bearing witness to her own state of becoming with the ecological landscape, walking also allows for exposure to a place beyond language, insofar as it delivers her back to the elements, and thus restores her.

Olivia Laing engages in fieldwork writing in her book *To the River: A Journey Beneath the Surface*. She maps a route and takes a planned walk following the river Ouse, in which Woolf committed suicide, weaving in elements of the autobiographical, describing the landscape idiosyncratically and precisely, and drawing on the history of place. The river Ouse is not a new landscape for Laing, rather it's a place she has returned to throughout the course of her life. She writes of approaching the river, specifically as the site of Woolf's drowning, but also as a means of processing her grief at the end of a long-term relationship.

> The thickening air was full of the scent of meadowsweet and if I looked closely I could make out a scurf of petals drifting idly along the bank. The river ran brimful at the edge of an open field, and as the sun dropped its smell became more noticeable: the cold green reek by which wild water betrays its presence. I stooped to dip a hand and as I did so I remembered Virginia Woolf drowned herself in the Ouse, though why or when I don't remember.[364]

Laing thereafter draws on Woolf's literary works, specifically her diaries: 'She was acutely sensitive to landscape, and her impressions of this chalky, watery valley pervade her work. Her solitary, often daily, excursions seem to have formed an essential part of the writing

---

[364] Laing, Olivia. 2011. *To the River: A Journey Beneath the Surface*. Edinburgh: Canongate. p. 29.

process.'³⁶⁵ Laing argues that Woolf's work is full of a desire to enter depths, which Laing's writing mirrors. And so, Laing goes beneath the surface, traces the riverbed like a scar tissue, as a means of attending to her own grief. The river is a vitality that heals her. Laing's book attests to walking specific landscapes as curative.

ii) Some European & American Urban Legacies

It seems poignant to briefly survey Leslie Stephen's essay 'In Praise of Walking', especially given that he was the father of Woolf who was undoubtedly influenced by his love of pedestrianism, and which he wrote about. He argues for the pleasures of walking in and of itself, but also praises the 'musings and imaginings' that are given rise to through undertaking this activity, and so for this reason he proposes that most 'men of letters' have been dedicated walkers. Women are clearly not part of his walker writer universe. For Stephen, the intellect (that women were historically thought not to possess) is effectively brought into balance by way of the meditative act of walking. 'Walking is the natural recreation for a man who desires not absolutely to suppress his intellect but to turn it out to play for a season.'³⁶⁶ He writes of Shakespeare, Captain Barclay, William Wordsworth, Swift, De Quincey and more. Though he proposes that: 'Opium-eating is not congenial to walking, yet even Coleridge, after beginning the habit, speaks of walking forty miles a day in Scotland, and, as we all know, the great manifesto of the new school of poetry, the *Lyrical Ballads*, was suggested by the famous walk with Wordsworth, when the first stanzas of the *Ancient Mariner*

---

[365] Ibid. p. 37.
[366] Stephen, Leslie. (1898) 2012. *Studies of a Biographer*. Cambridge: Cambridge University Press. p. 262.

were composed.'³⁶⁷ Stephen finds walking a highly favourable aid to composition, particularly in London where there's much stimulus, and this point of view certainly seems to have transposed into his daughter. Walking and encountering 'a stream of thought,' such that they become 'multitudinous,' shows up in Woolf's writing.³⁶⁸ This flux of thought brought about through walking is surely a precursor idea to the 'stream of consciousness' modernist technique taken up by Woolf, which I'll soon explore.

London has long been celebrated as an excellent city to perambulate, as has Paris. In fact in the early twentieth century, Walter Benjamin, inspired by the poetry of Charles Baudelaire, became intrigued by the figure of the flâneur wandering through urban Paris, and elevated *him* to the spectres of academic study, which he undertakes in his unfinished *Arcades Project* (written in the 1920s). It was Baudelaire who supposedly first coined the term 'flâneur.' Baudelaire pioneered the prose poem in relation to the theme of modernity and the urban metropolis, specifically Paris. According to him modernity needed a new language, which he set out to convey in *La Spleen de Paris*. I think this is poignant, especially in terms of unveiling the influence Baudelaire's new language had on Woolf, however it's important to distinguish the fact that the prose poem is a differentiated, albeit a somewhat cognate mode to poetic prose, and with its own organic development. Baudelaire's intention was to capture the modern city with an existential outlook. The idea that a certain perspective or school of thought can inform a consideration of landscape is therefore explored by Baudelaire.

---

[367] Ibid. p. 266.
[368] Ibid. p. 281.

For instance, in Baudelaire's poem 'Project,' collected in *La Spleen de Paris*, he writes of a man at leisure, walking through a 'great lonely park' in Paris. The man is daydreaming about a woman in a grand costume, such as a princess would wear. The man thereafter stops at a printshop and looks at a picture of a tropical scene, which makes him think of where the ideal place for him and his beloved would be to inhabit. He rejects the grandeur of a palace. His mind wanders further as he imagines 'a lovely wooden cabin by the sea' and he goes on painting a picture of this idyllic setting of his life with his beloved. Places and phenomena in the city prompt the man's digressive mental forays, and which Baudelaire incorporates into his writing. As the man walks on he notices a cosy inn. He watches seemingly happy people taking wine and food in there, and hypothesises that within this establishment there is even a cosy bed. He considers that he has imagined three various homes that day and in fact it is the project of imagining them that has brought him much satisfaction. No need to bother actually carrying out these projects. The project is that walking the modern city gives rise to mind wanderings, or vagabond thoughts, which is a kind of diversification strategy that brings pleasure in and of itself, a sense of liberation. The flâneur listens to the frequencies of his many divergent thoughts, ideas and observations, and records them.

In another prose poem collected in *La Spleen de Paris* titled 'Crowds,' Baudelaire writes of entering the crowded city, and encountering an immersion with others, albeit whilst simultaneously remaining apart in himself. He muses about the solitary 'roaming man' who delights in 'tak[ing] a bath of multitude.'[369]

---

[369] Baudelaire, Charles. (1869) 1970. *La Spleen de Paris*. Translated by Louise Varèse. New York: A New Direction Book. p. 20.

> Multitude, solitude: identical terms, and interchangeable by the active and fertile poet ... The poet enjoys the incomparable privilege of being able to be himself or someone else, as he chooses. Like those wandering souls who go looking for a body, he enters as he likes into each man's personality ... The singular and thoughtful stroller finds a singular intoxication in this universal communion.[370]

Walter Benjamin, writing on the flâneur, and specifically with regards to Baudelaire states that the crowd is his narcotic. 'The flâneur abandons himself to the crowd.'[371] He surrenders to this immersion with others. Perhaps the flâneur escapes his ego temporarily to enter into others—he frees himself in this way from a limited or fixed identity. In my view Baudelaire augurs this notion of fluid commune; a ceaseless entering into everything. He can cast himself off, recast himself anew with respect to the cityscape.

Benjamin considered Baudelaire to be a bohemian; an ideal of the political provocateur. He directly draws on Baudelaire in his *Arcades Project* to build up a picture of the modern flâneur '... strolling through the urban crowd as prosthetic vehicle of a new vision.'[372] He sketches the panorama of urban life, investigates the 'human types' around the marketplace, which he dubs 'physiologies.' He is a writer who studies with his gaze the mechanisms of a living system; a complex social and environmental ecology. The entire parade of bourgeois life in all its manifestations comes into view. And it was the invention of the arcade that made it possible for the

---

[370] Ibid.
[371] Benjamin, Walter, and Michael William Jennings. 2006. *The Writer of Modern Life: Essays on Charles Baudelaire*. Cambridge: Harvard University Press. pp. 85-6.
[372] Ibid. p. 9.

flâneur to stroll about because hitherto pavements were rare, and if they did exist they were often too narrow to be safe from vehicles (that might run a pedestrian down). The invention of the arcade, around 1852, transformed the boulevard into an interior. '... [A] glass-roofed, marble-paneled corridor extending through whole blocks of buildings, whose owners have joined together for such enterprises.'[373] In these terms the birth of the flâneur coincides with modernity, commodification, the city, and bourgeois existence.

And so, the flâneur is a chronicler of ideas, a recorder of modernity, most definitely a writer. For he carries around his notebook. He's never without it, although it might be tucked away out of view.

> The street becomes a dwelling place for the flâneur; he is much at home among house facades as a citizen is within his four walls. To him, a shiny enameled shop sign is at least as good a wall ornament as an oil painting is to a bourgeois in his living room. Buildings' walls are the desk against which he presses his notebooks; newsstands are his libraries; and café terraces are the balconies from which he looks down on his household after his work is done.[374]

He records Parisian life in his notebook. But, if the flâneur is a writer he is also an 'unwilling detective.'[375] The flâneur 'catches things in flight,' he grasps things with 'forensic knowledge' following some tract or another on a whim.[376] Benjamin argues that Baudelaire adopted the genre of the detective story, after Edgar Allan Poe, albeit

---

[373] Ibid. p. 68.
[374] Ibid. pp. 68-69.
[375] Ibid. p. 72.
[376] Ibid. p. 72.

within the frame of poetry. He's thinking of Baudelaire's *Fleur de Mal*.

As Karen O'Rourke points out in her book *Walking and Mapping: Artists as Cartographers*, Benjamin wasn't the only one thinking or writing about the flâneur. 'Benjamin's contemporaries Louis Aragon ("Paris Peasant," 1925), André Breton ("Nadja," 1928), and Philippe Soupault ("Last Nights of Paris," 1928) [also] put to paper their citywide ramblings. Like Baudelaire, they celebrated the inadvertent poetry of shop window displays, fleeting glances, elusive women, chance encounters, and mysterious pursuits.'[377] And yet, problematically, there is apparently no equivalent term for a woman. A google search brings up few results. And so, Lauren Elkin takes a highly pertinent look at the wanderings of women in urban landscapes in her book *Flâneuse: Women Walk the City in Paris, New York, Tokyo, Venice and London*. Elkin attempts to define the flâneause. She gives a fairly rudimentary definition: 'Flâneause [flanne-euhze], noun, from the French. Feminine form of flâneur [flanne-euhr], an idler, a dawdling observer, usually found in cities.'[378] Elkin points out that the idea of the flâneause has historically been dismissed by slew of women scholars on account of the fact that 'sexual divisions' of the nineteenth century would supposedly render her existence impossible, whereby the privileges of wandering the city were reserved only for men of certain means, that is to say bourgeois men. However, Elkin refutes the idea that 'the woman in the street ... was most likely a streetwalker,' since in fact the nineteenth century prostitute enjoyed very little freedom

---

[377] O'Rourke, Karen. 2016. *Walking and Mapping: Artist as Cartographer*. Cambridge: MIT Press.
[378] Elkin, Lauren. (2016) 2017. *Flâneuse: Women Walk the City in Paris, New York, Tokyo, Venice and London*. London: Vintage. p. 7.

of movement in the city. She was highly policed.[379] Elkin thus contends that the flâneause has been excluded from histories of walking the city because of 'the social conditions of women in the nineteenth century.'[380] For a nineteenth century bourgeois woman to venture alone into the street was to 'risk disgrace.'[381] She had to be accompanied by her mother, a suitable chaperone, or her husband. However, 'By the late nineteenth century, women of all classes were enjoying the use of public space in cities like London, Paris and New York.'[382] Women could ride their bikes around town, they worked in shops and offices. And yet, as Elkin advises: 'The *flâneause* is still fighting to be seen, even now, when, as we'd like to think, she more or less has the run of the city.'[383] Elkin explores the idea of the woman urban walker slipping the bounds of responsibility to wander the streets, i.e. to shirk work as much as domestic life to wander against the threat of sexual violence.

Woolf braved London's urban streets against the fear of criminal activity, such as sexual assault and murder, to encounter the crowd as a fully-fledged flâneause. She writes in her diary on the 3rd of November, 1918: '... rambled down to Charing Cross in the dark, making up phrases and incidents to write about. Which is, I expect, the way one gets killed.'[384] She tells Vita Sackville-West in a letter dated 9th November, 1924, that she is very fond of 'rambling the

---

[379] Ibid. p. 8.
[380] Ibid. p. 9.
[381] Ibid. p. 12.
[382] Ibid. p. 14.
[383] Ibid. p. 18.
[384] Woolf, Virginia. 1979. *The Dairy of Virginia Woolf: Volume 1: 1915-1919*. Editor Anne Olivier Bell. Harmondsworth, London: Hogarth Press. p. 35.

streets' of London for 'fresh air.'³⁸⁵ But, in addition to taking fresh air, Woolf wanders in the city to engage with human life in its myriad configurations. Woolf writes in her diary on 15th August, 1924:

> London is enchanting. I step out upon a tawny coloured magic carpet, it seems, and get carried into beauty without raising a finger. The nights are amazing, with all the white porticoes and broad silent avenues. And people pop in and out, lightly, divertingly like rabbits; and I look down Southampton Row, wet as a seal's back or red and yellow with sunshine, and watch the omnibus going and coming, and hear the old crazy organs. One of these days I will write about London, and how it takes up the private life and carries it on, without any effort. Faces passing lift up my mind; prevent it from settling, as it does in the stillness at Rodmell.³⁸⁶

And so, true to her word a couple of years later Woolf turns to writing 'Street Haunting: A London Adventure,' in which she likens wandering across London in the early evening for a pencil to encountering a temporary anonymity by way of immersion with the crowd—a peopling. She takes up this idea from Baudelaire. Woolf writes: 'Am I here, or am I there? Or is the true self neither this or that, neither here nor there, but something varied and wandering that it is only when we give the reign to its wishes and let it take its way unimpeded that we are indeed ourselves?'³⁸⁷ Her point is that

---

[385] Sackville-West, Vita and Woolf, Virginia. 2021. *Love Letters: Virginia Woolf and Vita Sackville-West*. With an Introduction by Alison Bechdel. UK: Vintage Classics, Penguin Random House. p. 15.

[386] Woolf, Virginia. 1978. *The Diary of Virginia Woolf; Volume 2, 1920-1924*. Editor Anne Olivier Bell. Assisted by Andrew McNeillie. New York: Harcourt. p. 301.

[387] Woolf, Virginia. 'Street Haunting: A London Adventure.' (1927) 1943. Collected in *The Death of the Moth and other essays*. London: The Hogarth Press: pp. 19-29.

we transgress the borders of our main being all the time to encounter other people and phenomena when we walk the city.

Woolf was also clearly influenced by Hope Mireless' wandering writing in Parisian streets in her groundbreaking project *Paris: A Poem*, a precursor text to TS Eliot's *The Wasteland* surveying post WWII Paris, which Hogarth Press published (Woolf's press with her husband). Mireless orchestrates a woman's gaze on Paris, albeit influenced by Freud, as well as the French poet Apollinaire. Apollinaire's *Calligrammes: Poems of Peace and War 1913-1916* was published the year before Mireless's *Paris*, and in it he explores an ideographic dimension of poetry. The spatial arrangement of the words on the page are a key element of the work, and are as significant as the meaning of the words, and which Mireless in turn takes up in *Paris*. In Apollinaire's 'It's raining,' he emulates rain with poetic sentences one of which says: 'It's raining women's voices as if they had died even in memory.'[388] It seems to me that Apollinaire's derailing of women's voices is something that Mireless seeks to redress, and which Woolf also critiques.

Mireless sets her poem *Paris* on a single day. Similarly, the plot of *Mrs Dalloway* is paced to her pedestrianism; her internal life unfolds on a ramble through London over the course of one day. The frisson of London enlivens Mrs Dalloway, and which is demonstrated in the famous early lines of the novel:

> In people's eyes, in the swing, tramp, and trudge; in the bellow and the uproar; the carriages, motor cars, omnibuses, vans, sandwich men shuffling

---

[388] Apollinaire, Guillaume . 2016. "It's Raining (Il Pleut)." Tumblr. April 3, 2016. https://www.tumblr.com/thepoetrytypewriter/142202742277/its-raining-il-pleut

and swinging; brass bands; barrel organs; in the triumph and the jingle and the strange high singing of some aeroplane overhead was what she loved; life; London; this moment of June.'[389]

And yet, whilst Mireless seeks a symbolic language that conveys her psychological state as a woman with respect to the modern city, specifically Paris, by contrast Woolf deploys a poetic prose approach to convey Mrs Dalloway's thoughts, a stream of consciousness, in the conveyance of the ongoing migrations of her internal life to the urban environment. Woolf sought a new language to convey a woman's experience in the city.

In her diary, Woolf informs us that London '... perpetually attracts, stimulates, gives me a play and a story and a poem, without any trouble, save that of moving my legs through the streets ... To walk alone through London is the greatest rest.'[390] Some of Woolf's favourite strolls included visiting the public gardens. She writes in her diary on the 6th of June, 1935 that: 'There is no doubt that the greatest happiness in the world is walking through Regents Park on a green, but wet ... evening ... & making up phrases.'[391] Woolf especially delighted in the activity of Oxford street, the Strand and the Thames. She writes in her diary on the 29th of March, 1940 of that which enlivens her: '... The river. Say the Thames at London bridge; & buying a notebook; & then walking along the Strand &

---

[389] Woolf, Virginia. 1925. *Mrs Dalloway*. New York: Harcourt, Brace and Company. p. 5.
[390] Woolf, Virginia. 2008. *Selected Essays*, edited by David Bradshaw. Oxford: Oxford World's Classics. p. x.
[391] Woolf, Virginia. *1982. The Diary of Virginia Woolf, Vol. IV, 1931—1935*. Edited by Anne Olivier Bell, assisted by Andrew McNeillie. London: Hogarth Press. p. 319.

letting each face give me a buffet.'³⁹² In David Bradshaw's lecture 'Virginia Woolf's London' he surmises that:

> If Cornwall captured Woolf's soul, London bagged her heart. Writing to a cousin from Hampshire on 18 August 1898, she confessed that she was 'counting the weeks till the 22nd September when we return to our beloved city'. Her love affair with London, and especially the City of London, would never cool, and when parts of it were reduced to rubble during the Blitz of 1940—41 she lamented its devastation like a grief-stricken widow.³⁹³

During the second world war Woolf wrote to her friend Ethel Smyth of walking through damaged parts of the city: 'And then, the passion of my life, that is the City of London — to see London all blasted, that too raked my heart. Have you that feeling for certain alleys and little courts, between Chancery Lane and the City?' And she adds: 'I walked to the Tower the other day by way of caressing my love of all that.'³⁹⁴ Like Wordsworth, she retraced a landscape in which specific damaging events had taken place, in order to process her grief, and thus restore herself.

Lauren Elkin rather poignantly mourns the fact that many contemporary psychogeographers, who take their cues from the figure of the flâneur, leave out women's experience of the city. And,

---

[392] Woolf, Virginia. *1984. The Diary of Virginia Woolf, Vol. V, 1936—1941*. Edited by Anne Olivier Bell, assisted by Andrew McNeillie. London: Hogarth Press. p. 276.
[393] Bradshaw, David. 2016. "Virginia Woolf's London." *The British Library*. https://www.bl.uk/20th-century-literature/articles/virginia-woolfs-london
[394] Woolf, Virginia. *1980. Leave the Letters Till We're Dead: The Letters of Virginia Woolf, Vol. VI, 1936—1941*. Edited by Nigel Nicolson. Assisted by Joanne Trautmann. London: Hogarth Press. p. 431.

as Merlin Coverley points out in his book *Psychogeography*, the term 'psychogeography' has fallen out of favour on account of this lack of inclusion of women. As Karen O'Rourke explains in her book *Walking and Mapping: Artists as Cartographers*:

> Graphy comes from the Greek graphein (to write), a decidedly polysemic word. If geographers 'carve,' 'draw,' or 'write' the earth (geos), what about psychogeographers? The Latin prefix psyche (breath) adds a zest of soul to the mix, linking earth, mind and foot. Psychogeographic writing can be thought of as an alternative way of reading the city. Wilfried Hou Je Bek calls it 'the city-space cut-up.' Just as William Burroughs and Brion Gysin cut and reorganized newspaper texts to reveal their implicit content, so too psychogeographers decode urban space by moving through it in unexpected ways.[395]

And so, psychogeography '... describes the point at which psychology and geography collide, a means of calibrating the behavioural impact of place.'[396] As O'Rourke enumerates: '... the term itself was first used by members of the Lettrist International, a Paris-based collective of radical artists and cultural theorists that was active in the early 1950s ...'[397] However, it was Guy-Ernest Debord, under the banner of Situationism (formed in the wake of surrealism), who came to define the term psychogeography. 'Writing in the Belgian surrealist journal *Les Lèvres Nues*, Guy-Ernest Debord [states that] ... psychogeography should examine the "specific effects of the geographical environment ... on the emotions and behavior of individuals." To accomplish this ambitious investigation, he and his

---

[395] O'Rourke, Karen. 2016. *Walking and Mapping: Artist as Cartographer*. Cambridge: MIT Press.
[396] Coverley, Merlin. (2006) 2018. *Psychogeography*. Harpenden, UK: Oldcastle Books. p. 116.
[397] O'Rourke, Karen. 2016. *Walking and Mapping: Artist as Cartographer*. Cambridge: MIT Press.

friends recommended drifting.'[398] Although, as Coverley points out, psychogeography was a fairly minor schema in Debord's Situationist agenda for radical social reform overall. Still, he attributed to it a 'pleasing vagueness' that has allowed multiple interpretations and iterations.[399]

> The principal tool at the psychogeographer's disposal is the aimless drift, or dérive; which enables its practitioner to ascertain the true nature of the urban environment as he passes through it. Hence, emotional zones that cannot be determined simply by architectural or economic conditions must be revealed by the dérive; the results of which may then form the basis of a new cartography characterised by a complete disregard for the tradition and habitual practices of the tourist ...[400]

The drift is non-purposive. As Karrie Higgis observes: 'Psychogeographers set out on derives (literally, driftings), forgoing all the usual motivations for movement, instead allowing themselves to be attracted or repelled by the world around them or through some element of chance.'[401] To allow '... the flow of myriad impressions—visual, auditory, physical, associative, and subliminal—that impinge on the consciousness of an individual and form part of his awareness along with the trend of his rational thoughts ...'[402] And, specifically while out for a walk. Clearly, this kind of straying has the potential to encourage radical digression from the prescribed patriarchal path. It is a means of enacting a resistance, which is clearly creatively charged.

---

[398] Ibid.
[399] Coverley, Merlin. (2006) 2018. *Psychogeography*. Harpenden, UK: Oldcastle Books. p. 116.
[400] Ibid. p. 117.
[401] Higgins, Karrie. 2007. "Senses of Place." Los Angeles Times. November 4, 2007. https://www.latimes.com/archives/la-xpm-2007-nov-04-bk-higgins4-story.html
[402] Britannica. 2019. "Stream of Consciousness | Literature." In *Encyclopædia Britannica*. https://www.britannica.com/art/stream-of-consciousness

Although, it's important to point out that the Situationist's brand of drifting had its roots in avant-gardism, specifically Surrealism and Dadaism, and was geared towards men.

The Situationists engaged in 'recreation drifting' in order to bring about 'disorientation.'[403] But they also drifted as a means of accessing the psychic atmosphere of the city. As O'Rourke elucidates:

> In recent decades, for poachers and protesters, artists, activists and drifters, walking has emerged as a means of reclaiming public space. From the Paris suburbs to London's ring road, pedestrians are reappearing (or springing up) in spaces dedicated to automobile traffic. For many of them walking is a process of self-education.[404]

For instance, a spate of British inheritors of the Situationists explore the urban environment pertaining to exploring psychological states, such as Ian Sinclair's *London Orbital*, in which he documents walking around the M25. Will Self too dapples in psychogeography. In *Psychogeography: Disentangling the Modern Conundrum of Psyche and Place* he describes a long walk across continents, of course impossible, he's helped out by a plane. Self walks from London to Heathrow airport and flies across to New York's JFK airport where he sets off on foot again for Manhattan. As Lyon comments in her article 'Psychogeography: a way to delve into the soul of a city': '... one cannot ignore some of the failures here, such as Self's "digression" that no female psychogeographers exist because women

---

[403] O'Rourke, Karen. 2016. *Walking and Mapping: Artist as Cartographer*. Cambridge: MIT Press.
[404] Ibid.

supposedly lack men's special infatuation with "orientation."'[405] This is of course sexist drivel. Clearly both Mireless and Woolf were early groundbreaking modernist flâneause come psychogeographers. Rebecca Solnit and Olivia Laing stand on their shoulders.

Solnit observes in *Wanderlust* that although rural walking has historically been more highly prized pertaining to the benefits of nature, that is it's been *morally* endorsed, by contrast: '[U]rban walking has always been a shadier business, easily turning into soliciting, cruising, promenading, shopping, rioting, protesting, skulking, loitering, and other activities that, however enjoyable, hardly have the high moral tone of nature appreciation.'[406] Solnit is a San Franciscan. In *Wanderlust* she writes of returning to her city after an extended period of absence and of seeing it anew. Solnit elucidates the enchantments of walking such a city—the eye candy. Here is a passage in which she describes the minutiae details of San Francisco.

> All along Divisadero keeping an eye on the other people and on the open venues—liquor stores and smoke shops—and then turned up my own street. At a cross street a young black guy in a watch cap and dark clothes was running downhill at me at a great clip, and looked around to suss up my options just in case—I mean if Queen Victoria was moving toward you that fast you'd take note. He saw my hesitation and assured me in the sweetest young man's voice, 'I'm not after you, I'm just late' and dashed passed me, so I said 'Good luck' and then, and then when he was into the

---

[405] Lyons, Siobahn. 'Psychogeography: a way to delve into the soul of a city.' *The Conversation* (June 19, 2017). https://theconversation.com/psychogeography-a-way-to-delve-into-the-soul-of-a-city-78032

[406] Solnit, Rebecca. 2001. *Wanderlust: A History of Walking*. London: Granta. pp. 173-4.

street and I had time to collect my thoughts, 'Sorry to look suspicious, but you were kind of speedy.' He laughed, and then I did, and in a minute I recalled all the other encounters I'd had around the hood lately that might have had earmarks of trouble but unfolded as pure civility and was pleased that I'd been prepared without being alarmed.[407]

Solnit augurs that the city is a place of community, of making personal connections, which walking provides access to. And Solnit draws on Woolf's seminal essay 'Street Haunting' pertaining to this notion of shedding the self to encounter the crowd—undergoing a peopling. As Woolf terms it becoming '... part of that vast republican army of anonymous trampers.'[408] Woolf also writes of a 'central oyster of perceptiveness, an enormous eye' on the street in 'Street Haunting' identifying a freedom and pleasure central to wandering, that of close observation, which accompanies this entering into encounters with others, and which also provides an access to trying on other identities. Solnit draws on further writers who have celebrated wandering in the city from Walt Whitman to the Beat poets. Frank O'Hara writes of 'becoming the street' in his poem 'Walking to Work.'[409] The path traversed itself lays down the narrative line.

To return briefly to Elkin's writing on the *Flâneuse*. In her chapter on New York Elkin describes her escape from the suburbs to the city, specifically New York as a university student.

---

[407] Ibid. p. 175.
[408] Ibid. p. 187.
[409] O'Hara, Frank (Feb 1969). 2025. "The Poetry Foundation." The Poetry Foundation. https://www.poetryfoundation.org/poetrymagazine/browse?volume=113&issue=5&page=42

Up and down the length of those avenues I went walking, Broadway, Amsterdam, Riverside, which turned into West End Avenue, down to 110th Street and across to Central Park, down Central Park West to the Museum of National History. I gaped at the gargantuan ornate apartment buildings, the wide boulevards, Zabar's, H&H Bagels, the Hungarian Pastry Shop with its sticky glazed croissants, the men selling books on folding tables on Broadway. To sit in a restaurant on Broadway with the world walking by and the cars and the taxis and the noise was like finally being let in to the centre of the universe, after peering in at it for so long.[410]

Elkin speculates that a society in which women don't walk is concerning, pointing to the suburbs, which are conceptually prefaced on the concept of the nuclear family unit: 'the neat grid, the nearby shopping centre, the endless loops of parkways, where the American adventure of the open road is tamed by the American dream.'[411] Elkin reflects on Marguerite Duras's hypothesis of suburban houses as apparatuses for curbing men and children's 'waywardness,' and to which she adds women. Carefully planned streets and shopping areas are antithetical to roaming, straying, getting lost. By contrast apartment living and rambling in a metropolitan environment like New York fosters digression, possibly even liberation. Of course, women may be exposed to violence in dark alleyways, and yet Elkin points out that cities are more populated than suburbs, and thus potentially safer. Of course it's not just women who face the threat of violence in urban environments.

---

[410] Elkin, Lauren. (2016) 2017. *Flâneuse: Women Walk the City in Paris, New York, Tokyo, Venice and London*. London: Vintage. p. 35.
[411] Ibid. p. 37.

Might you take a field trip? Might you record your experience in urban or rural spaces as an access to mind wandering? What are some of your maps? What impact do certain rural and urban landscapes have on your imagination? What comes up psychologically when you wander in a certain place in the city, but also beyond in rural places, or in the in-between suburban zones? Could you log a social and/or environmental ecology in detail in a journal? Might you undergo an immersion—experience yourself as migrated into a place? What is your sensuous embodied engagement with that place? Could you undertake stream of consciousness writing pertaining to places traversed? Could you visit certain places, in which pivotal events occurred to process certain psychological states—augur certain remnants of that past happening? Might walking become curative? What is the First Nations epistemology of a certain place? Might you seek to respectfully acknowledge, uphold, and celebrate that before finding your own embodied and sensuous connection to that place? Alternatively, in colonised countries such as Australia, might you seek to respectfully enter into truth-telling with regards to possible violence enacted on First Nations people in certain places, towards the exposure of past horrendous colonial injustices, and in full acknowledgement of ongoing suffering experienced by First peoples, and in the hopes of forging pathways of healing, and reconciliation. Can you charge the landscape with exactitudes as a means of safeguarding it? Protecting it? Could you deliberately drift, forgo a planned journey? Could this be a radical act? A means of shifting your identity in an affirmative sense, towards the fosterage of new paths of exploration psychically? Might you record your interaction with the living ecologies you are traversing? What is the spiritual potency of place? Might the artefacts or artistic documents that arise from these sojourns potentially transform you? If you take a poetical lens how might the reciprocal act, or the exchange engaged with, that is between human, more-than-human worlds, and taking in diverse environmental and social ecologies, become the focus for a new radical testimonial of planetary experience? Might you be lifted into relational aptitudes through an embodied and highly sensuous mode of poetical engagement with place?

Walking is potentially a radical approach to writing because it promotes greater awareness and reciprocity with place towards the cultivation of a sense of responsibility through practicing embodied poetical attention and imaginal diversification. Walking can also potentially promote affirmative identity deformation and reformation—effectively taking us outside of a limited concept of self towards the world and others—fostering an affirmative reschooling. To re-emphasise my opening remarks, when we record our journeys by foot, bear witness to our exchanges with diverse environmental and social ecologies, we gain a bit of latitude, even cure. We disengage a bit more from end time capitalisms mutations and fascist indoctrinations. And we must surely safeguard our liberty—walk towards it and a new planetary reality.

PART III

Feminist Bombs/New Maps

Chapter Seven

A Queer Morphology for Germaine Greer

Germaine Greer publicly stated, highly problematically, in 2015 that 'post-operative transgender men are not real women,' for which she was no-platformed. Greer petitioned to preserve a space of difference for women who have a womb on account of the fact that patriarchy has been targeting wombs as the source of potential danger and monstrousness, as well as magic and mana, for millennia. It has been a key *reason* for putting a door on women's mouths, prohibiting their voices, as Anne Carson reminds us in her essay 'The Gender of Sound.' So too, Greer has been sanctioned for her outpourings. Carson signposts the cultural anxiety associated with such unapologetic 'female ejaculation.'[412] She makes plain a connection between mouth and genitals in Ancient Greece, giving the example of Baubo whose face is on her torso, and therefore closer in proximity to the vulva. Greer is perhaps our contemporary Baubo. Bravely, if controversially, and sometimes reactively, giving voice to women's sexual difference, insisting on it, orchestrating her desires publically—unashamedly. Arguing for a *whole woman*. Not

---

[412] Carson, Anne. (1992) 1995. *The Gender of Sound*. New York: New Directions Books. p. 132.

a woman prefaced on a man's desire. Not a woman reduced to her womb—as a receptacle—a space to be colonised and pathologised. Rather, validating a woman as expansively, creatively, articulately enwombed—and with a corresponding imaginal trajectory, many in fact, which ought to be valued culturally. Consequently, she's been driven back into the woods, into the liminal spaces where such overtly creaturely women belong.

Surely preserving a space for a woman's embodied voice at the heart of cultural life is critical, vital even, albeit definitely not at the expense of another's embodied voice. And Greer did make a serious blunder—she tried to make trans people into eunuchs. She did to trans people what she accused men of doing to women—she attempted to castrate them or de-sex them. Whilst Greer clearly deserved to be called out for this, I think that to write her off, to sign her death warrant and put her six feet under before she's actually carked it, seems a bit on the nose. Actually, more than a bit on the nose. It reeks of misogyny In fact, in my view, the media have performed a hysterectomy on Greer's voice—they've been attempting it since the 70s. I can't help but think that in Australia at least, Thelma Forshaw's reaction to Greer's 1972 visit to Australia in *The Age* newspaper reverberates again today. 'King Kong is back … Save us from shaggy Germ, O Man.'[413] I mean, I think we need to ask ourselves why Greer hasn't been awarded an Order of Australia when her now dead male counterparts: Barry Humphries, Clive James, and Robert Hughes all were awarded one. Are we to ascertain that if you protest, go against-the-grain, advocate radical ideas, and

---

[413] Forshaw, Thelma. "Save us from Shaggy Germ O Man!" *The Age*. (15th January, 1972). https://blogs.unimelb.edu.au/librarycollections/2019/06/05/when-greer-came-home-january-march-1972-save-us-from-shaggy-germ-o-man/

generally buck the system, you are written off in Australian, or indeed out of historical relevance—becoming mere gap—or liminal discursive amendment?

Greer has demonstrated all her life how women may come to invest their desires in the world against-the-grain of patriarchal expectation. And I'd argue that women folk still stand on her tarnished and bruised feminist shoulders. She is a trailblazer who has strayed from the prescribed path for women—there have been a few not so well thought through maneuvers. From 'writing for counterculture publications Oz and Suck — an Amsterdam-based pornography magazine she'd co-founded in 1969 — that led her to the subject of women's liberation,' to penning the second wave feminist classic *The Female Eunich*, in which 'Greer argued the roles of wife and mother in the traditional nuclear family subordinated and oppressed women,'[414] and through which she sought to assign women sexual agency, and their own intellectual potency, to documenting her resuscitation of a portion of Australian environmental ecology in her book *White Beech*, not to dwell on the journalism and books reconfiguring the feminist project, and planting 'polemic bomb[s],'[415] as one Guardian article argued pertaining to *The Whole Woman*. Whilst Greer's relatively recent transphobic comments are off base I don't think it's fair to disregard her life's work. This kind of response reflects our contemporary inability to allow critical debate, which might be uncomfortable. I'd venture to suggest that Greer may have been responsible for the cancellation of one or two people along the way

---

[414] Heath, Nicola. "Germaine Greer's The Female Eunich had an enormous impact. It's still felt 50 years on." *ABC*. (4th February, 2025). https://www.abc.net.au/news/2025-02-04/germaine-greer-book-the-female-eunuch-feminist-blockbuster/104875722

[415] A review by Decca Aitkenhead from the *Guardian* featured on this site https://www.penguin.com.au/books/the-whole-woman-9781446497326

on account of some of her more thoughtless comments. In addition to the aforementioned trans-phobic comments I'm thinking of her insult to Julia Gillard, stating that she has 'a big arse,' which served to reduce the politician to her appearance—just diminishing and rude.

Still, Bob Hawke's remark on the impact of Greer's 1972 visit holds true to my mind: 'I think Germaine has been a refreshing experience; she has jolted many people into the unusual experience of thinking instead of jumping to conclusions.'[416] Although I certainly would not want to condone Greer's trans-phobic comments or several of her other thoughtless remarks, I believe her critiques have often been intended as a way to plant feminist bombs, mostly of the literary variety, to provoke radical thought, although her feminist activism in her later years has had a planetary focus. She's been far more concerned with planting trees and preserving a rainforest. Her avid interest in environmental ecologies probably took hold in Tuscany. Greer first visited Italy in 1965 whilst a postgraduate student at the University of Cambridge. From 1973-1994 she owned Pianelli, a stone house in Montannare di Cortona, Tuscany, close to the border of Umbria. It's this planetary tangent in Greer's career that piques my interest.

On wandering through Germaine Greer's archive at The University of Melbourne I discover *The Book of Pianelli* (documenting photographs and commentaries between 1973-1978), a red covered album that Greer prepared for her then best friend Gay Clifford. In the album, Greer reminisces about time spent together at what Italian filmmaker Federico Fellini referred to as her 'fairytale

---

[416] Ibid.

castle.'[417] That is until the area became encroached upon by an aspirational bourgeoisie—suburbanised by rich Americans who started cutting down trees and forced Greer elsewhere. Certainly, the Pianelli memento conveys an intimate exchange between two women, as well as their interactions with the environmental ecology of their part of Tuscany, and which seems to initiate an intriguing and divergent cartography.

Greer begins *The Book of Pianelli* by reminiscing about a working party in 1970, which she joined to ready the house for high summer. At the time, the house belonged to her friend Lyndell who owned several properties. It was Greer's favourite house because of its remoteness, and the fact that it was a bit of an oddity.

> We swept the mouse turds out of the corners, emptied their families out of the mattresses, plucked cobwebs from the beams and boiled caked fat and grime off the kitchen things. We didn't dare to attempt the extirpation of the brambles that were trying to grow through the walls.[418]

Pianelli was a house hemmed in by wilderness—encroached on by shrubbery. Greer noticed a Chestnut woods outback for rambling in. She writes that next time she visited Pianelli it was the summer of 1972. Clifford was already staying there with her friend Michael Miller. On arrival Greer found Clifford sunbathing naked 'on the ballatio, engulfed in fig and apple leaves, like Eve after the Fall.'[419] There is the sense of an against-the-grain friendship forged between

---

[417] Greer, Germain. *The Book of Pianelli, c.1973-c.1978*. The University of Melbourne Archives. Germaine Greer, Series 2014.0054 Photographs. Item number: 2014.0054.00536.
[418] Ibid. p. 2.
[419] Ibid. p. 3.

these two women in the vein of the Llangollen Ladies, an abiding kinship, albeit which was unlikely sexual.

Greer speculates that she never anticipated owning Pianelli. It was in fact Clifford who loved the house. Greer writes that she bought the house *for* Clifford, for them both, to keep it in the family. Although she suggests that Clifford may have had some ill feeling about that, maybe having wished to purchase it herself. There is an undercurrent of occasional misunderstanding, perhaps a thread or two of intimacy gone wayward, which Greer clearly hoped to reign in through her dedication. Nevertheless, *The Pianelli Book* is a kind of love letter from Greer to Clifford. Greer signs her letters to Clifford with a drawing of a love heart with bat wings and a small crown on top. Clifford responds with a heart and bat wings—no crown. Greer is the crowned one. But, as it becomes increasingly clear, the crown on Greer's heart signature intimates that she is crowned by virtue of knowing and loving Clifford.

Greer recalls the following summer of 1973 when she and Clifford were alone together at Pianelli. They planted white petunias. Greer surmises that they were likely extremely happy, but didn't realise it at the time. A polaroid of Clifford shows her nymph-like, a nipple touching the page of her book, her dark hair draped across her face, sitting in the sun reading atop several piled mattresses. On the next page there is a picture of Greer smiling broadly squatting out front of Pianelli nearby the *Iberis sempervines* planted on the second spring at Pianelli. Another polaroid shows the villa from behind a stone wall ledge and reveals the terrace of wild flowers leading up to the property. Three more portraits of '*Vipers Bugloss, Papaver rhoeas* and corn chamomile in the orchard' flowering at Clifford's window.[420] *Rosa floribunda* or 'Iceberg' grows over the gate in wild abundance. All is recorded at Pianelli by way of plantings.

In a letter from Greer to Clifford sometime post-summer in 1973 she writes to invite Clifford to Pianelli for the Christmas period. Greer talks of a possible excursion to Bologna, conveys that at the time of writing the letter she's using a borrowed typewriter, which flails under the strain of her literary will—the typeset is occasionally muddled. She ruminates about Italian carpenters at the house who likely think her a nouveau riche pig from Milano, unable to detect her Australian accent. (Greer is fluent in Italian). She comments on the fact that all of the flowering in the garden is overly white, as if a prodigious field of narcissus pre the fall into Hade's underworld. It prompts a friend, Enrico Tariffi, to gift Greer a red *Cerastium tormentosum* to plant. Nearby a polaroid depicts Greer's two white cats Bisi and Boogaloo—a feline flowering.

Greer informs Clifford of renovations underway at Pianelli, of camping out in the two thirds of the house not under construction, of drinking scotch and going to bed early. During this period Greer recounts an amusing episode of being pulled over by the Carabinieri (Italian military police) for driving her Cortina unlicensed with a small chimney in the back. Suffice to say that Greer was suitably unimpressed by the policeman's desire to bring her in line with the law. She quips to Clifford: 'You know what they say about carabinieri, they use the brick test, that is they bash him over the skull

---

[420] Ibid. p. 6.

with a brick—if the brick breaks he gets the job.'[421] Clifford writes back to Germaine accepting her invitation to Pianelli for Christmas.

A letter from Greer during winter addressed to 'My Sweet Gay,' tells her that 'The vegetable garden and all the plants and all the leaves have disappeared as if smitten by a giant hand.'[422] Greer laments that even the petunias are snap frozen and the cats refuse to go out in the snow. 'The sky is dead white, the wind blows a gale and it has begun to snow again.'[423] A polaroid of a domestic scene follows: Clifford on the sofa reading with Bisi and Boogaloo beside her contentedly. Greer thereafter writes a commentary on how much fun that Christmas together had been. 'We were comfortable, tidy, calm and busy.'[424] Serenity reigned supreme.

In a letter from Greer to Clifford after their shared Christmas, Greer writes of a 'bee army' enveloping Pianelli, likely in Spring. 'Lo—and—Behold, as I entered the house I discovered that various out-rider bees were reconnoitring, and the roar from the glade convinces me that bee-armies are on the move.'[425] She hastens around 'mopping up bees and hurling them outside' before shutting up the house.[426] Greer reports at length:

> The insect scene this year promises to be the liveliest for many a year, all along say the sages, of this year's mild winter and exaggerated rainfall. Appalling creatures appeared on the lilies and the potatoes, pink all

---
[421] Ibid. p. 11.
[422] Ibid. p. 13.
[423] Ibid. p. 14.
[424] Ibid. p. 16.
[425] Ibid. p. 17.
[426] Ibid.

over and hiding from the world under a pompadour of their own shit which they piped incessantly onto their heads. Then aphis descended on absolutely everything and ants appeared to herd them back and forth. I saw one little mean ant with its teeth sunk into a huge ants eye-socket, hanging on grimly while the big ant removed all his legs and his abdomen in the maddening effort to escape. Eventually they both died.[427]

She goes on to write of: 'Horse flies this year as they have never been my dear.'[428] And 'navy-blue bees' equipped with a kind of knife in front of their heads. 'I don't like them half so much now that I have actually had to watch the neat evisceration of my nasturtiums.'[429] A polaroid shows Clifford reclining naked on a mattress suspended on a metal frame sunbathing—pansies and wisteria behind her. Another polaroid depicts the Tuscan landscape covered in mist.

Greer reports that Clifford got sick the summer of 1974 when she went away to Romania for work. At this time, Clifford kept the Pianelli diary for Greer in her absence. Clifford writes in the red book of all the 'minutiae that engross [her]' at Pianelli over the course of the summer. She tells of getting rail thin (Clifford suffered from Crones disease). She ruminates on the wild yellow rose with two flowers, and of the 'pale whitey-purple verbera,' which has three new flowers, of 'melon progress,' the 'advent of new beans,' and of deluge.[430] Clifford writes of bad house guests who don't lift a finger to help. She informs Greer that 'The cats have buggered the fig-tree from playing in it and dismantling branches.'[431]

---

[427] Ibid.
[428] Ibid. p. 18.
[429] Ibid.
[430] Ibid. p. 22.
[431] Ibid. p. 23.

A picture with the subtitle 'great wall of Pianelli' appears to be a stone boundary wall built covered in *Hydrangea arborescens*. Another polaroid shows dog rose. Yet another reveals Clifford next to a man out front of Pianelli. The garden is in full bloom. An amusing commentary accompanies a picture of a sunken courgette souffle, which Clifford once taught Greer to bake 'even to the extent of blowing off your eyebrows and pubic hair.'[432] It makes the reader consider the pros and cons of nude baking, as well as ruminate further on the level of intimacy between these women. (Although, it was the 70s and nudity reigned supreme).

A final letter from Clifford in May, 1975, reads: 'If only you didn't have to make money and could be here. The garden is a wonder ... Huge heavy-faced papal poppies, delicate little marguerites, the jasmine and the broom collaborating towards intoxication on each inhalation.'[433] She writes of the ants eating the pansies, of the increasingly feral behavior of the cats. She reports that one of the cats has sunburnt flaky ears. A few polaroids follow the letter, one of Clifford wanly looking at the sky, another of labial wildflowers. Clifford's handwritten scrawl below reads 'Hurry up — nowhere could be as good as Pianelli.'[434] A small excerpt of text on the next page reads 'Best and beautiful Germaine, I do love you, and not "despite" anything.'[435] Signed as always with the love heart and bat wings minus the crown.

---

[432] Ibid. p. 26.
[433] Ibid. p. 27.
[434] Ibid. p. 29.
[435] Ibid. p. 30.

In the following pages there are pictures of the countryside dated 1977. Greer writes of a rift between her and Clifford, of some fall out over something or other, which she never fully understood. An hypnotic poetic love note in Clifford's handwriting states: 'The moon is full, the days are hot, the wind blows all the air like metempsychose honey everywhere: come quickly.'[436] Clifford evocation of metempsychosis induces a kind of poetic reverie, makes me sense transmigration underway. For *The Book of Pianelli* hereafter becomes somehow unintelligible—as Proust writes on the very first page of *In Search of Lost Time* with regards to a book Swann is reading, 'Then it began to grow unintelligible to me, as after metempsychosis do the thoughts of an earlier existence ...'[437] Greer is increasingly in pursuit of a life of reportage and eventually of conservation. Her great southern Queensland forest wins her in the end. But first, there is Pianelli and there is Clifford.

Whatever the quarrel it is clear that an abiding affection sutures Greer and Clifford's relationship, like the Llangollen Ladies immortalised in Wordsworth's poem, pottering about the garden, or entertaining leading minds of their age, exchanging letters. These women of profound friendship, 'sisters in love,' virago women, dodging marriage, and a life of servitude—seeking alms in the companionship of kindred other women. But, instead of Shelley, Byron or Wordsworth, Greer and Clifford counted Fellini among their house guests at Pianelli. It seems that Fellini propositioned Greer for a small part in his film *Casanova*, which she declined, albeit went on to act as unofficial consort to him on the film.

---

[436] Ibid. p. 32.
[437] Proust, Marcel. 2002. *The Way by Swann's*. Translated and with an Introduction and Notes by Lydia Davis. London: Penguin. p. 2.

The story goes that she visited the set of his film in Rome wearing neither bra nor knickers under her dress—suffice to say Fellini was impressed. He visited her at Pianelli and packed his best silk brown pajamas, rather confident. Greer tells an affectionate tale of Fellini in an hysterical moment presumably mid love-making when a bat flew into her bedroom and Greer feared that she would have to tell the papers he'd 'cark[ed] it in bed.'[438] Perhaps this explains Greer and Clifford's bat-winged heart sign to one another. Pianelli was their homely place of bats, close to the verdurous realms of fairy tale. Toward the end of *The Book of Pianelli* Greer writes Clifford a fairy tale like poem of rings, leopards, gazelles and pavilions. Theirs is a naïve phantasmagorical love already unhinged to the vast aphasia of *his*tory; it reads as gap, juncture, liminal poetical documentation of two women.

A photograph shows Greer smiling in the garden holding an umbrella while watering the garden with text accompanying it: 'Dr Greer's white magic involves watering when it rains, just to encourage it to keep on raining' is somewhat enchanting.[439] Then there's a succession of cat polaroids. Bisi 'genius loci' under a tree.[440] A poem penned by Greer in which guise is dedicated to her cats.

> On either side the poppies show
> In clumps beneath the violets grow
> The house is a slim brown ship

---

[438] Greer, Germaine. "Federico Fellini wanted to cast me in Casanova. We ended up in bed together." *The Guardian*, (Monday 12th April, 2010). https://www.theguardian.com/culture/2010/apr/11/germaine-greer-federico-fellini

[439] Greer, Germain. *The Book of Pianelli, c.1973-c.1978*. The University of Melbourne Archives. Germaine Greer, Series 2014.0054 Photographs. Item number: 2014.0054.00536. p. 36.

[440] Ibid. p. 38.

> Out of the rain on the hill.
> Two white cats flump and slip
> From grass to the door and into the slip
> One gold and wounded, where the herbs are dry
> The other earless, hunting, guards the hill.[441]

Another poem titled *Cats and All* by Greer addressed to Christina Gascoigne demonstrates her dedication to felines. Here's an excerpt:

> It has to be said first that all the best lovers
> Love cats. Perhaps it's their tact, perhaps it's
> Their grace, perhaps the fact that cats
> Have the art of being stupid but always a pleasure.[442]

Greer goes on to write that when she leaves the world she hopes to be led off by a cat, perhaps by Bastet. Then on the following page another round of cat polaroids, Boogaloo yawning. Boogaloo drinking from a stone bowl, which looks to be a mortar missing its pestle. Boogaloo with narrowed eyes lazing about. Boogaloo on a rock staring into the distance—blackish tiger striped tail slung down the rock.

A few pages later, Greer writes to Clifford of her motivation for assembling *The Book of Pianelli*, for she'd never before kept a photo album. It's in honour of Clifford's friendship. Greer writes a prose paragraph *Finalities* ahead of Clifford's July visit. All is winding up.

---

[441] Ibid.
[442] Ibid. p. 39.

> I don't just want you to remember everything about Pianelli, the raw Aprils, the serrano, the astonishments of June, the golden heat of July, the flash and the bombast of August storms (and our jewelry left in the garden to lure the rain) and the purple twighlights of the autumn, and our perfect Christmas, I want you to look forward to being there again. You're not coming on a visit to Pianelli, you're coming home to Pianelli. There you will see that it is not true that you have no past and no present, and we will still be there in the future. Together we can knit together the fragments and rebuild the continuity of your life, if you will only trust me. You must trust me enough to relax, to get angry when you feel angry, to be confused and tired when you need to be, and not to try to impress me or pretend that you aren't having difficulties. If I am doing things the wrong way, hurting you, or being insensitive, pushing you in the direction you are already moving in, you must say. I will make mistakes, but I can learn, if you will help me. You can't incur my displeasure, or contempt or anger because I love you. I love you in that old-fashioned Ladies of Llangollen way that literary females like us must keep alive and incorrupt by twentieth century sex-religion. Amor vincit omnia.[443]

Greer's friendship with Clifford is sacrosanct in this literary pledge. It is likely that Greer is shaken by Clifford's brain hemorrhage—wants to nurse her back to health. Greer writes on the next page. 'You shine beyond compliment, while my prosaic tongue stumbles on clumsy eulogy.'[444] A polaroid of Clifford looking over the balcony at Pianelli is positioned next to another poem in which Greer writes of an emptiness, a 'singing void.'[445] Clearly, Greer turns to poetry

---

[443] Ibid. p. 41.
[444] Ibid. p. 42.
[445] Ibid. p. 43.

to convey the plenitude of her emotions in relation to Clifford, but also potentially by way of homage to the fact Clifford was a poet.

On the last page of *The Book of Pianelli* Clifford's handwritten scrawl reads 'But the full moon at Pianelli was marvelous.'[446] A final polaroid shows a darkened mountain and then a cut and pasted child-like heart with angel wings and a crown. Greer signs her heart over to Clifford one last time—in perpetuity. Greer's work, as a journalist and author of books, thereafter took her elsewhere, motivated to abscond by the increasing popularity of Tuscany, and the clearing of much habitation in Cortona which bugged her. Greer strayed from Pianelli. She writes in the preface of her book *White Beech* that her forays into the woodlands proper began when she bought her Essex house, in England, in the late 1980s and planted a small wood, by way of extending her gardening habit, documented in her popular *Daily Telegraph* column 'Country Notebook' (begun in 1999 and ending in 2005). Greer's friends apparently predicted her purchase of an Australian piece of wilderness, even if she didn't divine it herself.

I spend hours in Greer's archive listening to her driving across the Australian landscape in pursuit of a bit of land she can rehabilitate, to restore biodiversity, do her bit.[447] She refers to this as a call to custodianship—her hearts work. She's a woman gone rogue, driving with a knot in her stomach, low on petrol, getting up at the 'crack.' It's like spending intimate time with her—listening to her engaging

---

[446] Ibid. p. 44.
[447] Greer, Germaine. 2007. *Travel Diary Cave Creek Rehabilitation Scheme to Melbourne*. The University of Melbourne Archive. Germain Greer, Series 2014.0040.00014 Audio Recordings. Item number: 2014.0040.00014.

ramblings about the Australian landscape. Past a bandicoot, brushtail turkeys, endless koala signs. Petitioning rain in the driest of continents. Cattle on the road vex her—she wants to pass and get on. She refers to the cows as beauties and ponders: 'Where's the fuckin' owner.' Reciting dozens of towns as she drives along—talking up the landscape. A dead wallaby by the side of the road—countless dead wallabies along the drovers' track. Wild non-native weeds like chicory and harebells disturb her. She names everything—notes plenty of eucalypts along the way. 'It's pretty dry' she bemoans. Then unexpectedly the wonderful sound of rain on the car. Naming creeks all the way: Oak Creek in the NSW Tablelands. Smatterings of 'bugger-all' and 'bastards' litter her laconic Australian accent with more than a hint of British defectiveness made into her voice. Musing on the colour of the earth 'deep mahogany—no, it's actually darker than that, dark chocolate.' She arrives one day in Coolah. Another day she drives on the Black Stump way. On another day she's headed to Mudgee.

Greer starts naming gullies. Dead man's gully is the first. She occasionally stops in a town for a pie and some petrol—notes the sad looking inhabitants in Dunedoo. Headed on the Goulburn Valley Highway up to Dubbo—a bloody long way. St John's Wort grows beside the road. She recites the names of purple flowers: Verbena, Clematis. Gets excited about driving on a graded road, loves the feel of rolling along quite contended, 'having a good time,' on the road to Wellington. Greer pontificates: 'Australian's have become more stupid than I remember them being ... I used to think of them as quite smart people, or did I, maybe I always thought they were slow-witted...' And then she happens upon an open woodland, which has clearly been logged and exclaims: 'Talk about slow-witted!' She reaches Wellington—crosses the Macquarie River. Greer traverses secret roads up the eastern part of Australia. Gets stuck behind a truck leaking steaming cow piss. In New South Wales there are many stone churches—'absolutely lovely' like the Adelaide Hills. But, the un-useable roads are 'fuckin madness.' She observes to herself bemusedly: 'I think it's going to take more than fixing the roads to fix Australia.'

Greer gives a commentary from the Bungle Bungle Ranges at dawn: 'You never saw country like this, it's fabulous. There's a wide sweeping valley surrounded by low hills and slightly higher ones, you've got a long vista over range after range towards the alps, and of course there's crap everywhere: I'm surrounded by pine trees, poplars and willows [introduced species], but I imagine it was sort of eucalypt scrub. But, probably pretty sparse, we're not yet in Mt Nash country, but it's gorgeous, amazing country ... Shangri-La.' Then on past the river flats. She rolls into Bungle. 'This is staggering country,' she tells as she drives along. Greer augurs that the grass trees need to be visited occasionally by fire to 'Do their thing.' She sees her first lantana—the good old pink and yellow variety. Driving nearby Grafton—sugar and banana country. Noting a pittosporum invasion choking out the forest along the way. More travelling—to Lachlan. 'There's a terrific amount of water around Forbes' she observes. Greer notes the 'Roly-poly rolling hills,' the burnt woods, the yellow acacia, the flowering wattles. Pressing on to Gilgandra— town of windmills. To Tamworth. To Armadale where she notes country 'enmeshed in mountains.' She laments the clearing of the country—the denuded of hills. Fields full of thistles and sedge make her shake her head in disgust. It is her task to restore the native vegetation in some minor stretch of wilderness—to do battle with 'fucking willows everywhere.' Oh the 'bombard' poplars, down with the maples, and the hateful copper beech. She spies red salvias on the side of the road near Mullumbimby. On her car journeys, Greer undertakes an important task of imagining the native landscape prior to colonisation. She discerns why Australia's 'so fucked'—'people keep trying to turn it into something else.'

Eventually Greer finds a bit of wilderness to rehabilitate: Cave Creek. Throughout her travels Greer observes that only 'a little bit of native vegetation remains …' She suggests that we ought to be grateful for it. Otherwise the vegetation is entirely encroached upon, 'driven back,' as our First Peoples have been. Greer wonders what an Australian actually even *is* and considers that they ought to become Aboriginal. But, she speculates, to do so Australians will need to give up their worst behavior. Greer notes: 'Aboriginality is Australia's only chance of survival … we have to change our values.' She ruminates about Australia as a country 'poor in spirit.' Greer puts her finger on a truth about Australian identity as only an expatriate returned can. She recognises the need for Australians to become custodians, to restore biodiversity by way of embracing First Nations epistemologies, which of course is a worldwide project. But, Greer notes that Australians will likely have to process their crippling white supremacist past, which remains a terrible stain on the country. As journalist Stan Grant told Australians in his 2015 speech on the impact of colonisation and ongoing discrimination in Australian culture, the so-called 'Australian dream' is fueled by racism, which originates with our murky colonial past.[448] And which was reiterated by the reprehensible 'No' vote for a First Nations voice to parliament. This might perhaps be the reason Greer doesn't yet have an Order of Australia, she's called out the persistence of a restrictiveness, a lack of vision, or innovative critical thought in Australia. But it's not actually parochialism, rather Australia's crippling filial ties to its coloniser, still failing to become a republic, which is at least partially responsible for this contemporary predicament. Certainly a new independent and affirmative story of Australia needs to emerge, which elevates and celebrates First Nations Australian lives and voices, and defers to First Nations ancestral knowledge pertaining to caring for Country, whilst also fostering connection for non-Aboriginal Australians with place, and towards its safeguarding.

In her book *White Beech: The Rainforest Years*, Greer petitions: 'Biodiversity is our real heritage as the ostentation of extinct aristocracies is not. We have inherited a planet that is richer and more various than could ever have been imagined.'[449] She goes on to point out that: 'The only way of keeping the extraordinary richness and exuberance of this small planet is to rebuild habitat.'[450] Greer tells of falling in love with the Australian landscape driving the Birdsville track to Alice Springs. She refutes the pastoral depictions of the Australian landscape as harsh, relentless, formless, and haunted, but rather embraces the landscape as a fountainhead of comfort which flourishes within her. For instance, she refutes Nicolas Rothwell's *Wings of the Kite-Hawk* in which he writes: 'Why do I feel "the stillness of the bush, pure and uncaring", or the "dull monotony

---

[448] Stan Grant's speech (2015). https://ethics.org.au/stan-grants-speech/
[449] Greer, Germaine. 2014. *White Beech: The Rainforest Years*, London: Bloomsbury. p. 3.
[450] Ibid. p. 5.

of tree and scrub", in this "inhuman", "unnatural", "alien" "world of suffering, exhaustion, danger and death", "the cruelest and most inhuman world that it was possible to conceive" under the "empty blueness of the sky?"'[451] Greer points out that there have been way too many disparaging literary descriptions of the Australian landscape. Pastoral mumbo jumbo.

Cave Creek is her haven of biodiversity which veritably sings its 'galaxies of rare plants.'[452] '*Ardisia bakeri, Rhodamnia maideniana, Tapeinosperma repandulum, Quassia* Mt Nardi, *Neisosperma poweri, Cupaniopsis newmannii, Lepiderema pulchella.*'[453] (And I note the irony of her listing of Latin plant names with sperm and new man genesis embedded). A whole forest assemblage of: '... liverwort and lichens, ferns and mosses, sedges and grasses, orchids and vines, thousands upon thousands of species ...'[454] No less than sixty species of trees in the canopy. And so, Greer the virago woman set up a charity called *Friends of Gondwana Rainforest*, conceived of as a rehabilitation scheme to 'highlight the plight of the remnant rainforests of the ancient continent of Gondwana' (as described on the website), albeit now seemingly defunct.[455] Our loud overbearing woman. A woman of great stature, strength, and courage. A shrew. An ill-tempered scolding woman—our provocateur. This invariably leads us to fury, harpy, harridan. So be it. A fury in-so-far as an avenging spirit for the usurpation of the rights/rites/writes of women. A tormentor of men who impudently try to straightjacket women into the role of marriageable termagant, and which might

---

[451] Ibid. p. 36.
[452] Ibid. p. 104.
[453] Ibid.
[454] Ibid. p. 107.
[455] https://register-of-charities.charitycommission.gov.uk/en/charity-search/-/charity-details/5023866

seem to be an historical phenomenon, but for the renewed rise of an aggressive mode of masculinity that seeks to dominate women, and which is demonstrably hostile to their empowerment. And it's for this reason that we must trace a path, suture a new planetary mapping that allows women their entire embodied reality, and which binds them to a diversity of environmental and social ecologies ongoingly.

On the last day in Greer's archive, I listen to an especially affecting recording of her exquisite documenting a beguiling storm at Cave Creek. She tells: 'I'm sitting here in the pitchy darkness finding my way about by the lightning flashes.'[456] She talks as the storm fulminates around her—installs herself on the patio beholding the vast sky full of stars. She just loves a storm. Blue lightening lights up the sky—Greer gasps. She lights a cigarette, watches 'the play of blue splashes,' and observes: 'Way down in the coastal plain the lightning is yellow flares like fire, it looks like Baghdad down there, but up here it's ice blue.' The thunderclouds roll in, but all is luminous. She goes on: 'I don't know of many other things on earth that are more wonderful than storms. I really love them. This is innocent violence. Most of the activity is behind me and I can see it very well except occasionally, well that was an electric white bit. It's sheet lightning, not chain lightning.' Greer rhapsodises about the 'mad magnesium radiance,' which lights up the entire bush—alliteration abounds. But, there's very little thunder and as yet no rain. The practised sound of amphibian habitat is meditative—the frogs sing along. A lightning strike of 'opaline.' 'Oh wow ... I'm inside an opal,' Greer ponders. But, still no thunder—it will come. Reflecting

---

[456] Greer, Germaine. 2007. *Travel Diary Cave Creek Rehabilitation Scheme to Melbourne*. The University of Melbourne Archive. Germain Greer, Series 2014.0040.00014 Audio Recordings. Item number: 2014.0040.00014.

on the 'turquoise light,' then jovially she gives herself a bit of a ribbing—'I'm probably fantasising now.' She continues to poetically comment on the weather system moving in—the rain finally starts. 'One large half pound drop at a time.' Greer is recording the 'calm velvet darkness.' She bemoans the 'waste light' pollution. Then the thunder starts. On the 'skirts' of the storm strobes of frozen green pour in. Greer petitions 'Come on shake your thunder sheet!' Pink flashes. Naples yellow. Pure white. The thunder cracks. 'That's not bad is it—eh!' An Australian visage—on the verandah watching the storm roll in. 'The clacker of the rain.' The storm at its 'full veracity.' Greer our outrageous thunderstorm. It is a poet's sensibilities that I apprehend here. Our harpy, part woman, part bird, singing her own song in the face of all haters—an almost extinct siren-like woman.

Chapter Eight

A Strange Hybridity in Italy; Or a Siren's Interlude

Why do I have to perform again the haus frau fuck hole? Barthesian absence, his lover's discourse, a textual enactment on my flesh, in which our love is validated.[457] A poetic fragment by which I'm othered, objectified, made subject, sedentary, faithful, immobile, giving shape to his absence, have time on my hands (as if) to sing his ordeal, his abandonment. Firstly his mother, soon to be lived out on my flesh. His feminine self enacted on my embodiment. In this configuration my pleasure cannot be given expression to. I am merely the colonised. But there were gaps, moments of disjuncture. When we first met and it was all shudder. And what of those times when we cast off into the 'night work,' as Don Paterson has it? When he held to me as if a part me, a working valve of my body? We were fluid then. We only had one another's skin; our logic. And it was illogical what we became, a kind of ecstatic dance; a mobility of pleasure in love.

A few years ago, during a three year stint living in Amsterdam, I had a particularly bad case of haus frau fuck-hole syndrome. My partner

---

[457] Barthes, Roland. (1977) 1990. *A Lover's Discourse: Fragments*. Translated by Richard Howard. London: Penguin books.

was travelling all over Europe for work while I raised our children mostly solo. He was in a high state of anxiety, working hard, partying hard, doing lines of cocaine off our kitchen bench on a Thursday evening while the children and I lay asleep in our beds—that kind of thing. I thought *fuck this* and purchased three tickets to Italy. I will never un-know Italy again. It is in me for the continuance. Haus frau fuck-hole syndrome is when you've been colonised by a patriarchal imperative and you've learnt to love your kidnapper because you've been hood-winkled into thinking you're making a contribution to a greater good; attempting to raise kind joyful citizens who thrive. You wake up one day and realise you're redundantly bourgeois, albeit with the heart of a punk feminist. You discover that you've been reduced to a domestic servant with an orifice that's temporarily lost its status as an erogenous zone.

You're in a relationship with a man you love—he's your best friend. You're extremely convenient to have around because you actually raise the byproducts of sexual desire. You even do it with pleasure most of the time. You do a lot of shit around the home—domestic shit. You're ok at it, not great. You wonder if you've possibly had a hysterectomy performed on your voice. You have a casual gig as an academic that has been fixed-term in the past, and with no time to write. You're somewhat exploited, underpaid for the work you do, that is once you calculate all of the unpaid preparation time, but you'd rather die than attend a tutorial unprepared. The institution relies on your work ethic. Add to that the situation of teaching a new subject almost every semester for six years—the pressure to get across a stack of new material ongoingly. And there's been a carrot dangled in front of you for a while now with the proposition of a more permanent gig that the institution never comes through with. You wonder how you've been coerced into a kind of peasantry that this kind of unstable casual work engenders, and which is after all the fascistic métier of end-time-capitalism.

Being a fuck-hole is a one-way street straight into the middle region, as in Michel Foucault's middle region, which brings about the possibility of disbanding the fundamental codes of culture—a place of deviation for a man. It's when men try to fuck themselves unconscious as a means of relocating the lost feminine counterpart of themselves. It's a physical and metaphysical drive. Of course, men want to perform this transgressive act onto a woman's body, and yet it doesn't have much to do with a woman's desire. But, I never signed up to be a Stepford wife, not even a new fandangle one who eats only organic food, un-schools my children, and lives in a gated community of anemic liberal replicants. Although I've tried my hand at homeschooling due to the crisis currently underway in the Australia state schooling system, likely a worldwide phenomenon. I am far more interested in using my imaginal capacities to build the emancipatory political future that is ecologically sustainable, to gain some agency through working towards disenabling the apocalyptic political thrust of end-time capitalism.

And so, I made a bid for Italy with my children along for the ride. At Bari airport close to midnight we lined up for a cab. I thought better of our predicament, hustled to the car hire, got us on the road. Next morning, after a good night's sleep at the hotel, we were back on the road headed for Alberobello, Puglia. We wandered up the slope to the trulli village of white washed conical-roofed houses displaying the sign of the sun, birds of flight, and crescent moons. Then in nearby Locorondo, we stayed in our own trullo for a few nights. The children roamed around the garden where hundreds of infinitesimal red spiders darted across the concrete, many unavoidably crushed, making faux-blood stains on the soles of their feet. Native poppies dotted the arid landscape, framed by rock walls. A ginger cat made exquisite sunlit dormancy—we named it Ginger-Stripe. It started to toy with a lizard, which was immobilised with fear. I took it, released it on a nearby potted succulent. We headed out for dinner to a local restaurant that we searched for down bidden laneways, sat alfresco, walked in a nearby garden afterwards and ate gelato, headed back to our trullo.

After a few days, we drove to Matera, saw a limestone church across the valley, toured the city by ape on the first day. My son suggested we go underground where we glimpsed the water mains built by earlier inhabitants of the city. It was the day of the workers, a festival was being set up. We heard music late into the night from our carpenter's studio built into the hillside. Next morning an insistent bird chirped, recapitulated its treble of chords at the open window persistently, interrupted my sleep, accompanied by the fridge, which grinded out its melancholy lung. I was reminded of my bad conscience. In a state of overtiredness I'd spoken harshly to my daughter the night before. Although I apologised, I felt ashamed as we drove up the coast to Vieste the next day, along winding coastal roads, and through the national park.

We arrived at our little terrace apartment to some wonderfully absurd retro vinyl being played at full pelt, echoing through the alleyways,

A Strange Hybridity in Italy; Or a Siren's Interlude

a callipso version of The Eagles' *Hotel California*. The old guy up high on the opposite terrace keen for a chat invited us up for a drink. I declined, he seemed a bit eager. Later, we met him walking his toy pooch named Lady Di in a nearby patch of weeds. He renewed his invitation to join him up on his terrace. Next day we drove through a rainstorm to a nearby beach, Spiaggia di Vignanotica. Once the rain stopped we descended to the beach by an old staircase made into the cliff. The waves thrashed the shore. My daughter was unsettled by the fierce winds. My son energetically scaled the cliff face. We hastily set about collecting strange elliptical rocks, which looked like glacial eggs, to take away as talismans of the journey—after asking for permission to the fractious winds. We meandered back up the rocky hill using the old rickety stairway and drove back to our little piazza. As the winds calmed I drank an aperitif at the wine bar nearby Co-cathedral, which rang out on the hour. The chiaroscuro light settled over us, slowly faded.

Next day, we lugged our overladen suitcases up calcareous alleys to the car. The children were happy to read quietly as I drove inland toward Umbria, down rugged dirt roads, past plentiful fields. We stopped, explored a private field where fava bean trees grew, ventured down the slope, picnicked a while. I thought to stay longer, knew innately somehow that we wouldn't see a rural landscape so idyllic again. But, I started to get uncomfortable about trespassing on someone else's property. So, we pressed on, northward, up the coast, stopped at an unmemorable beachside resort for the night, Francavilla el Mar, which felt like blasphemy in a land so flush. I'd simply plotted a midway point on a map, somewhere to rest from all the driving. To make up for it I bought us an extravagant dinner by the sea. Later, we hung out in the well decorated foyer, played the grand piano, read, drew for a while—turned in early for the evening.

We got back on the road early the next morning and headed to Spoleto. As the Umbrian hills came into view a tension in me began to let down. After several hours on the road we drove into Spoleto. We parked and rode the outdoor escalator to the top of the 12th century city, stood at the Rocco Albornoziana fortress, the highest point, marveled at the view. We glimpsed the cathedral in the distance, saw the monumental Roman bridge, then toured The National Museum of the Duchy, albeit briefly. We saw the impressive main courtyard, glimpsed a sarcophagus, some Roman jewels. The children were overtired from the travel—they couldn't be persuaded to stay. I begrudgingly departed with plans to return, although we never did. We stopped at a nearby supermarket, bought supplies, drove on. I accessed Massa Martena through a tunnelled highway leading to windy country roads. Finally we arrived at the rustic barn, took a walk, petted farm animals: Simba the dog, a pregnant goat, several lazy farmyard cats. From the window-arc in the kitchen I glimpsed an impressive vista of flower laden fields, and so we walked the dirt track, diverted into a glebe of wild poppies, almost got lost.

Next day we drove to Todi, a medieval city, ate gelato in the piazza, sat on the steps of the cathedral, bathed in the sun, then strode up and down alleys before heading to the gothic Duomo at Orvietta. Its alfresco depicted genesis. The children had fun listening on the retro telephone kits, on which the history of its stilted construction was recorded. Oh the magnitude—the vaulted space. Oh the abuses carried out under the name of the father—the *holy* catholic church.

A Strange Hybridity in Italy; Or a Siren's Interlude

I gave the children an education about corruption without specifics, told of abuses committed under its magnified domes to warn them off. The drive to Todi on the Amerina road, past the expansive Corbara Lake, followed by the Tiber river, was unparalleled.

After a week we said goodbye to the somnolent hills of Umbria, drove to San Gimignano, Tuscany, or so we thought. The satnav took us on mountain passes through charming villages to some arbitrary digital coordinate. After a lengthy detour we arrived at the villa located a few kilometers from the main village, a landscape of vineyards dotted with conifers, and a phantasmagorical castle perched on an opposite hill top. At the photography museum in San Gimignano, my daughter pulled her pants down in a show of disrespect for such places of purported high art. She pretended to touch paintings, veered too close. I got cross. We beat a hasty retreat back to the villa and the pool.

Next day we visited the Duomo in Forenze, paid like mugs to go up, witness the dome—vetted depiction of heaven and hell made us gasp. We glimpsed the entire city from that elevated post, a sea of terra cotta roofs, directly opposite the mountain where Leonardo tested his first light aircraft. We visited the Bargello museum, saw Michael Angelo sculptures. On to Lucca the next week, wrapped in a Roman wall, with its garden top tower. We rode bicycles, ate gelato, visited nearby mountains. I tasted truffle ravioli with sage butter sauce. On the last day in Lucca we attended a Puccini opera—*O Mio Babbino Caro*—lingered in the nearby piazza afterward.

Nothing But a Fine Nerve Meter

Italy is made into me—petitioning me always. My desire is inextricably bound to her landscapes. When looking for one's life the best course of action is to identify three films or books, or works of art that have been pivotal, seeking out major themes—there's usually a unifying strand. For instance, my three films: Merchant Ivory's *A Room with a View*, Bernardo Bertolucci's *Stealing Beauty*, and Luca Guadagnino's *I am Love*. A passionate love, desire fulfilled, Italy. And... in the final film... exile. As we know too well, often when women explore their multifarious desires they get excommunicated.

An amorous bird-woman may wish to lure her temporarily lobotomised partner (lobotomised on account of corporate slavery because no one wins under late patriarchal capitalism) to Italy, since out the other end of this patriarchal deadlock he's likely to become her lover again for the continuance. To the Strait of Messina specifically, located between the eastern tip of Sicily and the western tip of Calabria in Southern Italy. The Strait of Messina is a critical landscape for the migrations of birds each year. They cross the strait to reach their breeding grounds in northern Europe. The rock in the town of Scilla, Calabria, at the north of the straight is especially linked with the Greek myth of Scylla and Charybdis, where the Sirens lived according to Homer, also connected with the fairy Fata Morgana. For as Norman Douglas wrote in *Old Calabria*: 'I have never beheld the enchantment of the Straits of Messina, that Fata Morgana, when, under certain conditions of weather, phantasmagoric palaces of wondrous shape are cast upon the waters — not mirrored, but standing upright; tangible, as it were; yet diaphanous as a veil of gauze.'[458] Douglas is referring to a mirage seen in the Strait of Messina

---

[458] Douglas, Norman. 1915. *Old Calabria*. Boston & New York: Houghton Mifflin Company.

A Strange Hybridity in Italy; or a Siren's Interlude

linked with Morgan le Fay. Fata Morgana is the Italian translation of *Morgan the Fairy*. I digress. It's the Siren's voice, laden with desire, that I am angling to hear—a vital voicing in me.

After all, isn't it the Siren's embodied voice that is missing from the pages of *his*tory? Isn't it her singing that provides an access point to another story of humanity? In Homer's *Odyssey*, the goddess Circe warns of the Sirens' voices and their power to lure Odysseus and his crew from the Strait of Messina to their island. Circe is keen for Odysseus and his men to avoid any further 'trouble' or indeed 'suffering' having returned from the 'House of Death.' She warns Odysseus that he and his crew must make it past the Sirens and their beguiling voices at all costs.

> Your descent to the dead is over, true,/ but listen closely to what I tell you now/ and god himself will bring it back to mind./ First you will raise the island of the Sirens,/ those creatures who spellbind any man alive,/ whoever comes their way. Whoever draws too close,/ off guards, and catches the Sirens' voices in the air—/ no sailing home for him, no wife rising to meet him,/ no happy children beaming up at their father's face./ The high, thrilling song of the Sirens will transfix him,/ lolling there in their meadow, round them heaps of corpses/ rotting away, rags of skin shivering on their bones .../ Race straight past that coast! Soften some beeswax/ and stop your shipmates' ears so none can hear,/ none of the crew, but if you are bent on hearing,/ have them tie you hand and foot in the swift ship,/ erect at the mast-block, lashed by ropes to the mast/ so you can hear the Sirens' song to your hearts content./ But if you plead, commanding your men to set you free,/ then they must lash you faster, rope on rope.[459]

---

[459] Homer. 1996. *The Odyssey*. Translated by Robert Fagles. Introduction & Notes by Bernard Knox. New York: Penguin. pp. 272-3.

Nothing But a Fine Nerve Meter

The Siren's song is 'enchanting' and leads men to their certain death. Odysseus must be bound tightly to the mast by his crew to avoid straying to 'their meadow starred with flowers.'[460] Sure enough as the Sirens hear Odysseus' ship going by they cast out the lure of their song.

> Come, come closer, famous Odysseus—Achaea's pride and glory—/ moor your ship on our coast so you can hear our song!/ Never has any sailor past our shores in his black craft/ until he has heard the honeyed voices pouring from our lips,/ and once he hears to his heart's content sails on, a wiser man./ We know all the pains that the Greeks and the Trojans once endured/ on the spreading plain of Troy when the gods willed it so—/ all that comes to pass on the fertile earth, we know it all![461]

Odysseus cannot resist their 'ravishing' voices. All that he wishes is to be set free from the mast and stray to their island, to change his course, but his fellow crew who have beeswax in their ears do as they've been told, and more firmly secure the ropes keeping him held tightly to the mast. Still this desire to *not* listen to a bird-women persists: a liminality, a gap, a very *real* intervention.

The Siren's song exists only as threshold music of the hu*man* story. The world resists her wayward antithetical planetary knowledge at its own peril. The Siren's sounds come right up from her womb, which has been objectively separated out from the polis, the place of politics and cultural life, so as to forge instead a concept of hu*man* in close connection with a humanist discourse of so-called civilisation and its will to destruction. Beware the false liberation espoused

---
[460] Ibid. p. 276.
[461] Ibid. p. 277.

A Strange Hybridity in Italy; Or a Siren's Interlude

by democracies who seek to transform 'bare life' into a way of life for the benefit of hu*man*, albeit whilst still continuing to exclude women's embodied voices from that project.[462] Let women relocate womb sounds—a harpie-like protest that drives men mad. I am not re-invoking the hysteric here. Psychoanalysis is a dead language.

What nobody else can hear murmurs in me. Am I speaking me? Yes, this is my embodied voice. Check. Not madness. More real time emboldened woman torpor truth—here's proof. These words of incantatory verse. A trumpeter on the wind: O wild western lyrical tradition! Thou breath 'pestilence-stricken multitudes,' echoes of Earth's dying. O 'dark wintry bed.' 'Destroyer and preserver; hear, Oh hear!' my song—I am *not* your 'azure sister.' My hues are 'hectic red,' on a 'dim verge' dreaming over earth. A dirge. A dirge. A dirge. Our fire-waters and 'oozy woods.' [463] Our *blood jets*. Sylvia Plath's mouth shouts: 'Unspool human—rebirth yourself anew.' Not in a hu*man* image. I refuse the elements of canonical poetry—I prefer an alternative view. I weave the structures of: 'delegitimate, deconstruct, decenter, destroy, dismantle, displace, deform, explode.'[464] And resurrect this erotogenic cut; this life-giving voice. To Italy to speak vulva truths!

---

[462] Agamben, Giorgio. (1995) 1998. *HomoSacer: Sovereign Power and Bare Life*. Translated by Daniel Heller-Roazen. Stanford California: Stanford University Press. https://www.thing.net/~rdom/ucsd/biopolitics/HomoSacer.pdf
In *HomoSacer: Sovereign Power and Bare Life* Italian philosopher Giorgio Agamben argues that the inclusion of 'zoe' into the polis, or bare life, occurred with the advent of modernity, and which signals a radical transformation of public life. And yet, Agamben does not account for women's bodies. They are largely absent from his text. If bare life is in fact included in the modern state by means of its exclusion, this is still a phallocentric attempt to incorporate a threshold of animalism into human political life that cannot affirmatively account for difference.

[463] Shelley, Percy Bysshe. 1819. These last three lines are taken from 'Ode to the Westwind' by Percy Bysshe Shelley. https://www.poetryfoundation.org/poems/45134/ode-to-the-west-wind

[464] Rachel Du Plessis. 1990. *The Pink Guitar*. New York: Routledge.

And what about that other time when I absconded to Ibiza with the children—a place where the magnetic properties are strong. It was as if all of my imbalances were being brought to the surface. I felt overwhelmed, feared I'd made a mistake, wanted to go home. But after those first few days, a psychic pathway cleared. Then rejuvenation, a source, or fountain re-posited. The children and I jumped in a little red fiat and toured the island. To Portinax on the north coast. We tacked along the cliffs edge to Punta des Moscarter lighthouse and saw *Podarcis pityusensis* lizards dart through eroded hulls in primordial rocks. Another day we drove to Roca Llisa beach where people bathed nude, startled my son into a kind of liberty with his own body; less inhibited to change into his bathers in public. We entered crystalline waters—porpoise-like among the waves. Another day we drove to Figueral beach, admired mansions high on cliffs edge, swam below all day. Afterwards we drove to Sant Joan, ate ice-cream. Another day we hiked to Tanit's cave, Cova d'es Cuieram where the pythia sang, bounty of aleppo pines, *Juniperus Phoenicea*, almond trees, the sea was violet. Some noob-pagans gathered there—annoyed we'd stumbled on their holy grail. We entered the cave quietly, offered prayers to the swollen mother, her peaceable breasts full of rose milk cure. Next day we took a Venetian walk across from Formentera. We drove to a dazzling pebble beach, Cala d'Hort, sat across from the sacred rock Es Vedra. The children played an imaginary game—skirted the shoreline, energetically bounded up, down. We dined in a beachside restaurant, ate grilled fish, looked over azure sea waiting on the sunset mantra of Ibiza. On the last day we snorkeled at a little-known spot, Cala de Olivera. We saw lovers kiss tenderly. I now reinvoke Tanit, winged warrior goddess, sometimes lion faced, under the influence of Isis—a

A Strange Hybridity in Italy; Or a Siren's Interlude

sphinx-like goddess. I can re-learn her language if I let down this ladder into myself. So many bird-girl-women silenced.

In his A Portrait of the Artist as a Young Man (1916), James Joyce writes an epiphanic poetic passage, in which the central protagonist Steven Dedalus sees a bird-like girl by the sea with whom he seems to fall in love with at first sight. I'm particularly taken by this excerpt in the book on account of Joyce's poetic prose stylings, but also because this passage explores a strange mutation. Joyce deploys a sensuous language to explore a moment of soul-awakening.

> He was alone. He was unheeded, happy and near to the wild heart of life. He was alone and young and wilful and wildhearted, alone amid a waste of wild air and brackish waters and the seaharvest of shells and tangle and veiled grey sunlight and gayclad lightclad figures of children and girls and voices childish and girlish in the air.

> A girl stood before him in midstream, alone and still, gazing out to sea. She seemed like one whom magic had changed into the likeness of a strange and beautiful seabird. Her long slender bare legs were delicate as a crane's and pure save where an emerald trail of seaweed had fashioned itself as a sign upon the flesh. Her thighs, fuller and softhued as ivory, were bared almost to the hips, where the white fringes of her drawers were like feathering of soft white down. Her slateblue skirts were kilted boldly about her waist and dovetailed behind her. Her bosom was as a bird's, soft and slight, slight and soft as the breast of some darkplumaged dove. But her long fair hair was girlish: and girlish, and touched with the wonder of mortal beauty, her face.

> She was alone and still, gazing out to sea; and when she felt his presence and the worship of his eyes her eyes turned to him in quiet sufferance of his gaze, without shame or wantonness. Long, long she suffered his gaze and then quietly withdrew her eyes from his and bent them towards the stream, gently stirring the water with her foot hither and thither. The first faint noise of gently moving water broke the silence, low and faint and whispering, faint as the bells of sleep; hither and thither, hither and thither; and a faint flame trembled on her cheek.
>
> —Heavenly God! cried Stephen's soul, in an outburst of profane joy.[465]

Dedalus feels 'the riot of his blood'—his imminent rebirth from the 'peace' and 'silence' when he has witnessed the bird-girl-woman. He has come upon a new world of her creatureliness—a world of underwater 'glimmer.' He has copulated animal and saline thoughts. The wild ignoble beauty of breaking 'full crimson' in love. Oh life! 'On and on and on and on!' Joyce's evocation of Dedalus's awakening to another is miraculous. Yes, Dedalus' gaze is on the bird-girl-woman, though perhaps it is not a look that can possess, it does not wish to *take* anything, but more so to give. Dedalus perceives the bird-girl-woman and all of life is awakened in him—he fathoms another. His imagination encompasses something beyond himself. He has become more human by way of a bird-girl-woman. Ah, what medicine. Ah, revolution. And although Joyce too, like Levinas, conflates the 'feminine' other with a 'mystery' of 'not myself,' he manages to orchestrate a de-hierarchised notion of alterity based in love, which is emancipatory. He comes closer to the wild-heart-of-life.

---

[465] Joyce, James. (1916) 1943. *A Portrait of the Artist as a Young Man.* London: Jonathan Cape.

A Strange Hybridity in Italy; Or a Siren's Interlude

And what is the bird-girl's perspective? Let me now re-configure some of Joyce's text to deliver her perspective as a kind of prophecy text: *Alone amid light clad figures and brackish waters—she gazed out to sea. A wild hearted willful girl. She stood still, amid a tangle of air. Her heart swam in a slip-stream. A waste of sea harvest thought—her childish voice of shells and sunlight sang out. For her gayclad staleblue soul was happy and near to life—in the air. Her seabird kilted heart. A fringe of dark-plumaged brushed against her face—veiled her grey eyes. Bold magic changed the likeness of her strange long slender bare legs to a cranes. Her skirts plumed to fuller softhued ivory of a dove. Her dovetailed buttocks jutted. She was becoming woman-bird about to dive in. Her bosom struck at the nexus of action. To enter the seaweed ridden corpus—to wed the sea. To cry out with profane joy for the thither, hither and thither of her destiny. And was he starring at her? He was young and, and, and, and—beautiful. His gaze moved with the water at her feet—something she'd like to dive into. Something she'd like to believe in—the ecstacy of his flesh whispering her glory. Though she was no angel—the bells broke—and life rang out! His presence slipped thither, hither and thither into her. This nearby envoy of gently moving water. His soul, her soul—the advent of their soul leapt at the call. Her cheek aflame for the outburst of—on and on and on! For the blind persistence of life aglow with worshipped limbs. The advent of life—its error and ecstacy. 'On and on and on and on!'*

Here's the bird girl's perspective in yet another way—in the form of deconstructed villanelle. *Bird-girl couldn't stop thinking about the medicine—crying the advent of life, its dark plumage and heathen glamour. Her profound joy always tainted with sufferance of passion. Her soul leapt wild, epiphanic, an envoy specimen of hope, heart-faced, argus-eyed, trill-spirited-stammer. Bird-girl couldn't stop thinking about the medicine. She whirled round, fell on the sand, her heart refashioned by the burden of his gaze—drinking of her valor. Her profound joy was tainted with sufferance of passion. Bird-girl took to the ocean, porpoise-like, land jettisoned. The seashore now in the distance. She morphed into author oceanographer. Bird-girl couldn't stop thinking about the medicine. She propelled herself further— un-bidden by subjugation of the feminine. Her sex melted into a spill of brine splendor. Her profound joy—already tainted with sufferance of passion. Bird-girl swam shivers of flood, blood of adrenalin culminated in her veins, as persistent as a vital tremor. Bird-girl couldn't stop thinking about the medicine. Her profound joy was tainted with sufferance of passion.* But isn't Joyce's bird-girl-woman a kind of Siren? I must surely diversify from the precarious patriarchal path entirely—rewrite myself again pertaining to a Siren's topography.

For I'm a somewhat gender fluid variety of woman who has opinions and I often voice them publicly which frequently puts me on the side of the amorous and unruly bird women. The sanctioned, those who dare to screech in the polis, at the heart of political life no less. And if you think that women are no longer subject to denigrating attacks pertaining to a perceived regressive otherness, deliberately made liminal in negative terms on account of their reproductive organs, more broadly related to their mammalian status, then consider this tale of woe. I recently walked to my local post office with my dog, pausing at the entrance I asked if I could bring my dog inside with me, to which the owner replied: 'Your dog can come in, but you can't.' This micro-aggression brought up a memory of a debasing incident that occurred in my early twenties. Back then I

A Strange Hybridity in Italy; Or a Siren's Interlude

worked part-time behind a bar called The Vineyard in Acland Street, St Kilda, Melbourne. The proprietor thought it was hilarious to put a dog collar around my neck from behind as I crouched down at a fridge to restock it. I immediately tore it off—mortified. But, if I reframe myself not as victim of these patriarchal attacks I grasp my predicament as a woman of many thresholds.

For we *are* threshold creatures always undergoing transmutation—we are strange hybridities. Audre Lorde's testimony in 'The Transformation of Silence into Language and Action' delivered in a paper at the Modern Language Association's 'Lesbian and Literature Panel' back in 1977 seems on point, and worth mentioning here. Having encountered illness, Lorde became aware of the need to address her omissions in life. Subsequently, she issues an intersectional feminist rally call for women to speak their truths across difference:

> But my daughter, when I told her of our topic and my difficulty with it, said, 'Tell them about how you're never really a whole person if you remain silent, because there's always that one little piece inside you that wants to be spoken out, and if you keep ignoring it, it gets madder and madder and hotter and hotter, and if you don't speak it out one day it will just up and punch you in the mouth from the inside.'[466]

What do I need to say in acknowledgement of the whole truth about my embodiment to avoid being subjected to epistemological forces

---

[466] Lorde, Audre. 1977. 'The Transformation of Silence into Language and Action' delivered in a paper at the Modern Language Association's 'Lesbian and Literature Panel.' https://caps.sfsu.edu/sites/default/files/documents/Audre%20Lorde%20-%20Silence%20Into%20Action.pdf

that would subjugate me under patriarchy? I am writing back to, singing back to, my embodied desire. I am not yet an extinct species.

One day soon I will return to Italy with my daughter, son, and husband. I hope to bear witness to the environmental and social ecologies of that place in confluence with my own embodied desire as a woman, mother, life partner, and poet learning new ways to love beyond the bounds of patriarchy—more in accordance with the principles of *la dolce vita* perhaps. But the desire for Italy holds more than that for me, something in accordance with upholding a familial principle, adhering to kin, and notably in the wake of the loss of both of my brothers to untimely deaths. It might be a desire for pilgrimage—the need to find a safe trope in life—to guide my son and daughter toward a spiritually invested path. A sustainable planetary path—minus the religious dogma.

Chapter Nine

Re-Mapped in London

That first day in London we started out early from Kensal Rise, wandered up Portobello road tourist trap choked with souvenir shops. It was too early for the market stalls. We wended onward toward Kensington gardens where Virginia Woolf walked as a child. I marched my twelve and fourteen year old teens through the gardens against their occasional complaints about undertaking another one of my torture walks. We wandered toward the enormous golden monument of King Albert, his leg raised on a plinth, bearing the inscription: 'Queen Victoria and the People.' A gorgeous first morning, sun streaming before unheralded downpour. Then on the walk back to Kensal Rise I noticed some graffiti on the street: 'Just another rainy day. Kill D King.' Surely I'm not a subject of this Kingdomland, since I abhor nationalism in all of its guises. Still, there's a lineage in me that harks back to dear old England, albeit definitely not to British aristocracies. I'll never forget whilst living in Amsterdam, absconding to London for a weekend and feeling utter relief when the shop assistant at the off license smiled and enquired as I entered: 'Alright?' Despite the fact that she most certainly didn't expect a response, it was clear to me at that moment that I was with kin. I realised that despite the horror of Britain's colonial campaign around the globe, and my rightful inclinations towards the rebelliousness of the Irish, and the Scottish (and which also populates my bloodline), I am nevertheless a bit more Anglophile than I'd thought. And so, I'm on some kind of pilgrimage in part to explore my Romani heritage, but firstly this short stint in London, and onto nearby Kent. But, there's more to it than that.

My house in Melbourne's Yarra Ranges is under renovation both physically and metaphorically—I've left my husband to deal with it. He has persistently refused to consider the notion that we will not be able to live in the house during the winter whilst it's being deconstructed, and so I hatched a plan to do housesits with our children throughout England. The night before we departed from Melbourne we went as a family to the cinema and my husband was drinking wine whilst watching the film. When he dropped his wine glass and it smashed on the floor he didn't bother to pick it up. He just left it there for others to stand on. He's become messy, seeking to numb himself no doubt from the corporate malaise—the drudgery of capitalisms day to day. His death-drive is at the helm again. Maybe the truth is—and there are many truths—I need to stray again for a time to find another way. Perhaps I need to trace this genealogical tract in me toward a freedom.

After a couple of nights in London, we head to Ramsgate on the east Kent coast. Our Trusted Housesitter hosts have a three-story Victorian home a few blocks from the Royal Harbor and after giving us the lowdown on the particularities of their abode they depart. As Woolf's father wrote of the seascape albeit it was likely St Ives that he had in mind: 'The sea is always alive and at work. The hovering gulls and plunging gannets and the rollicking porpoises are animating symbols of a gallant struggle with wind and wave.'[467] The sea is chthonic. Part of my heart is surely sutured to this island place by dint of my genealogy. And yet, I am also not this, not this at all. From island to island. Genealogies gain and lose resonance under the English sun. I feel partially as if I've been sent to exile. I'm confused as to why I thought it was a good idea to come back to England when there is Italy.

My son turns thirteen the day after we arrive in Ramsgate and he plays the accordion to mark the occasion, which is a possession of our hosts. He puts the squeezebox to work—a trill of pleasant discordance exhales from its windbags. It sends the terrier who we've affectionately named Lazy Licey Lola (she's got fleas) yipping about at our heels. She's smelly, but sweet. We give her a wash and bring her along each morning to the harbor, past the record shop on the corner, down Anderson street, a quick peep into Paraphernalia which has an enviable collection of antique Kokeshi dolls. Once by the sea we descend the almost vertical staircase to the lower promenade built into the high red Roman wall. Tucked underneath are a series of cafes and an antique shop with large blue wooden arched doors. At the far end, buried in the Roman wall, is the Sailors Church founded 1878, historically used as a harbor mission and sailors home. Inside, it smells musty with disuse. Several glass cases display model ships—souvenirs of imperial Britain. We hastily head down toward Silverspoon Pavillion. 'An elegantly tapered ashlar stone lighthouse designed by John Shaw and built in 1842 stands at

---

[467] Stephen, Leslie. (1898) 2012. *Studies of a Biographer*. Cambridge: Cambridge University Press. pp. 254-285.

the end of the West pier.'[468] We pass a crackhead at the harbor who mutters something about my daughter's shorty shorts under his breath. My teens ask to go into the Boulevard Family Amusements; an old-fashioned arcade. I give them a few coins. They each take a turn to ride a shiny plastic red Ducati motorbike. After a few rounds of 'Angry Bird Coin Crash,' we're back walking the coastline. The wind is full of enormous gulls and pigeon coos.

Maybe we've come to 'Ramsgatize' under the English sun as Samuel Taylor Coleridge did. In his article 'Wish You Were Here: The Significance of Coleridge's Holidays at Ramsgate,' 1819-1833, Allan Clayson writes:

> Coleridge came to Ramsgate for the sea-cure, which involved, largely, fresh air and sea-bathing, and which held out prospects of relief for several of the ailments Coleridge had—or imagined he had. He and his house-companions exercised regularly along the cliff tops, and the seascape was to him almost as familiar in his declining years as was the landscape of the Quantocks or the Lake District in his prime.[469]

Clayson goes on to report that Coleridge '… regularly used the machines of the horse-drawn bathing-machine proprietor Philpott …'[470] In late summer it's warm enough for us to have a bit of a frolic in the sea. There's nothing like being reduced to an atom under the sun

---

[468] "Lighthouse by John Shaw, Senior (1776-1832)." 2025. Victorianweb.org. 2025. https://victorianweb.org/art/architecture/shaw/2.html
[469] Clayson, Allan. 2000. "Coleridge's Holidays at Ramsgate." Friendsofcoleridge.com. 2000. https://www.friendsofcoleridge.com/MembersOnly/Clayson_Ramsgate.html
In his article Clayson records that Coleridge wrote to his friend Gillman on 31 October, 1821: 'O I wish, you were here, and that we could all Ramsgatize till the midst of December!'
[470] Ibid.

followed by a cold plunge. After we've dried off we resume walking up the length of the promenade past the Victorian beach elevator towards King George VI Park and the Italianate Glass House, which dates back to the early nineteenth century. But on inspection the afternoon tea is a bit underwhelming and overly expensive so we head back to the house.

The next day, we visit local sculptor Anthony Padgett's Van Gogh bronze bust in Spencer Square. Van Gogh purportedly spent a couple of months as an assistant teacher in Ramsgate. A teen not more than thirteen sits nearby on a bench smoking a spliff. I want to tell him what my brother once warned his friend's son: 'Don't pull cones while your brain's still forming.' But, I tell my own teens instead. The sculpture of Vincent's head is set on a box of oil paints, and with a sunflower draped across the base. Vincent lived in a Georgian home, number 6, in 1876 according to the blue plaque across the square. We pop into the nearby Churchill Tavern, Vincent's local, before again walking the promenade with lovely, now not so licey, Lola. I ruminate as I walk about a whiff of impoverishment I get here—of damage inflicted by consecutive conservative governments. Britain has suffered grievously as Sam Knight writes in his article 'What Have Fourteen Years of Conservative Rule Done to Britain?'[471] It's been the worst period for wage growth since the Napoleonic wars, the average worker faces a precarious job market. All it takes is a trip to Aldi, which is situated opposite a housing commission, to get a sense that people are doing it a bit tough here.

---

[471] Knight, Sam. 2024. "What Have Fourteen Years of Conservative Rule Done to Britain?" The New Yorker. March 25, 2024. https://www.newyorker.com/magazine/2024/04/01/what-have-fourteen-years-of-conservative-rule-done-to-britain

The tube fare for four to London is unreasonable, so I bizarrely decide it might be a good idea to drive instead. We start out early one morning to London having taken the petrol guzzling option, which is a karmic blemish on the day. As we drive my daughter reads an afterword essay written by Jeanette Winterson, responding to Nan Shephard's re-issued *The Living Mountain* (by Canongate).[472] I've asked her to read this short essay because both she and my son love reading. Winterson's basic message is that a book can re-map you. It can enact things on you, that is, if it is imbued with being, an energy or force to shift your awareness out of yourself. Winterson makes special claims for poetry: 'Poetry is all about being, and because we are much less concerned with the subject matter or the story of the poem, it is much easier to understand Susan Sontag's remark: "A work of art is not just *about* something; it *is* something."'[473] That is to say that great poetry can migrate your soul—'that part of you that feels not obliged to materiality.'[474] When she experiences this herself, Winterson states that she's gained a language that can express her feelings; a language of the limbic system. Winterson vies for an abstract mediation engendered by great books, especially poetry, but also works of art. But my daughter and son could care less about what Winterson thinks.

We arrive in Bermondsey, London, in the street I'd planned to park in. I suddenly discover that my phone doesn't have enough data to undertake the requisite online registration for the carpark, and so I buy yet another international roaming data pack. Everyone starts to

---

[472] Shepherd, Nan. (1977) 2014. *The Living Mountain*. With an introduction by Brian McFarlane and a prologue by Jeanette Winterson. Edinburgh: Canongate.
[473] Ibid. p. 13.
[474] Ibid.

Re-Mapped in London

get a bit edgy, especially me on account of being sent into offline exile. I end up driving across London, at a glacial pace given the traffic, headed for Sloane Square carpark instead because it doesn't require registration, albeit costs fifty quid. This was to be the destination of the walk. In my haste to park I think to reverse the order of the walk instead. And so, rather than commencing at White Cube we start at Saatchi Gallery. Having finally parked the car we pop into a nearby bookstore, John Sandoe Books, on our way to the gallery. I notice a Sontag book close to the entrance of the shop. This brings about a Sontag rant from me (the ebullient book seller and I have a lively chat). I talk about how overtly polemic I find Sontag to be. How I prefer Adrienne Rich's generosity of spirit—her work radiates a warmth and is generally more on point for me. And how I see the two of these women working in tandem—rubbing up against one another over the course of the 1960s, 70s, 80s and 90s. My main two points:

1. To my mind, Rich emerges as more cogent, clear sighted, and politically astute than Sontag insofar as Sontag gets this polemic going. It's mostly about her flexing her critical theory muscles, rather than driving for a clarity of meaning. She's precocious about her own talents and abilities. I can't stand it when someone's name gains so much cultural capital that it becomes an intellectual weapon at the expense of doing any real good, like being canonised by a bunch of white men. On reading Benjamin Mose's Pulitzer prize winning biography on Sontag I was shocked by what an asshole she was. Mose reveals how much of a terrorist she'd been to poor Annie Lebovitz in addition to many others.

2. In Rich's essay 'Notes Towards a Politics of Location,' she argues that the writer ought to 'Pick up again the long struggle against lofty and privileged abstraction.'[475] So, drive for clarity of meaning. No abstraction for abstractions sake. Although I'm certainly not against abstraction. It just takes a delicate balance that's all, of anchoring the inarticulate, or invisible, in embodied material reality, and of course also with respect to social and environmental ecologies encountered. We women folk have to map our coordinates, show up on the new planetary cartographies, even if only as a trace.

In the book shop I spot Woolf's diaries, reissued by Granta and want to own them. But, noticing the price tag I shudder. I also know that I can't lug that kind of weight back to Oz. And besides, I don't think Virginia would want me to labour over her diaries. She'd want me to live life—make new maps. I head downstairs to the basement after my teens and of course to where the poetry lives. The least important subjects are set side-by-side: poetry and teenagers. I can't find the Jorie Graham collection I want. I see a bunch of relatively unloved Faber classics—the usual suspects. Across the basement on the other side of the store I quickly thumb through Freud's *Civilization & Its Discontents*, and think of Professor Barbara Creed warning me when I was writing my doctoral thesis: 'What do you want to give him more airplay for?' i.e. do not defer to Freud and his man authored death-drive. We leave the store not having purchased anything—a rarity.

---

[475] 2015. "Notes toward a Politics of Location (1984)." The Critical Flame. 2015. https://criticalflame.org/notes-toward-a-politics-of-location/

We walk on to the Saatchi Gallery Exhibition. The ground floor exhibition *Beyond the Gaze: Reclaiming the Landscape* is perhaps meant to offset the upstairs exhibition—to focus on a woman's perspective on landscape.[476] I wander past Kirsty Harris' tapestries depicting atomic explosions, which also look like brain hemispheres. These eloquent spare desert landscapes depict human predation and the destructive human impulse. However, the work that I find most enchanting is Lisa Ivory's small figurative painting series, which have a folkloric quality. In the first painting of the sequence 'Chance Meetings' (2023), a white skinned woman meets a black and hairy creature, twice her size, in an underworld of sorts. An even larger skeletal figure stands over them observing them. The woman has her black hairy creature by a rope. Is she attempting to capture her creatureliness? In the next painting of the series 'Juggernaut' (2023) four children stand on the back of a huge black stallion, which seems to me to be a celebrated figure of male sexuality. The sea is in the distance. An elemental force is being conveyed, perhaps a creationary force, albeit possibly destructive. In the next painting 'Magical Thinking' (2023) the black stallion stands in the middle of a white horse outline mapped on the ground. Ivory seems to be playing with the principles of yin/feminine and yang/masculine in her work, whereby she has reversed them, and so disturbed the binary. In the next painting 'Tourist in Your Town' (2023) a woman straddles a tree, encircles it. The tree is legged, a face can also faintly be made out. The woman figure copulates with the tree. She shares a reciprocity with the landscape, is in commune with it. In the next painting 'Slippage' (2023) the oversized skeleton has returned, but with elongated arms, revealing that it has far reach—a symbol of

---

[476] Saatchi Gallery. 2023. "Beyond the Gaze: Reclaiming the Landscape." 14 July—23 September. https://www.saatchigallery.com/exhibition/beyond_the_gaze_reclaiming_the_landscape

death. The woman is a small figure beneath the skeleton. A fire burns nearby. It seems some kind of rebirthing ceremony is about to take place. In the next painting 'Unnature' (2023), the white horse has come to life hitherto having been cast in the earth. It is perhaps the birth of a woman's sexuality. The black stallion runs away—afraid. This seems to be a commentary on the treatment of women's sexuality as a threat, regressively animalistic, unruly, potentially monstrous.

In the next painting 'Theatre of Cruelty' (2023), the black stallion is about to be whacked by the skeleton with its elongated arm. The black creaturely being crouches nearby, observing, but is not involved. Some kind of drama of violence, of murderous impulse, on part of the masculine principle is being enacted. In the next painting 'Pale Horse' (2023) the white horse gives birth to a face. The black hairy creature is tracing it, has the chalk in its hand, in recognition of its existence. To my mind, this narration is a subversive folkloric story which tells of the birth of a creaturely woman's sexuality and/or desire, and her own point of view and/or difference. In 'Love & Communication' (2023), the woman copulates with the black hairy creature. She straddles it. The black stallion stands nearby watching. The skeleton figure has its arms raised. For this new woman is in reciprocity with the social and environmental ecologies that she encounters. She is a planetary woman.

By contrast, the upstairs exhibition *Civilization: The Way We Live Now* (2023), purports to 'highlight the complexity and contradictions' of contemporary so-called civilisation as depicted in 150 photographic works, and pertaining to eight thematic topics of

Re-Mapped in London

enquiry: 1. HIVE: where we live. 2. ALONE TOGETHER: how we relate to one another. 3. FLOW: how we move our bodies and goods. 4. PERSUASION: the power of influence. 5. ESCAPE: how we relax. 6. CONTROL: maintaining order and discipline. 7. RUPTURE: breakdown and disorder. 8. NEXT: new worlds on the horizon.[477] As we wander up the stairs I balk at the word *civilisation*. It insinuates progress for the collective 'betterment' of humanity. But, perhaps this exhibition seeks to expose through close photographic documentation 'civilization and its discontents;' a hu*man* death-drive or destruction impulse. For me, these works don't really resonate life so much as they represent a hu*man* drive to destruction; a capitalist mutation against planetary awareness of kinship making. I begin to realise that this exhibition is a stark and important testimony of hu*man*ities extinction. Ivory's work provides an insightful contrast to the upstairs exhibition because it's all about non-destructive engagement with landscape, rather than human endeavour or domination over landscape.

I'm most struck by the final section *Next*. I immediately notice Michael Najjar's iconic image of Ariane 5 rocket being launched (November 17, 2016), an enormous phallus shooting into space for the purpose of releasing satellites into orbit around the earth, colonising the cosmos with more space junk; intoxicating the Amazon rainforest below with poisonous gases as it launches.

> The milestone mission Flight Ariane VA233 brought up 4 Galileo satellites at once in orbit, making Europe's new civil global navigation system a constellation of 18 satellites. Galileo will enable users worldwide to know

---

[477] Saatchi Gallery. 2023. "CIVILIZATION: The Way We Live Now - Saatchi Gallery." August 8, 2023. https://www.saatchigallery.com/exhibition/civilization_the_way_we_live_now

their exact position in time and space with great precision and reliability. Once complete, the system will consist of 24 operational satellites and the ground infrastructure for provision of positioning, navigation and timing services. With the Galileo navigation system Europe will become independent of the American GPS system controlled by the US military.[478]

But what happens when the global navigation system fails us? How can we navigate life at the planetary turn against-the-grain of this hu*man* death drive to *civilisation*? And which underwrites our patriarchal predicament.

We exit the exhibition and sit on the steps of the Saatchi gallery, eat our picnic lunch, staring all the while at the perfectly manicured lawns in front of us, and which we'd planned to sit on to eat our lunch, but which are being sprinklered—are just for show. We wander on toward the Thames through Chelsea. We cross the Albert Bridge and enter Battersea Park. My teens are again disgruntled about walking. Walks often start this way—they begin hating on it and end up being flooded by an endorphin rush. But, this walk has a distinctly dystopian vibe about it. The sun is uncharacteristically strong for England. My son is petitioning me about a computer game he wants to play, since all his friends play it, but he requires some kind of hardware, a steering wheel console. He's been on about it since the bookstore. His prodigiously obsessive ability to hold forth on a topic of interest to him is mirrored only by my own. However, underwriting this obsession is a capitalist desire to get more gaming stuff so as to keep up with his peers, to stay across the endless upscaling of games, the hundreds of new iterations, and

---

[478] Najjar, Michael. 2016. "Michael Najjar." Michaelnajjar.com. https://www.michaelnajjar.com/artworks/outer-space/works/orbital-ascent

recently released digital experiences, all of which his friends parents seem to pay for unendingly. He is at the effect of these capitalist imperatives. I start to wilt—to glaze over. After listening on and off for about two hours I ask him to please move onto another topic. He is offended. This sets the tone for his subsequent experience of the walk. And when I decline his request to ride the three-wheeler low slung bikes for hire in Battersea park (in a bid to save money) he becomes melancholic. I overly rigidly restate our mission is a Thames walk, which is ironic since the rather silly map we're following has us diverting through Battersea park away from the Thames. I stingily decline my daughter's request to enter the petting zoo. We wend onward.

A lone kid wanders up to us in Battersea Park. He speaks freely and openly about how he is going to swim in the fountain. We find his candid manner delightful. He wanders off. After a bit we start to twig to the idea he might be lost as he walks ahead of us intermittently speaking to random strangers in his wonderfully unaffected way. After walking the length of the park, past the peace pagoda, it becomes apparent that a man and his young son are trailing at quite a distance behind the boy, and so I ask the man if the boy is his child. He says yes and mentions something about how he likes to wander off ahead and makes some body language of slight bafflement. To witness a kid freely meander throughout a park, chatting to people completely blithe to *stranger danger*, having a blast, has become a sign of potential impairment. I check myself, wishing I'd actually congratulated the boy's father for fostering in his child this freedom to roam, and engage with people.

We walk on, back across the Albert bridge, and continue along the Thames. We notice Battersea power station in the distance. Past the Pimlico gardens in which a few people sit quietly in the shade. Onward past the Tate Britain. Walking beside rows of oaks, the mineral lick of sediment drifts up from the silt bed and evaporates in the heat. I keep gazing down at the rocky banks of the Thames wondering at the depth of the river. We wander on, passed The National Covid Memorial Wall on our way towards South Bank, and where the names of the deceased are written in love hearts. Words about contagion. My teens are utterly exhausted. I've pushed them too far in my quest to reach the Tate Modern to see the Hilma af Klint exhibition. The proposed final destination of White Cube gallery in Bermondsey seems highly unlikely. We sit down below The National Theatre beside the banks of the river and eat hot dogs and chips and drink coke. I buy fried stodge and sugar out of guilt for making them walk the Thames track through London against their will.

While they rest I quickly dash off to the Tate Modern to see a retrospective of af Klint's work, a Swedish artist who trained as a landscape painter in the nineteenth century before radically diversifying from figurative painting and drawing, mostly of flowers and plants, to create modern abstract works—developing an aesthetic language of 'thinking through' the interconnectivity of all forms of human life.[479] She predated Wassily Kandinsky's abstract works by around five years. As Ulrika af Klint writes in the Afterword of Hilma af Klint: A Biography:

---

[479] The Tate Modern. "Hilma Af Klint & Piet Mondrian | 20 April — 3 September 2023." https://www.tate.org.uk/whats-on/tate-modern/hilma-af-klint-piet-mondrian

> When she stopped painting representationally, she became both artist and researcher. Born into a family of naval officers and cartographers, she charted the spiritual dimensions of our existence. She received codes from the invisible world and made them visible. She turned these codes over to the future to decipher.[480]

I'm drawn to *The Ten Largest* (1907) works with their spherical shapes filled with flowers, spirals overlapping, and in a colour palette of subdued blue, purple, yellow, pink, white and orange. But it's the *Tree of Knowledge* (1913) works on paper which make me consider that af Klint offered a rhizomorphic tree of knowledge; an alternative understanding of the human situation on planet earth. Back at the turn of the century, these works would have seemed the drawings of an alien. In a way they were—she communed with spiritual entities. Af Klint was a medium and became a conduit for invisible forces. However, she understood that the world had very little capacity to understand her alternative perspective, and so after her death in 1944 her paintings went to her nephew Erik af Klint with the clear guidelines that they should not be shown for twenty years. It wasn't until 1986 that the curator Maurice Tuchman staged an exhibition including some of af Klint's work in Chicago and the Netherlands titled *The Spiritual in Art: Abstract Painting 1890-1985*. It took several more decades for the world to embrace her art, culminating in blockbuster shows at New York's Guggenheim Museum in 2018, and now this Tate Modern extravaganza. On leaving the Tate Modern I feel I've just exited the mothership.

---

[480] Ulrika af Klint writes this in the Afterword to a biography of Hilma af Klint.
Voss, Julia. 2022. *Hilma af Klint: A Biography*. Chicago & London: The University of Chicago Press.

I head back quickly to the Thames, remapped by af Klint's artwork. After collecting my somewhat rejuvenated companions we all climb up the nearby yellow spiral staircase, trundle past the spectacular brutalist architecture of The National Theatre, head to Waterloo where we catch the tube back to Sloane Square. When finally back in the car and on the road we discover that a section of the M20 is closed and the GPS can't re-route us—it gets stuck on the same loop—has us going around and around on the same circuit. It's getting dark and my phone is out of juice. We try plugging it into the car but it won't charge fast enough to cope with loading Google maps. We stop at a nearby service station and try to buy a paper map so that we can navigate to the coast and follow it back to Ramsgate. But they don't actually sell any physical maps of the area at the servo. And so the helpful attendant attempts verbal directions to the coast, which are useful, albeit complex, and slightly hard to follow. It takes four hours to get back to Ramsgate from London, instead of one hour, and a half tank of petrol—not tenable.

Later that evening my husband calls me from Australia and tells me he's crashed his car and has been taken to the police station on account of being found to be driving over the legal alcohol limit. He's thankfully not harmed, and neither is anyone else. His car is written-off. He's so ashamed. But, it turns out to be one of the best things that has ever happened to him, and us. He stops drinking—starts reprogramming his coordinates away from the death drive of so-called civilisations.

We need to destroy the patriarchal maps handed to us at birth, and which are after all detrimental to men too. We need to make new cartographies that chart communion over extinction. We need to tell new stories about kinship with social and environmental ecologies as Lisa Ivory and af Klint do. These planetary artists teach us to take into consideration our wild latitudes, our divergences, our abstract invisible governances on earth. We are more than just representable beings, or a set of identity coordinates, we are extra-representational. It is certain that we are all subject to colonial forces—to varying degrees—some are far more indoctrinated than others. I'm thinking of some of the more horrendous racist, misogynist, sexist, genderist, and heteronormative death drives of the twentieth and twenty-first centuries, hell bent on eradicating difference, and inflicting unfathomable trauma. And whilst I am somewhat subject to this ancestral tenor that sounds its music in me, this Britannia, I am also flying through the ether—I escape this location if I mutate myself. I am a planetary woman.

Chapter Ten
A Daughter of Exile, or A Ghost Flesh Sequence

I remember travelling in Eastern Europe back in the late 90s, watching the sun come up as I sat on my backpack at Poiana Brasov train station, Transylvania. I was transfixed by a few Romani orphans wandering around, left to fend for themselves—unconscionably young. A legacy of Ceausescu. It shocked me. I sat forlornly, watched the pack with a kind of fascination edged with terror for their welfare. A few days later I experienced 'the crush' as a small gang of Romani locals moved in around me in a small shop selling clothes, unzipped my backpack, attempted to steal my stuff. I managed to wrestle my way out of the situation, although with no help from the shop assistant who looked on with blithe disregard. I later uncovered my Romani heritage on a hunch—purportedly peg carvers in the Devon region of England.

Back home I became obsessed with Toni Gatlif's films commencing with *Latcho Drom* (1993), which depicts various Romani

A Daughter of Exile, or A Ghost Flesh Sequence

communities, also known as Roma and Travelling People, as well by as by the more pejorative term 'gypsies,' on their historic migratory journey from Northern India to Spain, via Rajasthan, Egypt, Turkey, Romania, Hungry, Slovakia, and France. There are many heart-rending laments in the film. In one scene a Romani musician plays his violin with a horse hair to produce a discordant melody, alternating with the bow. He sings the words:

> Ceausescu the criminal/ Green leaves, flowers of the field/ What are the people doing?/ They're taking to the streets/ Yelling and crying 'freedom'/ Green leaves flowers of the field/ What are the students doing?/ They're marching in Bucharest/ Yelling and Crying/ 'Sweep away dictatorship'/ Green leaves a million years/ On this 22nd day/ Here, the time for life has returned/ To live in freedom/ Green leaves, flowers of the fields/ There in Timisoara/ People are taking to the streets/ Yelling 'It's all over for the tyrant!'/ What are the men doing?/ They're taking out their guns/ They're shooting at the people/ Ceausescu hears them/ 'Tyrant, you have destroyed Romania.'[481]

On a train traveling across a desolate landscape in Europe enroute to Slovakia, a young girl sings of the world hating her people, of the Romani 'chased,' 'cursed,' and 'condemned to wander through life.' She tells: 'The mountain is green/ The forest is well/ Torture takes flight and then returns again/ The sword of anxiety cuts into our skin/ the world is hypocritical/ The Whole world stands against us/ We survive as hounded thieves, but barely a nail have we stolen/ At the foot of a bloodied Jesus/ God have mercy!/ Deliver us from our trials.'[482] In Slovakia, an old woman sings by a stream in the snow

---
[481] Gatlif, Tony, dir. 1993. *Latcho Drom*.
[482] Ibid.

with a cigarette between her fingers: 'At Auschwitz we die of hunger/ In huge sheds, they imprisoned us/ At Auschwitz, the kapo is cruel/ We can't find bread anywhere/ Life is so far off.../ And death is so close/ The black bird wants to tear out my heart.'[483] It is estimated that 250,000 European Roma were murdered by the Nazi regime during World War II, although devastatingly it could be as high as 500,000.[484]

Gatliff reveals an encoded language as one Romani group ties a bunch of wildflowers to a fence to notify a friend of the unexpected direction they've taken on the road. A musician has come in his Benz to take other musicians to the festival of Saint Sara in Saintes-Maries-de-la-Mer where a Romani procession carries an effigy of Saint Sara from the church down to the sea. It becomes increasingly clear whilst watching Gatlif's filmic survey of Romani communities that keeping culture through music and dance is critical—a safeguard against persecution. However, it also serves a cathartic function—a source of emotional release. At the end of *Latcho Drom* the Flamenco singer La Caita sings on the outskirts of a city, nearby community housing projects, somewhere in Spain. She is a liminal figure cast against firelight.

> Me, I'm a blackbird who has taken flight/ Why does your wicked mouth spit on me?/ What harm is it to you that my skin is dark and my hair is gypsy black?/ Why does your wicked mouth spit on me?/ From Isabelle the Catholic ... from Hitler to France/ We have been the victims of their

---

[483] Ibid.
[484] Information about the Romani Holocaust can be found at: https://encyclopedia.ushmm.org/content/en/article/genocide-of-european-roma-gypsies-1939-1945

A Daughter of Exile, or A Ghost Flesh Sequence

wars/ Some evenings (repeat)/ Like many other evenings/ I find myself envying the respect that you give to your dog.[485]

I found Gatliff's other films: *Gadjo Dilo* (1997), *Vengo* (2000), and *Swing* (2001), in which he explores Romanian, Spanish and French Roma communities, compelling.

In further pursuit of the Romani diaspora I read Frederico García Lorca who was enamored with the Spanish Romani community, although it's not likely that he had an ancestral connection. He was born in Granada, 'O city of the gypsies,' and this is the place he sought to build up a mythos of Romani life. Lorca composed *The Gypsy Ballads,* his most famous work, in which he invokes Spanish 'gypsies,' the moon, horses, the wind, and Andalusian folksong to create a fantastic world of 'love and death, sex and destruction.'[486] If the terrain seems a bit haunted, over-worked, and racially essentialist that's because clearly it is. In the first poem of the collection 'The moon, the moon,' the Romani are romantically bequeathed a potency, a lunar-depth, akin to the owl's screech.[487] In 'Preciosa and the Wind' the Romani girl named Preciosa has possession of the moon. She plays it as she walks an 'amphibian path,' albeit which is depicted as antithetical to the English '[g]uarding the towers of white.'[488] Preciosa knows another way—the richness and resonance of wildscapes—an exile's terrain.

---

[485] Gatlif, Tony, dir. 1993. *Latcho Drom*.
[486] Lorca, Frederico García. (1953) 1963. *The Gypsy Ballads*. With an Introduction by L.R. Rind. Translated by Rolfe Humphries. Bloomington: Indiana University Press. p. 13.
[487] Ibid. p. 19.
[488] Ibid. p. 21.

My ancestral connection to the Romani is not derivative of Spain, at least not directly, but rather purportedly of England. And I don't know if I have the right to write about this lineage even though it is somehow made into my blood work. I find myself travelling with my teens to Cullompton in Devon, which is where a cousin named Olive has traced my father's lineage. I have very little information. All I know is that I descend from the Grey/Gray clan. As I drive into town I notice a pub 'The Weary Traveller,' opposite a designated place for Roma, or Romani, to park their mobile homes and cars. A local informs me that 'Travelling People' have been coming to this town for a very long time. The main street of Cullompton is pretty downtrodden. We discover a monument to The Great War 1914-1918 and the Second World War 1939-45. I notice E.H.C. Dyer listed as Sergeant Air Cunner and wonder if we're related, although what I'm seeking here is unrecorded genealogy. We meander down the street to the medieval church yard and take a look at the gravestones, long since eroded to wordless moss hewn tablets. There's no lineage for me here. No Grey or Gray clan. Anyway, my Romani ancestors wouldn't have been given graves in a cemetery designated for the most distinguished citizens of Cullompton. We rapidly head out of town, back past The Weary Traveller, enroute to Dartmoor National Park, which is only one hour drive away.

The 1531 British act of parliament expelled 'outlandish people calling themselves Egyptians,' which is where the racially pejorative

A Daughter of Exile, or A Ghost Flesh Sequence

word 'gypsy' derives from. This act was thereafter amended in the Egyptians Act 1554, although only partially, since the main thrust of the law still ordained that 'gypsies' who were described as 'naughty, idle and ungodly,' ought to be made to leave the territory, or be put to death if they weren't complicit.[489] Skip ahead roughly five centuries and racism toward 'Travellers, Roma or Romani' people in the United Kingdom persists. Haroon Siddique writes of prejudice and racism in *The Guardian*:

> ... The Council of Europe committee said the GRT community suffer 'shocking' amounts of bullying in the education system, prejudiced reporting in the media and threats to their legal status and rights, including as a result of recent legislative changes.

> ... There is also a systematic shortage of sites resulting either from local authority unwillingness, opposition from local residents, and this new definition reducing the number of sites required in needs assessments.[490]

Neither my teens nor I are weary travellers. We are fortunate enough to not be in need of a house, just temporary accommodation on our travels, and which we can afford (with some fancy tap dancing). I presently have insecure casual employment at a leading Australian

---

[489] The Statutes Project. 2020. "1530: 22 Henry 8 C. 10: The Egyptians Act." The Statutes Project. April 7, 2020. https://statutes.org.uk/site/the-statutes/sixteenth-century/1530-22-henry-8-c-10-the-egyptians-act/

[490] Siddique, Haroon, and Haroon Siddique Legal affairs correspondent. 2023. "Gypsy, Roma and Travellers Suffer 'Persistent' Discrimination in UK." *The Guardian*, May 25, 2023, sec. World news. https://www.theguardian.com/world/2023/may/25/gypsy-roma-travellers-suffer-persistent-discrimination-uk

university with no guarantee of ongoing employment. Still, I have the resources and sufficient education to seek further employment. I have a few safety nets to help catch me if I should start to fall from my perch. I certainly wouldn't want to over-write my desire for release from subjection, my own need to speak or register my embodied desire onto the textual body of the Romani, and which may in some way preclude them from achieving self-identity. I don't intend to re-invoke Jack Kerouac in *On the Road*—wishing he was not white, as Maggie Nelson perceptively points out in her book *On Freedom*. Kerouac fetishises non-white others in *On the Road* by '… projecting onto Black and brown bodies all of the irrationality, disobedience, heathenism, and open rebellion that constitutes the underside, or the "outside," of so-called civil society and reason.'[491]

The desire to stray, to transgress, in order to emancipate the self is a valid urge. However, I certainly don't want to idealise or homogenise Romani existence, which is far less nomadic than it used to be, and comes with its own cache of problems, such as the ongoing threat of racism, prejudice more broadly, ongoing marginalisation, and a lack of access to resources. Although there clearly seems to be a Romani way, an approach to living that is indelibly linked with a freedom to roam, to cultivate self-governance, to pursue a heightened state of being through music and dance, and which speaks to me on sublimated levels. Still, I am acutely aware of Rosi Braidotti's comment: 'A misreading of the conditions of our un-freedom reduces our ability to become freer.'[492] My freedom must not come at the expense of another's freedom. But my freedom must come.

---

[491] Nelson, Maggie. 2021. *On Freedom: Four Songs of Care and Constraint*. Minneapolis: Graywolf Press. p. 151.
[492] Braidotti, Rosi. 2019. *Posthuman Knowledge*. Cambridge: Polity. p. 47.

A Daughter of Exile, or A Ghost Flesh Sequence

In Damian Le Bas's *The Stopping Places; A Journey through Gypsy Britain*, he traces his Romani diaspora to the days of wagons and 'bender' tents in the United kingdom when his forebears roamed the country stopping at various places sometimes with and sometimes without permission. Le Bas explores this liminal Traveller trajectory of the stopping places as an access point to a Romani philosophy.

> This is the Gypsy belief — the core belief of the culture — that it is possible to live in a different way; in your own way, part of the world, but not imprisoned by the rules. That you can know the ropes and yet not be hemmed in by them. That you can dwell alongside the mainstream, whilst not being part of it. Otter-like, you can live in the bank of the river and swim and hunt there when you need to, and then climb back out with equal ease and alacrity. There is no better symbol of this belief than the network of atchin tans [stopping places] laced across Britain; they are historical, topographical proof that the Gypsy philosophy has existed here, that it still does, that it still can.'[493]

Le Bas undertakes a journey in his van to visit key stopping places and finds that he gradually becomes more and more responsive to the environment that he is traversing, whether guided by the weather conditions, animals, or indeed other humans. His 'quest' to embrace a nomadic way of life offers 'a beginning, a fresh start with new capabilities.'[494] He gains a measure of sovereignty, of self-government, through his nomadic experiment, and comes to

---

[493] Le Bas, Damian. 2018. *The Stopping Places: A Journey Through Gypsy Britain*. London: Chatto & Windus. p. 26.
[494] Ibid. p. 288.

feel far less hemmed in by the machinations of his everyday capitalist existence. Le Bas attains latitude—a bit of Romani divergence. He no longer has to quibble with himself over whether his ancestral claims to Romani culture are authentic for instance, albeit which they undeniably seem to be to me. I suppose I too am hoping to gain some latitude in my life by attending to this Romani lineage. I am a settler poet living on stolen lands in Australia. I sometimes find it hard to align myself with a place that voted no to a First Nations voice to parliament, or a government that refuses to take a political stand against homelessness, the atrocious mental health crisis, the assault on Palestinians in Gaza, and so on. Although Australia is a landscape of home to me, is intimately made into me, and as such I have become with it, it is not *of* me—at least not ancestrally. But it is devoutly in me.

As we drive through Dartmoor National Park we're elated by the moors that roll out on either side of the road. We check in at Bovey Castle in Dartmoor National Park, which is a neo-Elizabethan mansion built in 1906-7 by Delmar Blow for WFD Smith. It's now a hotel. Perhaps, this luxury I've afforded us, of staying a couple of nights at Bovey Castle, is a small nod to Vita Sackville-West who so lauded her Romani heritage. Back in the car we drive the distance that opens up between Bovey Castle and Warren House Inn, glimpsing volcanic vegetation that descends into a valley, then rolls off into the distance toward a Tor. We take in the flowering gorse, sedge, heather variants and brown fern foliage cast against granite boulders partially submerged in the earth, and notice intermittent patches of

A Daughter of Exile, or A Ghost Flesh Sequence

iridescent green pasture which black footed sheep and brown ponies graze on. It suddenly dawns on me that I'm in Ted Hughes country. A poet can become a mouthpiece for country as Hughes has been for Dartmoor, as Heaney has been for all of Ireland really. But, can a settler poet become a mouthpiece for the Australian landscape? Even if they practice light-footedness in the landscape? Even if they intuit the place—bring its orchestrations right through their embodied voice against romantic iterations? Even when they take a post-pastoral and decolonial lens to apprehending the landscape they will never apprehend an ancestral register—although some perhaps intuit a spiritual tenor.

Back at the hotel I make plans to hike to the memorial spot on the moors where a boulder is placed to celebrate Hughes' legacy. Hughes served as an early mentor poet for me. I took him as a model to ventriloquise, so to speak. To get a literary transference, advice I got from W. H. Auden, specifically in his essay *The Dyer's Hand*.[495] I soon replaced Hughes with Audre Lorde, Sharon Olds, Don Paterson, Natalie Diaz, and so on, as a means of finding my craft. Though Hughes remains special perhaps because he was my first mentor poet. Neither my daughter or son want to accompany me on the hike. They prefer lounging in the castle and wandering in its surrounding grounds.

There are kindred places that unlock something in the body and the soul, with which we enter into a correspondence. Dartmoor

---

[495] Auden, W.H. (1948) 1962. *The Dyers Hand*. London: Faber & Faber.

is such a place for me. I think of Emily Brontë's poem 'Loud Without the Wind was Roaring,' in which she writes of walking the granite covered and wind ravaged English moors, albeit in another part of England, West Yorkshire. Brontë tells of an autumnal sky, of approaching winter, her exiled spirit grieving, till she hears the '[w]ild words of ancient song' and adds: 'For the moors! For the moors, where the short grass/ Like velvet beneath us should lie!/ For the moors! For the moors, where each high pass/ Rose sunny against the clear sky!'[496] Perhaps like Emily my spirit is exiled too.

What if I'm ghost flesh—speaking jibber-jabber holler-articulate wyrd-speak—closer to the understory of capitalism—dealing in this other currency—poetry. A subject ejected—fallen from the ivory tower—descendent also of a savage place of redhead poetries. The other side of my lineage, my mother's side, is Scottish. My grandfather Alec had to walk through snow bare foot. He refused monarchial English. He got to Australia by boat. To escape poverty he read philosophy. He was a boiler maker all his life. I'm one of the first to be university educated in my line.

The next day we seek out Wistman's Wood in the Dartmoor National Park. I want to encounter the sanctuary of trees, which is purportedly central to my Romani ancestors, on account of the

---

[496] Brontë, Emily (1846). 2025. "Loud without the Wind Was Roaring | Poems of Emily Brontë | Emily Brontë | Lit2Go ETC." Usf.edu. 2025. https://etc.usf.edu/lit2go/75/poems-of-emily-bronte/5643/loud-without-the-wind-was-roaring/

A Daughter of Exile, or A Ghost Flesh Sequence

fact they were peg carvers. And so, we drive to Two Bridges Hotel and walk directly across the road to the farm gate, starting off down the well-worn path towards Crockern Farm. Old Crockern is said to be guardian spirit of the moor. The myth states that he rides out at night on a skeleton horse. The Wistman's Wood is supposedly the kennel for his hounds of hell. But the woods are hidden from view for at least two miles of the walk. To the left of the path is a hand built stone wall beyond which the West Dart River streams down the valley, running parallel with the path, a tributary of the River Taw much documented in the poetry of Hughes. 'It spills from the Milky Way, spiked with light/ It fuses the flash-gripped earth —' and in the next stanza of 'The West Dart' Hughes adds 'The spiky torrent, that seems to be water/ Which is spirit and blood.'[497] Yes, this is discernably Hughes country.

On the right side of the path I observe native grasses, dried ferns, gorse and granite boulders amidst a scattering of contorted tree branches in various states of decomposition. Hills roll out expansively, ascending beyond the valley. A mature pine wood stands high on a ridge ahead. The path gradually becomes more grass laden and lined with large flattened granite rocks, which gives the impression of stepping stones. The sun has bite in it—it solders us as we walk. We notice heather growing liberally across the moor, its hot pink downturned bell petal uplifts us as we go along.

Suddenly Wistman's wood reveals on the horizon. We continue walking toward the ancient oak wood. As we come to the entrance more rapidly than expected we are blown away. It speaks to a

---

[497] Hughes, Ted. *River*. 1983. New York: Harper & Row. p. 39.

canonical concept of fairy tale wood, which seems somehow regressive to me given that Australian rainforests such as Tasmania's Takayna Rainforest, a refuge for ancient Huon pines, are thought to be around 3000 years old. By contrast, Wistman's wood is said to be 500 to 600 years old and is considered a 'dwarf habit,' albeit likely part of a much vaster ancient wood dated 7000 BC. The trees appear uncannily all of a similar height, stunted in their growth. There's no disputing the otherworldly aesthetic of this high-altitude wood; a vast ecosystem of Atlantic mosses and lichen that covers the granite boulders and climbs the Pendunculate oaks, a few Rowan oaks too, as well as some Holly, Hawthorn, Hazel and Eared-willow varieties. The canopy stretches far into the distance. The effect is of a somewhat iridescent velvety green sea draped across the granite boulders and enveloping the tree trunks. Nowadays the wood covers only around three hectares of West Dart Valley and is protected by the National Nature Reserve.

A small handwritten sign at the entrance says not to enter. Although we want to desperately we resist—not wanting to disturb the reified habitat. Instead, we skirt the edge of the wood, walk up the moor towards Longford Tor; a cluster of granite teeth. We peer into the wood as we walk, veering close to its edge. We eventually meander back to the entrance and consider entering the wood again despite the sign. My son notices that the moss growing on the boulders nearby the woods entrance has been disturbed by human activity. Suddenly a strong foreboding comes over me—the wood seems to whisper for us to go away. Maybe there's nothing here for us after all. No Romani heritage to defer to—no tractable Devon.

A Daughter of Exile, or A Ghost Flesh Sequence

According to Eliza Bray, a nineteenth century local historian, 'druids conducted human sacrifice in the woods eight centuries ago.' Jonathan Evans recounts in his article about Dartmour's haunted wood that: 'Devon folklore claims the devil and his hellhounds, with blood-red eyes and fearsome yellow fangs, roam the land looking for wayward travellers.'[498] I reflect on how the woods would have been at times the only resting place for Travelling people, which makes me wonder if the myth of Old Crockern and his hell hounds is a tale designed to ward off my Romani ancestors, so as to safeguard the resources of this wood. As The South West Heritage Trust reveals the wood: '... is a relic of once widespread coppice woodland that was used to make charcoal for smelting tin.'[499] And now it is increasingly necessary to prevent all human interaction with the wood for fear of damaging the habitat.

In *The Tree*, John Fowles narrates his exploration of Wistman's wood's coppices whereby he comes across a rarified amphitheatre of green, in which he sits for a moment.[500] Fowles attempts to account for his exchange with the wood, which he realises is beyond the domain of words. He writes: 'So I sit in the nameless, the green phosphorous of the tree, surrounded by impenetrable misappellations.'[501] The secret of the wood is antithetical knowledge. Fowles reflects on the value of trees beyond any utility value. He emphasises that our only currency

---

[498] Evans, Jonathan. 2021. "Human Sacrifice and Pagan Rituals: A Walk through Dartmoor's Haunted Wood." The Independent. March 11, 2021. https://www.independent.co.uk/travel/uk/devon-wistmans-wood-dartmoor-haunted-b1814603.html

[499] St Austell, Carnmenellis. 2005. "Geology and Landforms Dartmoor Factsheet Dartmoor National Park Authority Geology and Landforms Factsheet March 2005 Page 1 of 8 Seven Stones Land's End Isles of Scilly Bodmin Moor." https://www.dartmoor.gov.uk/__data/assets/pdf_file/0019/72109/lab-geology.pdf

[500] Fowles, John. (1926) 1983. *The Tree*. Ecco Press: New York. pp. 89-90.

[501] Ibid. p. 90.

with trees is to be present with them—to honour the exchange. An 'internal peace' overcomes him and a feeling that the wood is harmless after all, having at first felt warded off by it, thinking it haunted.[502] But this place doesn't want us, so we head back to the Two Bridges Hotel.

The next day, my moor guide cancels our hike to Hughes' memorial stone on account of a knee injury. She informs me that this particular trek to the boulder is rugged terrain and boggy in sections—pretty hard going. And so, we have to contend ourselves with walking the Ted Hughes poetry trail in Stover Park, Newton Abbot, although I'm desperate to walk the moors more extensively. Stover Park is a heathland that lacks species diversity, but has rare plant variants that includes all seed, marsh gentian and petty whin.[503] Other marshland plants that can cope with infertile soil are: bilberry, heath bedstraw, and sheep's fescue because they get a slow rate of growth. Otherwise, heather is predominant. Ling and bell grow freely near other shallow root plants like tormentil and purple moor grass. I notice a lot of low-lying ferns scattered about. Wildflowers spill amongst the grasses: common spotted orchid, ragged robin, meadowsweet, fleabare. Insects are plentiful: glowworms, butterflies, field grasshoppers. Squirrels scamper across the path sporadically. We encounter ducks and swans whilst walking. At the beginning of the trail we spot a kingfisher in the wetlands, which is a rare sighting. Spiders are especially abundant in the heathland. Crickets, craneflies, beetles,

---

[502] Ibid. p. 89.
[503] Devon County Council. 2016. "Stover Country Park." Https://Www.devon.gov.uk/Stovercountrypark/. January 26, 2016. https://www.devon.gov.uk/stovercountrypark/

A Daughter of Exile, or A Ghost Flesh Sequence

dragonflies, silver-studded blue butterflies, emperor moths, bees and wasps dart about.

Along the trail I re-read the Hughes poems on display: 'Wren,' 'The Warm and the Cold,' 'An Otter,' 'A Cormorant,' 'To Paint a Waterlily,' 'Rose-Deer,' 'The Thought-Fox,' 'Work and Play,' 'Pike,' 'Fern,' 'The Harvest Moon,' 'Nightjar,' an excerpt from The Ironman, 'The Coming of the Ironman,' 'Kingfisher.' As Yvonne Reddick points out in her book *Ted Hughes: Environmentalist and Ecopoet*: 'Hughes was an environmental writer ahead of his time, yet the brand of environmentalism in his poetry is subtly different from conventional ecological thinking, being at once more aesthetic and more mystical.'[504] He invoked a shamanic world lore in his approach to the poet's role and mode of working—conjure a mythological figure, a warrior who must undergo a conflict between lightness and darkness in his work. He's been criticised for his poetic meditations on the 'predatory' and 'destructive' aspects of 'nature,' an overly masculine inflected point of view.[505] Although as Hughes work progressed he clearly developed his exploration of 'nature' with respect to a 'feminine' aspect, albeit which might now be considered pretty gender reductive.

A grafter among the elements
he posts new observations from
a primordial frontier. His dictation of

---

[504] Reddick, Yvonne. 2017. *Ted Hughes: Environmentalist and Ecopoet*. New York: Palgrave.
[505] Gifford, Terry and Roberts, Neil. 1981. *Ted Hughes: A Critical Study*. London: Faber and Faber. p. 14.

Nothing But a Fine Nerve Meter

rain swears backwards as
clouds burst ironies, his heart
shudders dead stones. Flowers grow
arrowheads of song. Butterflies cry
panic, their near far voices weave across
rapturous sea in sleepy drafts—
He is healed by swollen honey sums,
by sexual skirts of petals, by desire
wrenched out of the throats of violets.
His crystal amulets of blood and milk,
almost too esoteric, but then he makes it all
stick to the earth somehow with a yolk
of Om—with a skulk of Elmet.
His chant doesn't stop until the thought-fox
manifests itself, until crow outspeaks
a death, and the un-cage-able jaguar reports
a violence known to Man. Oh the grey horses
standing in a field sentient with gloam,
weighted by horizon. The crush of life
assembles for his dictation. Making nature into
a feminine ground in which he sows his
wild seeds. Still, no one else can
penetrate the dawn with a flourish of
stars tearing in their throat—oh the
un-mannered hawk reducing life
to an ensemble of kills. In love with Ted,
loathing him for raking the wild moor,
his Devon-tomb, in search of womb.

A Daughter of Exile, or A Ghost Flesh Sequence

Whilst Hughes came to live in Devon for the majority of his life, and it became the main landscape in which his poetry unfolded, he originally hailed from Yorkshire—Brontë country. I too am seeking an unwritten archive here—attempting to decode and remember a lost ancestral strain. I try to decipher these tremors of voice in the landscape. They come to me via Hughes and Plath too.

Since we're in the general vicinity, we visit Court Green in North Tawton—an unexpected literary pilgrimage to Hughes and Plath's hallowed, if haunted, territory. This is where they lived together after they were married and it is where Hughes remained living his entire life. Court Green has a thatched roof and is positioned adjacent to St Peters Church, the local parish, which was built in the thirteenth and the fifteenth century, restored in 1832, and again afterwards in 1842. Some of the second story windows of Court Green have a view to the church and its broach spire, which rings out twice on the hour. I notice that Plath's yew tree still stands in the church yard. At the rear of the medieval church there's a gate to an elegant low-walled path lined with silver birch trees, which we walk up towards the rear wooden church door. It appears shut up. And so we sit on the edge of the walled path and I read Plath's 'The Moon and the Yew Tree' on my iPhone to my daughter and son who are hungry and want to go back to Bovey Castle. I sense Sylvia in the vapor. I can even see where she probably sat by the second story window, looking over the gravestone tablets as she wrote the first drafting of her poem. A kind of hauntology laces the late afternoon air.

'The Moon and the Yew Tree' opens with the line: 'This is the light of the mind, cold and planetary.'[506] Plath's poem is about not being able to see her way forward. She explores the graveness of the English landscape, to which she attributes a gothic residue, and which she finds un-homely. The yew tree is an arrow, it augurs a dark passage pointing toward the moon. The yews message is 'blackness' and 'silence,' which reflects the poet's state of mind. Plath has lost her way. The moon is *not* a door, rather it is 'the O-gape of complete despair'—'bald' and 'wild.' It has its own face, but it is not 'sweet like Mary,' rather it wears 'blue garments' that 'unloose' bats and owls. The moon is a 'white knuckle and terribly upset/ It drags the sea after it like a dark crime.'[507] It brings no access—no safe passage for Plath in her planetary predicament. She aligns the moon with a maternal power, which doesn't bring comfort, but rather grief. It seems that Sylvia longs for a tenderness to replace the cold reality of the harsh graveyard and her marriage too.[508] She needs a map out of patriarchy. She wants an effigy of candles burning, lighting the way forward, toward a safe and kindly home on earth. But, she does not need religion—no holy stiffness. I think Plath is exploring her nostalgia for a lost future in this poem. And perhaps she divines a nostalgia for our lost future on a planetary level too.

---

[506] Plath, Sylvia. (1965) 1990. *Ariel.* London: Faber and Faber. p. 47.
[507] Ibid.
[508] Ibid.

A Daughter of Exile, or A Ghost Flesh Sequence

Still in search of an English wood, we decide to drive to Wiltshire's Savernake Forest to visit the 1,100 year old Big Bellied Oak, although after closely following a map claiming to track key specimens of oak in the wood we realise we've been given a bum-steer. The Big Belly Oak is extremely hard to access—there's no clear pathway to it. Even with our hiking boots, wet weather jackets, and jeans on we're still not suitably attired, so a friendly local walker we meet along the way informs us. We head for the Grand Avenue instead, starting to notice mature oaks everywhere. We also notice silver birch, mature elms, and chestnut trees. It is a relief to be walking in a wood again—my entire nervous system relaxes as I begin to communicate on sublimated levels with the trees. As Peter Wohlleben points out, environmental conservation is self-care. He advocates sensuous engagement with trees, arguing for the existence of a sixth sense, for instance which reacts to electromagnetic fields such as altered weather patterns.[509] Wohlleben also discusses a seventh sense that stems from our nervous system, the interplay of nerve cells with the brain which interprets data it receives. Our nerves cells talk with trees and renew themselves. This is surely part of nomadic philosophy—becoming more responsive to the ecologies that we are in confluence with—sympoetically. Becoming good stewards of place—custodians. But also traveling to gain a measure of self-governance—even for a time. And of course, there are ways to do travel more affordably, and to that end we have undertaken house sits with Trusted Housesitters, but for this luxurious stint at Bovey Castle.

---

[509] Wohlleben, Peter. 2021. *The Heartbeat of Trees: Embracing our Ancient Bond with Forests and Nature.* Translated by Jane Billinghurst. Canada: Graystone Books.

We drive away from the Savernake Forest, finally catch sight of the Black Belly Oak close by the 346 roadway. It is impossible to stop, so I u-turn and do a few slow drive-by maneuvers whilst my daughter haphazardly attempts to snap a photograph with my iPhone. Not exactly an experience of commune. The girth at the base of the Black Belly Oak is set in wide ripples of gnarled aged bark. Moss and lichen cover the trunk higher up near to the branches where an iron band is placed around the tree, constricting it, perhaps to stop squirrels climbing up it. I count two major limbs with a couple of thick branches creeping skyward, scarcely covered in leaves. It's the wood base of greyish brown that impresses—its foundation is quixotic. If I have strayed back to England with my daughter and son to retrace a distant Romani genealogy in the family tree, perhaps I've regained a font of knowledge. England, not *my* England. Like Preciosa I too refute these towers of white. And yet, this England is part of me, made into me alongside Scottish and Irish echoings.

Chapter Eleven

On Becoming the Wave at St Ives

We walk the Cornwall coastline starting at Perramporth and head towards St Agnes. The expansive Perramporth beach and its grassy clifftops are at our backs. On either side of the rocky coastal path gorse and heather, native grasses, and wildflowers grow in abundance. Monumental hills roll out to our left—Poldark territory we joke. Scalings of jagged cliff descend dramatically to our right, veering from silver grey to russet tones, cast against glittering azure waters. Waves hemorrhage against the cliffs below, forming undulating trails and rivulets in their wake. Twelve, thirteen successive waves ripple into the headlands. It is easy to make out the waves' birthings from this aerial post—each inauguration. We pass several walkers along the way towards St Agnes with whom we exchange a few kindly words. We stick close to the cliff's edge with Ziggy the spaniel labrador cross we've agreed to dog sit in exchange for a place to stay in Cornwall. He tugs the lead with an unnerving strength as my daughter and son begin to learn the coasts encoded language. My mother has joined us on our trip, and we're pleased to have her with us. As we press on, inevitable clouds start to roll in—still the day has some heat in it.

After making it halfway to St Agnes we learn from some fellow walkers that it is around six and a half miles there and back by foot, which wouldn't be a problem for me, in fact it would be a joy to walk it, but my teens baulk at the idea of persisting especially given the undulating rocky terrain. My mother is seventy-five years old and very fit, but I'm conscious of not pushing her too far. So, we head back to Perramporth and drive on to St Ives by way of St Agnes. I recall as I drive that Saint Agnes was purportedly a martyr, which makes me reflect on the lingering legacy of the martyr imposed on me to some extent, as well as on many mothers in post-Christian societies. Agnes was the second name of my grandmother. I don't want to be a martyr mother and come to resent my children's desire for my time and presence. It's a constant challenge to square away my need to walk and write with being a nurturing and present mother who actively fosters her children's learning along divergent lines. I want to embody the best parts of St Agnes, to be a woman of nobility, of charitable deeds. And as the German poet Hrosvitha wrote in her poem 'The Passion of St Agnes,' I also want to be a woman '... whom our Muse sings in strains uncultured,' siren-like sounds from coastal paths that explode patriarchy.[510]

We arrive in St Ives and head to the Tate. I'm struck by Picasso's *Head of a Woman* (1924). His late modernist portrait is startlingly simple with its spare burnished sienna lines filled in with a subdued colour palette of mostly salmon pink, peach, and white which compose the woman's face. The woman has a crustacean hand, which seems to be taking off the white side of her face. Is she taking off a portion of herself that no longer serves her to reveal her infinite

---

[510] Wiegard, Sister M. Gonsalva. 1936. *The Non-Dramatic Works of Hrosvitha: Text, Translation, and Commentary.* Saint Lewis, Missouri: The Abby Press. p. 237.

identity? Surely we live, we die, in life as Edna St Vincent Millay prophesied in her poem 'Renascence.'[511] We get reborn, reformed ongoingly in relation to everything and everyone all our lives. And what if the woman in the painting's pincer-like claw is meant to signal deformity—yes that's it. I am undergoing deformation and reformation again. The world shapeshifts me. It is for the best. I'm at least one hand crustacean. I am creaturely and I have a scar body. This is the only stable knowledge I can hold to—the simple startling fact of my ongoing transformation.

Picasso's genius here lies in the fact that he depicts a woman undergoing metamorphosis. Maybe what he meant by: 'Women are machines for suffering' is that on account of having reproductive organs women have access to something that he does not (albeit which has historically problematically been align with a regressively animality under patriarchy). In her article 'The Enduring Appeal of the Misogynist Picasso' Liz Hobday reminds us that it wasn't especially safe to be a woman in Picasso's universe. 'One of his muses lost her mind, another became reclusive. Two more took their lives.'[512] Perhaps Picasso was a bit jealous of women. Clearly patriarchal societies have historically been threatened by women, trans men, and nonbinary people with a womb because they have access to the rites of birth (should they choose to, want to, or be able to access this experience). Patriarchal societies have tried to

---

[511] To read Edna St Vincent Millay's poem (917) Renascence visit: https://www.poetryfoundation.org/poems/55993/renascence

[512] Hobday, Liz. 2022. "The Enduring Appeal of the Misogynist Picasso." *Australian Financial Review*. June 9, 2022. https://www.afr.com/life-and-luxury/arts-and-culture/the-enduring-appeal-of-the-misogynist-picasso-20220609-p5asm4

In this article Liz Hobday reminds us that Picasso reputedly told one of his many lovers: 'Women are machines for suffering.'

take over the means of production—to deny the importance of the mother and her influence. Freud was hell bent on doing this. And yet, 'Freud wrote in a letter to Wilhelm Fleiss, dated December 6, 1896, of the mother as "the prehistoric, unforgettable other person who is never equaled by anyone later." Unfortunately, Freud didn't care to [further] explicate his early illuminating comprehension of the mother's pivotal influence on human development.'[513] But, as I've already pointed out in *A Room of One's Own* Virginia Woolf told us*:* 'to think back through our mothers.'[514]

To my mind, Virginia was a trailblazing *not* Freudian, an architect of desires that are otherwise; contra to the entire patriarchal enterprise. Or rather, perhaps her desires intersected on the patriarchal, but couldn't be absorbed wholly, for they demanded to be spoken, or written as the case may be. So, what is this mammalian truth that Virginia highlighted, which has been so undervalued and denied in western epistemology? Picasso sensed it—he wanted to access this chrysalis singing sensuous in the body of a woman. He too wanted to give birth to worlds. His umbilicus plugged into her planetary nexus. He got a life raft off his muse. Crossed over. For the desires of this *Head of a Woman*, this thinking woman, are embodied desires—mammalian or perhaps creaturely antithetical knowledge tracks that connect to everything—a way of mediating the planetary. We can't erase this awareness, although patriarchy has been trying hard to for centuries. I'm certainly not trying to re-reduce a woman to her womb, but I don't want a hysterectomy performed on my

---

[513] Dyer, Natalie Rose. 2020. *The Menstrual Imaginary in Literature : Notes on a Wild Fluidity*. Cham, Switzerland: Palgrave Macmillan. p.137. And Dyer cites Widawsky, Rachel. 2014. Julia Kristeva, Reliance, or Maternal Eroticism. *Journal of the American Psychoanalytical Association* 62 (1): 69—87.

[514] Woolf, Virginia. (1931) 1992. *The Waves*. Introduction by Kate Flint. London: Penguin. p. xix.

voice anymore, nor on any woman's voice for that matter. After all, a poet's voice comes from their body and I am a woman poet. I am not a man poet. I don't belong to a canon—I don't show up on those mappings of patriarchal desire. I exceed that designation.

St Ives is an impenetrable tourist town, especially in the summer during the school holidays. Although now a tad overcast, the weather is unseasonably warm. England is encountering its hottest September on record and so we quickly head to Porthminster beach where my teens can play amongst the waves. I notice a baby boy nearby squealing with delight as he's rinsed off and dried with a towel by his father. I watch a girl kick the waves at the shoreline, turning cartwheels, sun bronzed. After a while I leave my teens swimming under the supervision of my mother and walk to nearby Talland House. I recall my partner's observation as I walk that homeschooling is another form of domestic servitude. Clearly the nuclear family model is frequently more damaging than institutional frameworks. And yet, my daughter and son tell me repeatedly that they do not feel that they have any autonomy at school. I'm aware that they're largely being taught to tow a corporate line, confined to doing the curriculum, over and above uncovering what they're interested in pursuing, or even what they know intuitively. They're denied agency to some extent or access to learning through play. My teens seem to be learning that institutions are often intolerant of their difference and their ability to learn in diversified ways. They're being coerced into performing a version of themselves that is socially sanctioned or culturally approved, to trim off the excess liberties— the mind wanderings. My son is chastised for daydreaming in class. My daughter apparently asks too many questions. Both are subject to a capitalist system that is broken—on the verge of collapse. Children go to school, learn to fit in, to not make waves. They are not allowed to *become* the wave as Virginia was as a child in St Ives.

'From 1882, when she was only a few months old, to 1894, when she was 12 — the year before her mother died — Virginia spent a few months each year at Talland House, situated on the outskirts of St Ives ...'[515] The death of Virginia's mother and the end of her yearly trips to St Ives are inextricably bound. However, St Ives is also the spiritually invested place in which she gave birth to her voice, began to adhere to her own artistic vision. In *Moments of Being: Autobiographical Writings* Virginia writes: "I could fill pages remembering one thing after another. All together made the summer at St Ives the best beginning to a life conceivable."[516] She records experiencing a poignant moment in St Ives. It is her first memory as a human being.

> It is of lying half asleep, half awake, in bed in the nursery at St Ives. It is of hearing the waves breaking, one, two, one, two, and sending a splash of water over the beach; and then breaking, one, two, one, two, behind a yellow blind. It is of hearing the blind draw its little acorn across the floor as the wind blew the blind out. It is of lying and hearing this splash and seeing this light, and feeling, it is almost impossible that I should be here; of feeling the purest ecstacy I can conceive.[517]

---

[515] Tep, Ratha. 2018. "In Search of Virginia Woolf's Lost Eden in Cornwall." *The New York Times*, February 26, 2018, sec. Travel. https://www.nytimes.com/2018/02/26/travel/virginia-woolf-cornwall.html

[516] Woolf, Virginia. (1940) 1985. *Moments of Being: Autobiographical Writings*. Edited with introduction and notes by Jeanne Schulkind. Second Edition. Harcourt Brace Jovanovich Publication: San Diego, New York & London. p. 128.

[517] Ibid. pp. 78-9.

On Becoming the Wave at St Ives

Virginia experienced being lulled by the waves that acted as an abstract secret woven into her physical being. Didn't our mothers first communicate this to us in the womb and thereafter whilst nursing us and caring for us ongoingly? Perhaps, we carry this antithetical pre-linguistic relational mode of communication within us—as code. Virginia in fact alights us to a radically other kind of schooling, similar to Julia Kristeva who highlights a maternal influence re-accessed cathartically by way of poetry, which exists prior to language—a sensuous mode of communication associated with sound, touch, smell, and even probably thoughts, bacterium, cellular drives and so on.[518] And yet, in her essay on the sexual life of women 'Professions for Women', Virginia rather startlingly expresses the view that she doesn't think she achieved '... telling the truth about my own experiences as a body.'[519] But, surely she tells the truth about our embodied experience in a fuller capacity than anyone before her. She manages to elucidate that: '... one's life is not confined to one's body and what one says or does; one is living all the time in relation to certain background rods or conceptions.'[520] Our lives are mediated. We alight to our existence, the fact of being, when we register ourselves in other phenomena—when we become the wave.

I sit on the concrete gutter across from Virginia's childhood holiday home looking at the perfectly rectangular manicured and hedged front lawn that slopes down toward me. It is the picture of haute bourgeois privilege. I take a photograph of the chalk-white Edwardian

---

[518] Kristeva, Julia. (1974) 1984. *Revolution in Poetic Language*. New York: Columbia University Press. p. 2.
[519] Woolf, Virginia. (1942) 1961. *The Death of the Moth and Other Essays*. Middlesex: Penguin Books. p. 210.
[520] Ibid.

Talland house and notice I've captured some kind of oracular day time moon; the sun is shadowed by clouds and casts a rarified silvery light over the house. I think of Sylvia Plath's mother-moon, which is 'bald' and 'wild,' but by contrast this mother-sun-moon looms tenderly over the house. I sit a moment longer to collect my thoughts, although I feel increasingly inhibited by nearby holiday makers on their balconies taking tea, politely ignoring me. After a few minutes I descend back down the driveway, wend along the busy road towards the Barbara Hepworth Gallery, noticing the Godrevy lighthouse off in the distance. I descend through alleys, pass the memorial gardens, and the clock tower. I think of Virginia as a child in her bed at Talland house listening to '... the waves breaking—one, two, one, two ...'[521] And I begin to feel cleansed by the salty windy balm on my skin. Something starts to let down in me. I pass a child who chastises his mother for drinking from his water bottle: 'Mummy, I told you that was mine.' Internal eye-roll. The tireless, thankless toil of mothers. I bask in this moment of respite—inhale deeply—enjoy my own private meandering thoughts. I feel grateful for my mother's support on this trip. I consider how important it is to value my mother, although I am different to her, and perhaps represent a model of womanhood that is divergent to hers. Onward through the alleyways, past mostly hack-galleries, one interesting shop selling retro wares, a couple of designer clothes boutiques.

In Ratha Tep's article 'In Search of Virginia Woolf's Lost Eden in Cornwell,' she writes that: '*To the Lighthouse* encapsulates Woolf's love and longing for her mother — as well as her conflicted view of

---

[521] Woolf, Virginia. (1940) 1985. *Moments of Being: Autobiographical Writings*. Edited with introduction and notes by Jeanne Schulkind. Second Edition. Harcourt Brace Jovanovich Publication: San Diego, New York & London. p. 66.

her mother's vision of Victorian womanhood. All those bottled-up feelings, seemingly suspended in time after the family gave up Talland House following Julia Stephen's death, found their release in the novel.'[522] The plot of Virginia's novel unfolds in a seaside location, the Isle of Skye, Scotland, purportedly drawing heavily on Woolf's childhood summers spent in St Ives. Virginia discloses in 'A Sketch of the Past' of experiencing an 'involuntary, rush' whilst walking in Tavistock square nearby her London home, at which time the novel flooded her being. She says: '... I wrote the book very quickly; and when it was written, I ceased to be obsessed with my mother. I no longer hear her voice; I do not see her.'[523] Virginia goes on to speculate that perhaps she gave herself some kind of talking cure, not akin to psychoanalysis though, divergent: 'I expressed some very long felt and deeply felt emotions. And in expressing it I explained it and then laid it to rest.'[524] She attended to a maternal lineage within herself—penned a world suffuse with her mother. *To the Lighthouse* is dedicated to the figure of the mother keeping 'the panoply of life.'[525] Virginia paid homage to her tireless toil—released herself from an ancestral hold. She cured herself of this patriarchal matriarch after writing *To the Lighthouse* and became able to finally pursue her own path, to go her own way, embracive of her own notions of womanhood—to become the creator *not* the muse. In *To the Lighthouse* Virginia conveys Lily Briscoe's self-doubt pertaining to her capacity to perceive things and articulate them as a woman

---

[522] Tep, Ratha. 2018. "In Search of Virginia Woolf's Lost Eden in Cornwall." *The New York Times*, February 26, 2018, sec. Travel. https://www.nytimes.com/2018/02/26/travel/virginia-woolf-cornwall.html

[523] Woolf, Virginia. (1940) 1985. *Moments of Being: Autobiographical Writings*. Edited with introduction and notes by Jeanne Schulkind. Second Edition. Harcourt Brace Jovanovich Publication: San Diego, New York & London. p. 81.

[524] Ibid.

[525] Ibid.

painter up against a masculine world view, such as that of Mr Tansley who states that 'Women can't paint, women can't write.'[526] Virginia manages to convey Lily's courage, her desire to win out, to keep on with her creative pursuit. When we become the author of our own destinies we heal ourselves. We write ourselves a new lineage.

St Ives is a place where the bowl of sea reflects the light exceptionally well and so has become a haven for artists. As I wander along downhill toward the Barbara Hepworth Museum and Sculptural Garden I wonder if perhaps I might borrow some of this St Ives light—illuminate my way forward. I must think back through my mother towards a wisdom about the human situation on planet earth. I remember, yes, I remember that I am the wave—I integrate that abstract secret of infinitum into my material being. The crashing waves tell me of my first home—a maternal haven. If part of a teen's learning is to tear away from the maternal influence, so as to forge their own identity, which persists into early adulthood, then in later adulthood we perhaps again return to uncover a vital truth about our beginnings on planet earth—the importance of the mother as first teacher of kinship structures. We give thanks to the mother, even as we gradually release ourselves from ancestral strongholds. And yet, within me this persistent tremor, this longing for my mother, on account of the fact she was taken from me at age twenty-four when my brother first became ill. His continual annual hospitalisations plunged us all into grief ongoingly, took her again and again. She retreated into herself—a survival mechanism. I suppose in a way asking my mother to come to England with me, to walk the coast, is a bid to restore our kinship. To suture this wound.

---

[526] Woolf, Virginia. (1927) 2023. *To the Lighthouse*. Foreword by Patricia Lockwood. Introduction by Hermione Lee. Edited with notes by Stella McNichol. UK: Penguin Books. p. 42.

On Becoming the Wave at St Ives

To perceive things as they really are by the light of one's soul in St Ives, in late summer. Upon entering Trewyn Studio where Hepworth, one of Britain's most celebrated sculptors, lived and worked, I firstly survey the contents of the ground floor room, in which a series of cabinets display photographs of Hepworth and her artworks, accompanied by quotations on her practice.[527] I'm particularly taken in by a photograph in which Hepworth looks out the window contemplatively—the light cast onto her face. Nearby, there's a quote from Hepworth on display that emphasises: 'the woman's approach [to the visual arts, and especially sculpture] presents a different emphasis.' Hepworth fell in love with the 'pagan' Cornish landscape—she becomes the landscape to sculpt as must the writer—as did Virginia. In the upper room I find an early sculpture titled *Infant*, (1929), which is carved in Burmese wood. The sculpture depicts an infant with arms raised by its head and legs drawn back, the way my daughter used to lie in the tiny bathtub we bought for her—lotus like. It was a position of utter peaceability. The infant's eyes are mere indents, by which Hepworth perhaps emphasises the child as a sensuous perceptual being who does not experience the world through the primacy of vision alone, but rather by way of the entire embodied self, through sound, smell, touch, thought, and imaginal transmutation. Hepworth alerts us to this mammalian perspective.

The next day on a walk to Zennor Head, a little further along the coast from St Ives, I wonder to myself if Virginia walked this coastal path and make a silent wish to some unknown divinity to bring me a butterfly if she did. Apparently Virginia visited Zennor to

---

[527] Tate St Ives. 2019. "Barbara Hepworth Museum and Sculpture Garden | Tate." Tate. 2019. https://www.tate.org.uk/visit/tate-st-ives/barbara-hepworth-museum-and-sculpture-garden

recuperate after writing *The Voyage Out*, age 28. She purportedly returned repeatedly to the area with Leonard—to vivify herself. Zennor is a picturesque village with a small church and a charming pub called *Finners Arms*. My mother, son, daughter, and I walk the Zennor Head National Trust path towards St Ives close to sunset, although we accidentally take a wrong turn and head out over the fields. Suddenly we notice cows and then a bull streaming slowly into the field. We carefully edge away. The bull is in fact disinterested in us—chewing its cud meticulously. I think of Picasso's lithograph series *La Taureau*. No, I am not *a machine for suffering*. But, I am part animal—part mammal. Like Susan in *The Waves*:

> I like to walk through wet fields alone, or to stop at a gate and watch my setter nose in a circle, and to ask: Where is the hare? I like to be with people who twist herbs, and split into the fire, and shuffle down long passages in slippers like my father. The only sayings I understand are cries of love, hate, rage and pain ... I shall never have anything but natural happiness. It will almost content me. I shall go to bed tired. I shall like a field bearing crops in rotation; in the summer heat will dance over me; in the winter I shall be cracked with the cold. But heat and cold will follow each other naturally without my willing or unwilling. My children will carry me on; their teething, their crying, their coming to school and coming back will be like the waves of the sea under me. No day will be without its movement. I shall be lifted higher than any of you on the backs of the seasons. I shall possess more than Jinny, more than Rhoda by the time I die. But on the other hand, where you are various and dimple a million times to the ideas and laughter of others, I shall be sullen, storm-tinted and all of one purple.

On Becoming the Wave at St Ives

> I shall be debased and hide-bound by the bestial and beautiful passion of maternity.[528]

All of these migrations in Susan—in me. I am all of one purple. I am in St Ives on a poet's pilgrimage to listen to the waves—to learn to abort reason. To unburden myself from patriarchy. To reconnect with my mother. To teach my teens that there is another way.

After finding the correct path we fairly rapidly approach the English Channel. Three headlands stand to our left, black rock rolls out in an undulating vertical curtain hewn in moss. We look for the seal colony we've read might be here, but see none. Heather, thistle, gorse, dried fern, native grasses, wild carrot, and summery wild flowers grow in abundance. Up high on the right side of the path there is a rocky outcrop of sienna-coloured earth. Granite boulders scatter the landscape—an archaic geological scaffolding. Below us the turquoise sea crashes the shore in a foamy gauze. An exceptional contrast of grey granite, burgundy flowers, purple heather, and green grasses unfurl to our left—the spectrum is astounding. Unsurprisingly, we see an artist sketching the scene. This is the most beguiling stretch of coast I've yet witnessed in Cornwall. The granite is taken by the wind into lyrical contours. I can see Hepworth's work here as my teens climb a ledge of granite—flirting with the edge to find the best vantage point. Further along the coast a cluster of monolithic boulders make an excellent place to hike up and take in the panoramic expanse. My son and daughter urge me to climb too, and so I scale up the rockface. I notice intricate patternings on some of the boulders, cartographies of the wind. We finally head

---

[528] Woolf, Virginia. (1931) 1992. *The Waves*. Introduction by Kate Flint. London: Penguin. pp. 98-99.

back towards the pub. Fields of cows graze to our right—no sign of the Picasso bull. No, I am not *a machine for suffering*. I undergo metamorphosis—to write myself anew, to love, to thrive.

> My many scarred, scared
> scriptures, under my belly
> a downward spell. But logical,
> stoical, in an upright womb
> and enwombed, a signature.
> Compartment and safehold.
> Held together by a tension.
> A free hold of hope. Bespoke.
> Getting stricter, never compliant.
> Getting older, holding well like hell.
> An exile sentence—too long.
> But, mostly a seat at my breast,
> a living archeology, articulate
> molecular, a helix text. Blessed.

On a second walk along Zennor coastal path we head the other way toward three successive headlands. The terrain is more rugged. I begin to hear the waves more ardently on account of my son's chatter about gaming. I ask him to take a moment to just listen for the soundings of this place. There's an elegant seam of water that lays down through this landscape on its way to the ocean. We cross over it via a small wooden bridge. There's a fair bit of blackberry prickle to negotiate on the path, grasses burst over granite mounds, and small delicate pink flowers proliferate. From our position on the hill we can see the many currents in the distant ocean—its gentle steering. Soon we glimpse an idyllic cove, in which a couple bathe naked. We wonder how they managed to navigate a path down there. Both my son and daughter chart possible courses. I spot an inert skink on the rocky path, pick it up, hand it to my son. It appears to be dead, although I wonder if it's frozen as a defense mechanism, an instinctual response to a hovering predator. Still, as skinks usually dart off at high speed when they come into contact with humans, I'm pretty sure it's likely to be dead. My son holds it all the way back along the coastal path to Zennor village, making a studying of it, whispering things over it—trying to coax it back to life. His tenderness is moving. All the while the soothing sound of the waves are lapping. Suddenly a peacock butterfly appears in front of my daughter on the path. It is dark brown with markings of purple, red and yellow, flitting along the hedgerow as we advanced toward Zennor village. Perhaps Virginia did walk here. It is a wonderful moment at sunset as the butterfly wafts airily on an updraft of sea current—guides us. The suck and lap of saline augurs something migratory. There's a great migration going on in me.

On the last day in Cornwall, we visit Kynance Cove where my daughter, son, and I play in the waves together. We laugh and float a while, observe the granite cliffs of black, burgundy, grey, brown and olive hews. But my mother doesn't swim, instead she sits quietly on the rocks sunning herself, a little withdrawn. She watches over us. I wonder if she is perhaps grieving the loss of my brother, which is how grief takes us, in ebbs and flows, after the initial tidal wave. My daughter, son, and I continue to float, and listen to the waves, returned to granite, returned to this ledge of green, an outstretched grassy plain beyond the cliff's edge. In this ancestral place the waves compose a melody of stray lineage and deference, which is somehow made into me, but from which I'm also exiled. I'm re-learning these tidal soundings of wave and wind. I'm leaning into these deformations and reformations of the self as the wave does. Nothing but a fine nerve meter. The waves seem to offer me a valuable maternal voicing. They say: 'Refuse to turn away. Bear witness. Attest to the lives with which you are entangled. Attest to our planetary kinship.'

Bibliography

ABC News. 2023. "Israelis Describe 'Nightmare' as Hamas Gunmen Take Hostages at Music Festival and Roam the Streets," October 8, 2023. https://www.abc.net.au/news/2023-10-08/hamas-hostages-captives-music-festival-gaza-israel/102948950.

Agamben, Giorgio. (1995) 1998. *HomoSacer: Sovereign Power and Bare Life.* Translated by Daniel Heller-Roazen. Stanford, California: Stanford University Press. https://www.thing.net/~rdom/ucsd/biopolitics/HomoSacer.pdf

Alfred Russell, Wallace. 2019. "The Origin of Human Races and the Antiquity of Man, by Alfred Russel Wallace." Wku.edu. 2019. https://people.wku.edu/charles.smith/wallace/S093.htm.

Allen, Chadwick. 1999. "Blood (And) Memory." *American Literature* 71 (1): 93—116. https://doi.org/10.2307/2902590.

Ammons, A R. 1987. *The Selected Poems (Expanded Edition)*. W. W. Norton & Company.

Andrews, Kerri. 2020. *Wanderer: A History of Women Walking*. London: Reaktion Books.

Bibliography

Apollinaire, Guillaume . 2016. "It's Raining (Il Pleut)." Tumblr. April 3, 2016. https://www.tumblr.com/thepoetrytypewriter/142202742277/its-raining-il-pleut.

Araluen, Evelyn. 2021. *Dropbear*. St Lucia: University of Queensland Press.

Artaud, Antonin , and Susan Sontag. 1988. *Antonin Artaud, Selected Writings*. Berkeley: University Of California Press.

Auden, W.H. (1948) 1962. *The Dyers Hand*. London: Faber & Faber.

Bailey, T. Grahame. 1927. "The Position of Romani in Indo-Aryan. By R. L. Turner. 9¾ X 6; 45 Pp. Gypsy Lore Society, 1927." *Journal of the Royal Asiatic Society* 59 (3): 601—3. https://doi.org/10.1017/s0035869x00058470.

Barthes, Roland. (1977) 1990. *A Lover's discourse: Fragments*. Translated by Richard Howard. London: Penguin books.

——. 2006. "The Death of the Author." http://tbook.constantvzw.org/wp-content/death_authorbarthes.pdf.

Basso, Keith. 1996. *Wisdom Sits in Places: landscape and language among the Western Apache*. Albuquerque: University of Mexico.

Baudelaire, Charles. (1869) 1970. *La Spleen de Paris*. Translated by Louise Varèse. New York: A New Direction Book.

Bausells, Marta. 2016. "Why We Read: Authors and Readers on the Power of Literature." The Guardian. The Guardian. April 23, 2016. https://www.theguardian.com/books/2016/apr/23/why-we-read-authors-and-readers-on-the-power-of-literature.

Belka, Olga. 2020. "The Silent World 1956. Jacques Cousteau. FULL HD 1080P. Original Movie. Le Monde Du Silence." *YouTube*. https://www.youtube.com/watch?v=xr4FrELKfvk.

Benjamin, Walter. 1968. *Walter Benjamin: Essays and Reflections*. With introduction by Hannah Arendt. Translated by Harry Zohn. New York: Schocken Books.

Benjamin, Walter, and Michael William Jennings. 2006. *The Writer of Modern Life: Essays on Charles Baudelaire*. Cambridge, Mass.: Harvard University Press.

Bennet, Jane. 2010. *Vibrant Matter: A Political Ecology of Things*. Durham: Duke University Press.

Bennett, Andrew, and Nicholas Royle. 2004. *An Introduction to Literature, Criticism and Theory*. London: Longman Publishing Group.

Bergvall, Caroline . 2004. "Via 48 Dante Variations." http://carolinebergvall.com/wp-content/uploads/2018/08/VIA.pdf.

——. 2015. "VIA (48 Dante Translations) Mix W Fractals." SoundCloud. 2015. https://soundcloud.com/carolinebergvall/via-48-dante-translations-mix.

Beta, Germano. 2021. "Os Motivos Que Tornam a Vulva 'Diva' Tão Polêmica." Vogue. January 7, 2021. https://vogue.globo.com/Vogue-Gente/noticia/2021/01/os-motivos-que-tornam-vulva-diva-tao-polemica.html.

Birch, Tony. 2015. *Ghost River*. Brisbane: Univ. of Queensland Press.

——. 2019. "'There Is No Axe': Identity, Story and a Sombrero." Meanjin. March 5, 2019. https://meanjin.com.au/essays/there-is-no-axe-identity-story-and-a-sombrero/.

——. 2020. "Six Walks Episode One: Tony Birch on the Birrarung." ACCA. 2020. https://acca.melbourne/whos-afraid-of-public-space/offsite/six-walks/six-walks-episode-one-tony-birch/.

———. 2022. "Indigenous Places (Video)." Writers Victoria. February 21, 2022. https://writersvictoria.org.au/resources/writing-tips-and-tools/indigenous-places-video/.

Blair, Kirstie. 2004. "Gypsies and Lesbian Desire: Vita Sackville-West, Violet Trefusis, and Virginia Woolf." *Twentieth Century Literature* 50 (2): 141. https://doi.org/10.2307/4149276.

Bob Brown Foundation. n.d. "Takayna / Tarkine." Bob Brown Foundation. https://bobbrown.org.au/campaigns/takayna/.

Borges, Jorge Luis. (1967) 1974. *The Book of Imaginary Beings*. Translated by Norman Thomas di Giovanni. New York: Avon.

Bourgeois, Louise. 1998. *Destruction of the Father, Reconstruction of the Father: Writings and Interviews 1923-1997*. Edited and with texts by Marie-Laure Bernadae and Hans-Ulrich Obrist, MIT Press: Cambridge, Massachusetts.

Bradshaw, David. 2016. "Virginia Woolf's London." *The British Library*. https://www.bl.uk/20th-century-literature/articles/virginia-woolfs-london.

Braidotti, Rosi. 2011. *Nomadic Subjects: Embodiment and Sexual Difference in Contemporary Feminist Theory*. Second Edition. New York: Columbia University.

Braidotti, Rosi. 2015. "Punk Women and Riot Grrls. ." Performancephilosophy.org. 2015. https://www.performancephilosophy.org/journal/article/view/32/63.

———. 2019. *Posthuman Knowledge*. Cambridge: Polity Press.

Brakhage, Stan. 1963. *Metaphors on Vision*. U.S.A: Film Culture Inc.

———. 1989. *Film at Witsend*. London: Polygon.

———. 2009. "Mothlight (1963)." YouTube. June 4, 2009. https://www.youtube.com/watch?v=Yt3nDgnC7M8&list=PLfTaZIagMDn6_SuMT-CzeBBKmOo8KoRCy&index=11.

———. 2012. "Window Water Baby Moving (1959) Part 2." YouTube. January 15, 2012. https://www.youtube.com/watch?v=Q_MA8h8PXQM.

———. 2013. "Dog Star Man (1959)." *YouTube*. https://www.youtube.com/watch?v=NA0THILzheo.

———. 2007. "Window Water Baby Moving (1959) Part 1." YouTube. July 25, 2007. https://www.youtube.com/watch?v=-drSrvTtZ1k&list=PLfTaZIagMDn6_SuMTCzeBBKmOo8KoRCy&index=7.

———. dir. 1959a. *Sirius Remembered*.

———. dir. 1959b. *Window, Water, Baby. Part 2*.

Bristow, Tom. 2015. *The Anthropocentric Lyric; An Affective Geography of Poetry, Person, Place.* London: Palgrave.

Brönte, Charlotte. (1847) 1848. *Jane Eyre*. London & Glasgow: Collins' Clear-Type Press.

———. (1846). 2025. "Loud without the Wind Was Roaring | Poems of Emily Brontë | Emily Brontë | Lit2Go ETC." Usf.edu. 2025. https://etc.usf.edu/lit2go/75/poems-of-emily-bronte/5643/loud-without-the-wind-was-roaring/.

Brown, Brené. 2018. *Dare to Lead: Brave Work. Tough Conversations. Whole Hearts.* London: Vermilion.

"Buninyong." 2004. The Sydney Morning Herald. February 8, 2004. https://www.smh.com.au/lifestyle/buninyong-20040208-gdkqra.html.

Cameron, Liz. 2022. "Indigenous Ecological Knowledge Systems — Exploring Sensory Narratives." *Ecological Management & Restoration* 23 (S1): 27—32. https://doi.org/10.1111/emr.12534.

Camus, Albert. (1947) 2015. *The Plague*. London: Penguin.

BIBLIOGRAPHY

Carson, Anne. (1992) 1995. *The Gender of Sound*. New York: New Directions Books.

Cave, Nick. 2021. "Happy Red Hand File Anniversary! Three Years! How Time Flies When You Are Answering Multiple Questions At..." The Red Hand Files. September 15, 2021. https://www.theredhandfiles.com/happy-anniversary-three-years/.

Cixous, Hélène. 1993. 'The School of the Dead' in *Three Steps on the Ladder of Writing*. New York: University of Columbia Press.

Cixous, Hélène and Clément, Catherine. (1975) 1986. *The Newly Born Woman; Theory and History of Literature, Volume 24*, trans. Betsy Wing. Introduction by Sandra M. Gilbert. Minneapolis: University of Minnesota Press.

Cixous, Hélène, with Susan Sellers. 1993. *Three Steps on the Ladder of Writing*. New York. N.Y.; Chichester: Columbia University Press.

Cixous, Hélène. 'The Laugh of the Medusa' in *Signs*. Volume 1, Number 4 (Summer 1976). Chicago: University of Chicago Press. pp.875-893.

Clayson, Allan. 2000. "Coleridge□S Holidays at Ramsgate." Friendsofcoleridge.com. 2000. https://www.friendsofcoleridge.com/MembersOnly/Clayson_Ramsgate.html.

Clément, Catherine. (1975) 1986. "The Guilty One." In *The Newly Born Woman; Theory and History of Literature, Volume 24*. Hélène Cixous, and Catherine Clément, Translated by Betsy Wing. Minnesota Press: University of Minneapolis.

Corballis, Michael C. 2015. *The Wandering Mind: What the Brain Does When You're Not Looking*. Chicago, Il: University Of Chicago Press.

Cott, Jonathan. 2010. "John Lennon: The Last Interview." Rolling Stone. December 23, 2010. https://www.rollingstone.com/feature/john-lennon-the-last-interview-179443/.

Cousteau, Jacques. Y. 1977. *The Silent World*. New York: Ballantine Books.

Coverley, Merlin. (2006) 2018. *Psychogeography*. Harpenden, UK: Oldcastle Books.

Crosby, Jon. 1998. "Vast — Touched." Genius. 1998. https://genius.com/Vast-touched-lyrics.

David, Bradshaw. n.d. "Virginia Woolf's London | the British Library." British Library. https://www.britishlibrary.cn/en/articles/virginia-woolfs-london/.

De Certeau, Michel. 1988. *The Writing of History*, translated by Thomas Conley. New York: Columbia University Press.

Deleuze, Gilles. (1969) 1990. *Logic of Sense*. Translated by Mark Lester with Charles Stivale. Edited by Constantine V. Boundas. London: The Athlone Press.

——. (1993) 1998. *Essays Critical and Clinical*. Translated by Daniel W. Smith and Michael A. Grew. London: Verso.

Deleuze, Gilles and Félix Guattari. (1975) 1986. *Kafka: Toward a Minor Literature*. Translated by Dana Polan. Minneapolis: University of Minnesota Press.

——. (1980) 1987. *A Thousand Plateaus: Capitalism and Schizophrenia*. Translated and with a foreword by Brian Massumi. Minneapolis: Minnesota Press.

Dell, Marion and Whybrow, Marion. 2004. *Virginia Woolf and Vanessa Bell: Remembering St Ives*. Cornwall: Tabb House.

Devon County Council. 2016. "Stover Country Park." Https://Www.devon.gov.uk/Stovercountrypark/. January 26, 2016. https://www.devon.gov.uk/stovercountrypark/.

Dickens, Charles. 1867. "Oliver Twist." https://ia802300.us.archive.org/23/items/books_202205/oliver-twist.pdf.

Didion, Joan. (1979) 2009. *The White Album*. New York: Farrar, Straus and Giroux.

Doherty, Maggie. 2020. "The Long Awakening of Adrienne Rich." *The New Yorker*, November 23, 2020. https://www.newyorker.com/magazine/2020/11/30/the-long-awakening-of-adrienne-rich.

Douglas, Norman. 1915. *Old Calabria*. Boston & New York: Houghton Mifflin Company.

Rachel Du Plessis. 1990. *The Pink Guitar*. New York: Routledge.

Dyer, Natalie Rose. 2008a. "Song for the Boatman." YouTube. February 10, 2008. https://www.youtube.com/watch?v=TPr6-Zr91Uk.

———. 2008b. "Stranger than Kindness." YouTube. February 12, 2008. https://www.youtube.com/watch?v=1NLtc0HZrSE.

———. 2009. "The Lamenting Wife - by Natalie Rose and the Pantomime Horse." YouTube. January 19, 2009. https://www.youtube.com/watch?v=v21wgz7AJ10.

———. 2020. *The Menstrual Imaginary in Literature: Notes on a Wild Fluidity*. Cham, Switzerland: Palgrave Macmillan.

Eliot, T.S. [1944] 1974. *Four Quartets*. London: Faber and Faber.

Elkin, Lauren. (2016) 2017. *Flâneuse: Women Walk the City in Paris, New York, Tokyo, Venice and London*. London: Vintage.

Estes. C.P. 1992. *Women Who Run With the Wolves: Myths and Stories of the Wild Woman Archetype*. New York: Ballantine Books.

Evans, Jonathan. 2021. "Human Sacrifice and Pagan Rituals: A Walk through Dartmoor's Haunted Wood." The Independent. March 11, 2021. https://www.independent.co.uk/travel/uk/devon-wistmans-wood-dartmoor-haunted-b1814603.html

Eve, K. (2020). *Julia Stephen: From Freshwater Bay To The Lighthouse — Journal of Victorian Culture Online*. [online] Oup.com. Available at: https://jvc.oup.com/2020/10/22/julia-stephen/ [Accessed 28 Feb. 2025].

Ferguson, Donna. 2020. "Letters Reveal Postnatal Crisis of Barbara Hepworth." *The Observer*, April 19, 2020, sec. Art and design. https://www.theguardian.com/artanddesign/2020/apr/19/letters-reveal-postnatal-crisis-of-barbara-hepworth.

Fitch, Toby. Editor. 2021. "Australian Poetry Chapbook Transforming My Country." https://emergingwritersfestival.org.au/wp-content/uploads/2021/06/Transforming-My-Country_AP2021.pdf

Forshaw, Thelma. "Save us from Shaggy Germ O Man!" *The Age*. 15th January, 1972.

https://blogs.unimelb.edu.au/librarycollections/2019/06/05/when-greer-came-home-january-march-1972-save-us-from-shaggy-germ-o-man/

Foucault, Michel. (1966) 1970. *The Order of Things: An Archeology of the Human Sciences*. Translated from the French. London: Tavistock Publications.

——. 1982. *The Subject and Power*. Chicago: Chicago University Press.

Foundation, Poetry. 2021. "Wilderness by Carl Sandburg." Poetry Foundation. March 12, 2021. https://www.poetryfoundation.org/poems/53233/wilderness.

Fowles, John. (1926) 1983. *The Tree*. Ecco Press: New York.

Freeman, Robin, and Karen Le Rossignol. 2011. "Clarifying Creative Nonfiction through the Personal Essay." *TEXT* 15 (2): 1—11. https://doi.org/10.52086/001c.31345.

Gadsby, Hannah. 2018. "Hannah Gadsby: Nanette (2018)." *IMDB*. https://www.imdb.com/title/tt8465676/.

Gardner, Thomas. 2020. "The Art of Poetry No. 85." The Paris Review. February 24, 2020. https://www.theparisreview.org/interviews/263/the-art-of-poetry-no-85-jorie-graham.

Gatlif, Tony, dir. 1993. *Latcho Drom*.

——, dir. 1997. *Gadjo Dilo*.

——, dir. 2000. *Vengo*.

——, dir. 2001. *Swing*.

Gifford, Terry and Roberts, Neil. 1981. *Ted Hughes: A Critical Study*. London: Faber and Faber.

Gilbert, S.M. (1975) 1986. 'Introduction.' *The Newly Born Woman; Theory and History of Literature, Volume 24*. Hélène Cixous and Catherine Clément. Trans. Betsy Wing. Minneapolis: University of Minnesota Press.

Gillian Gill. 2019. *Virginia Woolf: And the Women Who Shaped Her World*. Boston, Massachusetts: Mariner Books (Imprint of Harper Collins).

Glausiusz, Josie (Cites Marcus Raichle). 2013. "Living in an Imaginary World." *Scientific American* 23 (1s): 70—77. https://doi.org/10.1038/scientificamericancreativity1213-70.

Glendinning, Victoria. 1998. *Vita: the Life of Vita Sackville-West*. London: Weidenfeld & Nicolson.

Goldsmith, Kenneth. 2011. *Uncreative Writing: Managing Language in the Digital Age*. New York: Columbia University.

——. 2013. "Plagiarism: Maybe It's Not so Bad | on the Media | WNYC Studios." WNYC Studios. 2013. https://www.wnyc-studios.org/podcasts/otm/segments/plagiarism-maybe-its-not-so-bad.

Graham, Jorie. 1992. "'Notes on the Reality of the Self,' by Jorie Graham." The New Yorker. August 17, 1992. https://www.newyorker.com/magazine/1992/08/24/jorie-graham-poem-notes-on-the-reality-of-the-self.

Greer, Germaine. "Federico Fellini wanted to cast me in Casanova. We ended up in

bed together." *The Guardian*, Monday 12th April, 2010. https://www.theguardian.com/culture/2010/apr/11/germaine-greer-federico-fellini

——. 2014. *White Beech: The Rainforest Years*, London: Bloomsbury.

——. 11th April, 2016. 'Q&A: Germaine Greer revives an old controversy about what

constitutes a real woman.' https://www.abc.net.au/news/2016-04-11/q&a-germaine-greer-weighs-in-sexuality-transgender/7318024

Quinn, S. "Germain Greer: 'Saucy Feminist that Even Men Like.'" *The Washington Post as cited*

in *Women's Agenda*. 7th May, 1971. https://womensagenda.com.au/latest/germaine-greer-life-of-the-party/

Haraway, Donna. 1991. *Simian, Cyborgs, & Women: The Reinvention of Nature*.

New York: Routledge.

——. 2016. *Staying with the Trouble: Making Kin in the Chthulucene*. Duke University Press.

Haynes, Suyin. 2019. "A New Virginia Woolf Biography Deals with the Author's Experience of Childhood Sexual Abuse." Time. December 17, 2019. https://time.com/5750614/virginia-woolf-biography/.

Hazlitt, Sarah Stoddart. 2022. "The Sarah Stoddart Hazlitt Project | about SSH." Theproject. 2022. https://sarahstoddarthazlitt.wixsite.com/theproject/about-ssh.

Hazlitt, William. (1821) 1918. *Twenty-Two Essays of William Hazlitt*. Selected and Edited by Arthur Beatty. Boston, New York, Chicago: University of Wisconsin. D.C. Heath & Company Publisher.

Heaney, Seamus. 1966. "Digging." Poetry Foundation. Poetry Foundation. 1966. https://www.poetryfoundation.org/poems/47555/digging.

——. [1975] 2001. *North*. London: Faber and Faber.

——. 2002. *Finders Keepers: Selected Prose 1971-2001*. London: Faber & Faber.

Heath, Nicola. "Germaine Greer's The Female Eunich had an enormous impact. It's still felt 50 years on." *ABC*. (4th February, 2025). https://www.abc.net.au/news/2025-02-04/germaine-greer-book-the-female-eunuch-feminist-blockbuster/104875722

Higgins, Karrie. 2007. "Senses of Place." Los Angeles Times. November 4, 2007. https://www.latimes.com/archives/la-xpm-2007-nov-04-bk-higgins4-story.html.

Hobday, Liz. 2022. "The Enduring Appeal of the Misogynist Picasso." Australian Financial Review. June 9, 2022. https://www.afr.com/life-and-luxury/arts-and-culture/the-enduring-appeal-of-the-misogynist-picasso-20220609-p5asm4.

Hoffmann, Edith. 1965. "Karel Appel at Amsterdam." *The Burlington Magazine* 107 (750): 484—482. https://doi.org/10.2307/874653.

Homer. 1996. *The Odyssey*. Translated by Robert Fagles. Introduction & Notes by Bernard Knox. New York: Penguin.

Hughes, Ted. *River*. 1983. New York: Harper & Row.

Huxley, Aldous. (1959) 1989. *The Human Situation*. London: Grafton Books.

Irigaray, Luce. (1977) 1985. *This Sex Which Is Not One*. Ithaca, N.Y.: Cornell University Press.

Irigaray, Luce. (1977) 1985. *This Sex Which is Not One*. Translated by Catherine Porter with Carolyn Burke. Ithaca, New York: Cornell University.

Jahan Ramazani, Richard Ellmann, and Robert O'Clair. 2003. *The Norton Anthology of Modern and Contemporary Poetry*. W W Norton & Company Incorporated.

James, William. 1890. *The Principles of Psychology*. New York: Holt.

Jamie, Kathleen. 2005. *Findings*. London: Sort of Books.

John Durham Peters. 2015. *The Marvelous Clouds : Toward a Philosophy of Elemental Media*. Chicago ; London: The University Of Chicago Press.

Joyce, James. (1916) 1943. *A Portrait of the Artist as a Young Man*. London: Jonathan Cape.

——. 2001. "The Project Gutenberg EBook of a Portrait of the Artist as a Young Man, by James Joyce." Gutenberg.org. 2001. https://gutenberg.org/files/4217/4217-h/4217-h.htm.

Kafka, Franz. 1977. *Letters to friends, family, and editors*. Translated by Clara and Richard Winston. New York: Schocken Books.

Keller, Helen. 1908. *The World I Live In*. London: Hodder & Stoughton.

Kelley, Joyce. 2018. "Virginia Woolf's Appreciation for Walt Whitman's Leaves of Grass: Book Making/Reading, Intimacy, Collectivity." In *Virginia Woolf and the World of Books*, 254—59. Liverpool: Liverpool University Press.

Knight, Rebecca Dinerstein. 2020. "The Fabulous Forgotten Life of Vita Sackville-West." The Paris Review. March 31, 2020. https://www.theparisreview.org/blog/2020/03/31/the-fabulous-forgotten-life-of-vita-sackville-west/.

Knight, Sam. 2024. "What Have Fourteen Years of Conservative Rule Done to Britain?" The New Yorker. March 25, 2024. https://www.newyorker.com/magazine/2024/04/01/what-have-fourteen-years-of-conservative-rule-done-to-britain.

Kristeva, Julia. (1974) 1984. *Revolution in Poetic Language*. New York: Columbia University Press.

———. (1977) 1985. *Stabat Matter*. Translated by Arthur Goldhammer. Durham: Duke University Press.

———. 1982. *Powers of Horror: An Essay in Abjection*. Trans. Leon S. Roudiez. New York: Columbia University Press.

———. 1991. *Strangers to Ourselves*. New York: Columbia University Press.

Kudláček, Martina, dir. 2002. *In the Mirror of Deren* .

Kwaymullina, Ambelin. 2024. "Walking Many Worlds: Aboriginal Storytelling and Writing for the Young." The Wheeler Centre. June 29, 2024. https://www.wheelercentre.com/wlr-articles/e221876968a8/.

Laing, Olivia. 2011. *To the River: A Journey Beneath the Surface*. Edinburgh: Canongate.

———. 2016. *The Lonely City*. Edinburgh: Canongate Books.

Laster, Pail . 2017. "Karel Appel and the Influence of Outsider Art." Whitehot Magazine of Contemporary Art. October 2017.

https://whitehotmagazine.com/articles/karel-appel-influence-outsider-art/3796.

Le Bas, Damian. 2018. *The Stopping Places: A Journey Through Gypsy Britain*. London: Chatto & Windus.

Le, Ursula. 1986. "We Are Volcanoes." Speakola. May 1986. https://speakola.com/grad/ursula-le-guin-we-are-volcanoes-bryn-mawr-1986.

Leane, Jeanine . 2023. "Ngurambang Yali — Country Speaks." Red Room Poetry. 2023. https://redroompoetry.org/poets/jeanine-leane/ngurambang-yali-country-speaks/.

Lehrer, Jonah. 2012. "The Virtues of Daydreaming." The New Yorker. June 5, 2012. https://www.newyorker.com/tech/frontal-cortex/the-virtues-of-daydreaming.

Lethem, Jonathan. 2007. "The Ecstasy of Influence | Harper's Magazine." Harper's Magazine. February 2007. https://harpers.org/archive/2007/02/the-ecstasy-of-influence/.

Levertov, Denise. 2025. "The Poetry Foundation." The Poetry Foundation. The Olga Poems (1965). 2025. https://www.poetryfoundation.org/poetrymagazine/browse?contentId=30054.

Levinas, Emmanuel. 1989. In *The Levinas Reader*, ed. Seán Hand. Oxford: Basil Blackwell.

"Lighthouse by John Shaw, Senior (1776-1832)." 2025. Victorianweb.org. 2025. https://victorianweb.org/art/architecture/shaw/2.html.

Lorca, Frederico García. (1953) 1963. *The Gypsy Ballads*. With an Introduction by L.R. Rind. Translated by Rolfe Humphries. Bloomington: Indiana University Press.

Lorde, Audre. 1977. 'The Transformation of Silence into Language and Action' delivered in a paper at *The Modern Language Association's Lesbian and Literature Panel*. https://caps.sfsu.edu/sites/default/files/documents/Audre%20Lorde%20-%20Silence%20Into%20Action.pdf

Lyons, Siobhan. 2017. "Psychogeography: A Way to Delve into the Soul of a City." *The Conversation*, June 18, 2017. https://theconversation.com/psychogeography-a-way-to-delve-into-the-soul-of-a-city-78032.

MacFarlane, Robert. 2012. *The Old Ways: A Journey on Foot*. London: Penguin Books.

——. 2015. *Landmarks*. London: Penguin Books.

——. 2025. *Is a River Alive?* London: Hamish Hamilton, Penguin Books

Maclean, Caroline. 2020. *Circles and Squares: The Lives and Art of the Hampstead Modernists*. London and New York: Bloomsbury.

Macmillan, Jade, and Joanna Robin. 2022. "'The Whole Thing Has Been Such a Circus': How the Jury Reached Its Verdict in the Johnny Depp-Amber Heard Case." *ABC News*, June 1, 2022. https://www.abc.net.au/news/2022-06-02/johnny-depp-amber-heard-verdict-explained/101117404.

Marland, Pippa. 2015. "The Gannet's Skull versus the Plastic Doll's Head: Material 'Value' in Kathleen Jamie's 'Findings.'" *Green Letters* 19 (2): 121—31. https://doi.org/10.1080/14688417.2015.1024156.

Mauss, Marcel. (1902) 2001. *A General Theory of Magic*. Translated by Robert Brain. London: Routledge.

Melville, Herman. [1851] 1930. *Moby Dick*. With illustrations by Rockwell Kent. Chicago: The Lakeside Press.

Millsapps, Jan.L. 1986. 'Maya Deren, Imagist.' *Literature/Film Quarterly; Salisbury*. 14 (1):
22-31.

Mireless, Hope. (1920) 2020. *Paris: A Poem*. London: Faber & Faber.

Mocatta, Gabi. 2021. "The Guide to Travelling the Tarkine." Australian Geographic. June 11, 2021. https://www.australiangeographic.com.au/travel/travel-destinations/tasmania/2021/06/the-tarkine-natural-tasmanian-wonder/.

Money, Jazz. 2021. *How to Make a Basket*. St Lucia: University of Queensland Press.

Muecke, Stephen. 2021. "'What Country Have You Walked?' Why All Australians Should Walk an Indigenous Heritage Trail." The Conversation. July 2021. https://theconversation.com/what-country-have-you-walked-why-all-australians-should-walk-an-indigenous-heritage-trail-162519.

Najjar, Michael . 2016. "Michael Najjar." Michaelnajjar.com. 2016. https://www.michaelnajjar.com/artworks/outer-space/works/orbital-ascent.

Nelson, Maggie. 2021. *On Freedom: Four Songs of Care and Constraint*. Minneapolis: Graywolf Press.

NGV. 2023. "Live and in Conversation After-Hours: Tracey Emin | Triennial | NGV." Vic.gov.au. 2023. https://www.ngv.vic.gov.au/program/keynote-tracey-emin-in-conversation/.

North, Michael. 2013. "The Making of 'Make It New.'" Guernica. Guernica Magazine. August 15, 2013. https://www.guernicamag.com/the-making-of-making-it-new/.

Notari, Juliana . 2020. "Julia Notari's Post on Facebook." Facebook. December 31, 2020. https://www.facebook.com/juliana.notari/posts/10219401789651753.

O'Hara, Frank (Feb 1969). 2025. "The Poetry Foundation." The Poetry Foundation. 2025. https://www.poetryfoundation.org/poetrymagazine/browse?volume=113&issue=5&page=42.

O'Riordan, Adam. 2009. "Why Are Poets so Fascinated with Birds?" *The Guardian*, April 28, 2009, sec. Books. https://www.theguardian.com/books/booksblog/2009/apr/28/poets-birds-poetry.

O'Rourke, Karen. 2016. *Walking and Mapping: Artist as Cartographer*. Cambridge, MA: MIT Press.

"Os Motivos Que Tornam a Vulva 'Diva' Tão Polêmica." n.d. Vogue. https://vogue.globo.com/Vogue-Gente/noticia/2021/01/os-motivos-que-tornam-vulva-diva-tao-polemica.html.

Ostriker, Alice. 1988. "That Story: The Change of Anne Sexton." In *Anne Sexton: Telling the Tale*, 263—88. Ann Arbour: The University of Michigan.

Parke, Erin. 2016. "Aboriginal People Move to Reclaim Art That Sparked Extra-Terrestrial Theory." *ABC News*, December 4, 2016. https://www.abc.net.au/news/2016-12-05/aboriginal-people-move-to-reclaim-sacred-wandjina-drawings/8049978.

Parr, Adrian. 2017. *Birth of a New Earth: The Radical Politics of Environmentalism*. New York: Columbia University Press.

Phillips, Tom. 2021. "The Vagina Dialogues: 33-Metre Artwork Draws Far Right's Ire in Brazil." The Guardian. January 3, 2021. https://www.theguardian.com/world/2021/jan/03/the-vagina-dialogues-33-metre-artwork-draws-far-rights-ire-in-brazil.

Plath, Sylvia. (1965) 1990. *Ariel*. London: Faber and Faber.

Proust, Marcel. 2002. *The Way by Swann's*. Translated and with an Introduction and Notes by
Lydia Davis. London: Penguin.

Pussy Riot. 2016. "Pussy Riot - Straight Outta Vagina (Feat. Desi Mo & Leikeli47). Official Music Video." Www.youtube.com. 2016. https://www.youtube.com/watch?v=Bp-KeVBNz0A.

Reddick, Yvonne. 2017. *Ted Hughes: Environmentalist and Ecopoet*. New York: Palgrave.

Reddick, Yvonne. 2018. "Yvonne Reddick." Yvonne Reddick. February 27, 2018. http://yvonnereddick.org/blog/towards-taw-tor-sources-ted-hughess-inspiration/.

Rhook, Nadia. 2021. "Review of 'Dropbear' by Evelyn Araluen." Westerly Magazine. August 12, 2021. https://westerlymag.com.au/dropbear/.

Rich, Adrienne. 1972. "When We Dead Awaken: Writing as Re-Vision." *College English* 34 (1): 18—30. https://doi.org/10.2307/375215.

——. 2010. "Someone Is Writing a Poem by Adrienne Rich." Poetry Foundation. May 12, 2010. https://www.poetryfoundation.org/articles/69530/someone-is-writing-a-poem.

——. 2015. "Notes toward a Politics of Location (1984)." The Critical Flame. 2015. https://criticalflame.org/notes-toward-a-politics-of-location/.

——. (1976) 1995. *Of Woman Born: Motherhood as Experience and Institution*. New York: W.W. Norton & Co.

——. 1986. *Blood, Bread and Roses*. New York: W. W. Norton & Company.

Rousseau, Jean-Jacques. (1782) 1992. *The Reveries of a Solitary Walker*. Translation by Charles E. Butterworth. Indianapolis/Cambridge: Hackett Publishing Company.

Ryan, Tom. 2015. "They Do Not Realize We Are Bringing Them the Plague - the Other Journal." The Other Journal. June 29, 2015.

https://theotherjournal.com/2015/06/29/they-do-not-realize-we-are-bringing-them-the-plague/.

Saatchi Gallery. 2023a. "CIVILIZATION: The Way We Live Now - Saatchi Gallery." August 8, 2023. https://www.saatchigallery.com/exhibition/civilization_the_way_we_live_now.

———. 2023b. "Beyond the Gaze: Reclaiming the Landscape - Saatchi Gallery." Saatchi Gallery. August 9, 2023. https://www.saatchigallery.com/exhibition/beyond_the_gaze_reclaiming_the_landscape.

Sackville-West, Vita. 1926, *The Land*. London: William Heinemann.

———. (1937) 1986. *Pepita*. London: Virago.

Sackville-West, Vita and Woolf, Virginia. 2021. *Love Letters: Virginia Woolf and Vita Sackville-West*. With an Introduction by Alison Bechdel. UK: Vintage Classics, Penguin Random House.

Santilli, Nikki. 2002. *Such Rare Citings: The Prose Poem in English Literature*. New Jersey:

Fairleigh Dickinson University Press.

Saunders, Kirli. 2023. "'Go Rogue', a New Poem by Kirli Saunders." Australian Book Review.

September 23, 2023. https://www.australianbookreview.com.au/abr-online/current-issue/994-october-2023-no-458/11085-go-rogue-a-new-poem-by-kirli-saunders.

Self, Will. 2007. *Psychogeography: Disentangling the Modern Conundrum of Psyche and Place*. USA: Bloomsbury.

Shepherd, Nan. (1977) 2014. *The Living Mountain*. With an introduction by Brian McFarlane and a prologue by Jeanette Winterson. Edinburgh: Canongate.

Siddique, Haroon, and Haroon Siddique Legal affairs correspondent. 2023. "Gypsy, Roma and Travellers Suffer 'Persistent' Discrimination in UK." *The Guardian*, May 25, 2023, sec. World news. https://www.theguardian.com/world/2023/may/25/gypsy-roma-travellers-suffer-persistent-discrimination-uk.

Siegal, Nina. 2016. "Shedding New Light on the Late Dutch Artist Karel Appel." *The New York Times*, February 4, 2016, sec. Arts. https://www.nytimes.com/2016/02/05/arts/international/shedding-new-light-on-the-late-dutch-artist-karel-appel.html.

Sister M. Gonsalva Wiegard. 1936. *The Non-Dramatic Works of Hrosvitha: Text, Translation, and Commentary.* Saint Lewis, Missouri: The Abby Press.

Solnit, Rebecca. 2001. *Wanderlust: A History of Walking*. London: Granta.

———. (2005) 2017. *A Field Guide to Getting Lost*. Edinburgh: Canongate.

———. 2014. *Men Explain Things to Me and Other Essays*. London: Granta.

Sontag, Susan. 1966. *Against Interpretation; And Other Essays*. New York: Farrar, Straus, Giroux.

Spivak, Gayatri Chakravorty. 2003. *Death of a Discipline*. New York: Columbia University Press.

St Austell, Carnmenellis. 2005. "Geology and Landforms Dartmoor Factsheet Dartmoor National Park Authority Geology and Landforms Factsheet March 2005 Page 1 of 8 Seven Stones Land's End Isles of Scilly Bodmin Moor." https://www.dartmoor.gov.uk/__data/assets/pdf_file/0019/72109/lab-geology.pdf.

Stephen, Leslie. (1898) 2012. *Studies of a Biographer*. Cambridge: Cambridge University Press.

Swan, Michael. 1954. "Lorca's Gypsy." The Atlantic. September 1, 1954. https://www.theatlantic.com/magazine/archive/1954/09/lorcas-gypsy/640534/.

Tate Modern. n.d. "Hilma Af Klint & Piet Mondrian | Tate Modern 20 April — 3 September 2023." Tate. https://www.tate.org.uk/whats-on/tate-modern/hilma-af-klint-piet-mondrian.

Tate St Ives. 2019. "Barbara Hepworth Museum and Sculpture Garden | Tate." Tate. 2019. https://www.tate.org.uk/visit/tate-st-ives/barbara-hepworth-museum-and-sculpture-garden.

Tep, Ratha. 2018. "In Search of Virginia Woolf's Lost Eden in Cornwall." *The New York Times*, February 26, 2018, sec. Travel. https://www.nytimes.com/2018/02/26/travel/virginia-woolf-cornwall.html.

The National Gallery of Victoria . 2019. "Keith Haring | Jean-Michel Basquiat | NGV." Www.ngv.vic.gov.au. December 1, 2019. https://www.ngv.vic.gov.au/exhibition/keith-haring-jean-michel-basquiat/.

The Statutes Project. 2020. "1530: 22 Henry 8 C. 10: The Egyptians Act." The Statutes Project. April 7, 2020. https://statutes.org.uk/site/the-statutes/sixteenth-century/1530-22-henry-8-c-10-the-egyptians-act/.

Theoretical Puppets. 2021. "Gilles Deleuze on Chaos and Creativity." YouTube. May 23, 2021. https://www.youtube.com/watch?v=bqV1uXy0Ny8.

Thoreau, Henry David. (1851) 1994. *Walking*. San Francisco: Harper San Francisco.

Tony, Gatlif, dir. 1997. *Gadjo Dilo*.

Tranter, Kirsten. May 10, 2014. Interview with Alice Walker. "I'm still writing in the Dirt with a Twig." *The Age Good Weekend*.

Ushigua, Manari. 2020. "Of the Forest." Granta. November 19, 2020. https://granta.com/of-the-forest/.

Van Dooren, Thom, and Matthew Chrulew. 2022. *Kin : Thinking with Deborah Bird Rose*. Durham: Duke University Press.

Van Neervan, Ellen. 2020. *Throat*. St Lucia: University of Queensland Press.

Voss, Julia. 2022. *Hilma af Klint: A Biography*. Chicago & London: The University of Chicago Press.

Whitman, Walt. (1892) 1979. *Leaves of Grass*. Pennsylvania: The Franklin Library.

Wiegard, Sister M. Gonsalva. 1936. *The Non-Dramatic Works of Hrosvitha: Text, Translation, and Commentary*. Saint Lewis, Missouri: The Abby Press.

Wilson, James. 1999. *The Earth Shall Weep: A History of Native America*. America: Pan Macmillan.

Winfrey, Oprah. 2018. "'Their Time Is Up': Oprah's Inspiring Golden Globes Speech." The Irish Times. January 8, 2018. https://www.irishtimes.com/culture/film/their-time-is-up-oprah-s-inspiring-golden-globes-speech-1.3348262.

Wohlleben, Peter. 2021. *The Heartbeat of Trees: Embracing our Ancient Bond with Forests and Nature*. Translated by Jane Billinghurst. Canada: Graystone Books.

Woolf, Virginia. 1925. *Mrs Dalloway*. New York: Harcourt, Brace and Company.

——. (1927) 1958. 'The Narrow Bridge of Art' collected in *Granite and Rainbow: Essays by Virginia Woolf*. New York: Harcourt, Brace and Company. pp.11-23.

——. (1927) 2023. *To the Lighthouse*. Foreword by Patricia Lockwood. Introduction by Hermione Lee. Edited with notes by Stella McNichol. UK: Penguin Books.

——. (1928) 2006. *Orlando*. Annotated and with an introduction by Maria DiBattista. New York: Harcourt.

——. (1931) 1992. *The Waves*. Introduction by Kate Flint. London: Penguin.

——. (1940) 1985. *Moments of Being: Autobiographical Writings*. Edited with introduction and notes by Jeanne Schulkind. Second Edition. Harcourt Brace Jovanovich Publication: San Diego, New York & London.

——. (1942) 1961. *The Death of the Moth and Other Essays*. Middlesex: Penguin Books.

——. 1978. *The Diary of Virginia Woolf; Volume 2, 1920-1924*. Editor Anne Olivier Bell. Assisted by Andrew McNeillie. New York: Harcourt.

——. 1979. *The Dairy of Virginia Woolf: Volume 1: 1915-1919*. Editor Anne Olivier Bell. Harmondsworth, London: Hogarth Press.

——. *1980. Leave the Letters Till We're Dead: The Letters of Virginia Woolf, Vol. VI, 1936—1941*. Edited by Nigel Nicolson. Assisted by Joanne Trautmann. London: Hogarth Press.

——. 1980. *The Diary of Virginia Woolf; Volume 3, 1925-1930*. Editor Anne Olivier Bell. Assisted by Andrew McNeillie. New York: Harcourt.

——. 1980. *The Diary of Virginia Woolf; Volume 4, 1931-1935*. Editor Anne Olivier Bell. Assisted by Andrew McNeillie. New York: Harcourt.

——. 1982. *The Diary of Virginia Woolf, Vol. IV, 1931—1935.* Edited by Anne Olivier Bell, assisted by Andrew McNeillie. London: Hogarth Press.

——. 1984. *The Diary of Virginia Woolf, Vol. V, 1936—1941.* Edited by Anne Olivier Bell, assisted by Andrew McNeillie. London: Hogarth Press.

——. 2006. *The London Scene: Six Essays on London.* Introduction by Francine Prose. New York: Ecco.

——. 2008. *Selected Essays*, edited by David Bradshaw. Oxford: Oxford World's Classics.

——. 'Street Haunting: A London Adventure.' (1927) 1943. Collected in *The Death of the Moth and other essays.* London: The Hogarth Press: pp.19-29.

Wordsworth, Dorothy. 1971. *Journals of Dorothy Wordsworth. The Alfoxden Journal 1798 and The Grasmere Journals 1800-1803.* 2nd Edition. With an introduction by Helen Darbishire. Oxford: The Oxford University Press.

——. 1997. *Recollections of a Tour Made in Scotland.* Edited by Carol Kyros Walker. London: New Haven.

Wright, Alexis. 2019a. "Telling the Untold Stories: Alexis Wright on Censorship." Overland Literary Journal. February 8, 2019. https://overland.org.au/2019/02/telling-the-untold-stories-alexis-wright-on-censorship/.

——. 2019b. "A Journey in Writing Place." Meanjin. June 17, 2019. https://meanjin.com.au/essays/a-journey-in-writing-place/.

——. 2022. "The Inward Migration in Apocalyptic Times — Alexis Wright." Emergence Magazine. October 26, 2022. https://emergencemagazine.org/essay/the-inward-migration-in-apocalyptic-times/.

Wright, Judith. 1994. "Train Journey" in *Judith Wright: Collected Poems*. N.S.W. Australia:
Angus and Robertson.

Archive Material:
Greer, Germain. *The Book of Pianelli, c.1973-c.1978*. The University of Melbourne Archives. Germaine Greer, Series 2014.0054 Photographs. Item number: 2014.0054.00536.

Greer, Germaine. 2007. *Travel Diary Cave Creek Rehabilitation Scheme to Melbourne*. The University of Melbourne Archive. Germain Greer, Series 2014.0040.00014 Audio Recordings. Item number: 2014.0040.00014.

www.ingramcontent.com/pod-product-compliance
Lightning Source LLC
Chambersburg PA
CBHW020517080526
44583CB00013B/635